Contents

Introduction

Welcome to this guide on **Amazon Neptune Analytics** – a powerful in-memory graph analytics engine designed for deep insights and real-time exploration of complex relationships in graph datasets.

This book is built to help you understand, use, and master Neptune Analytics through clearly written explanations, feature overviews, and practical guidance. It walks you through everything from getting started and loading data, to running powerful graph algorithms and performing advanced queries with openCypher.

> **Note:**
> This guide focuses on **text-based explanations only**. To keep the material streamlined and accessible, we've intentionally left out diagrams, flowcharts, and schema visuals.
> Instead, you'll find:

- Clear breakdowns of Neptune Analytics concepts

- Practical usage scenarios and feature walkthroughs

- Code samples and examples for hands-on learning

If you're a data engineer, data scientist, architect, or developer looking to leverage graph analytics in the AWS ecosystem, this guide will provide the foundation you need to work confidently with Neptune Analytics.

Let's dive in!

Chapter 1: What is Neptune Analytics?

Introduction to Neptune Analytics

In the evolving world of data analytics, where interconnected data plays a pivotal role in delivering insights, **Neptune Analytics** emerges as a powerful tool in the Amazon Web Services (AWS) ecosystem. Neptune Analytics is a **memory-optimized graph database engine** specifically designed for **analytics workloads on large-scale graph data**. Built for speed, scalability, and versatility, it enables users to run **graph analytics algorithms**, execute **low-latency queries**, and even perform **vector searches** seamlessly.

This chapter introduces Neptune Analytics, explores its core architecture and capabilities, and lays the foundation for understanding when and why to use it. Whether you're a data scientist, software engineer, or business analyst, this chapter will help you grasp the significance of Neptune Analytics in modern data analysis pipelines.

Why Graph Analytics?

Graphs are a natural way to model complex relationships between entities, such as social networks, fraud detection patterns, cybersecurity threats, and recommendation systems. Traditional relational databases struggle to process deeply interconnected data efficiently. Graph databases, on the other hand, allow for **high-performance traversal**, **pattern matching**, and **relationship-centric queries**.

However, most graph databases are optimized for **transactional workloads**—they're great for reading and writing small amounts of data frequently. But when it comes to **analyzing large volumes of graph data**, particularly in data science workflows, there's a need for

analytical engines that can ingest, process, and analyze massive graphs rapidly.

This is where Neptune Analytics fits in.

Core Definition

Neptune Analytics is a **fully managed graph analytics engine** that:

- Stores graph datasets **in memory** for high-speed analytics.

- Supports a **library of built-in graph algorithms** for out-of-the-box insights.

- Integrates seamlessly with **Neptune Database**, Amazon's transactional graph DB, and **Amazon S3**, making it easy to source data.

- Provides a **"Graph-as-a-Service"** experience— abstracting infrastructure management so users can focus on data and insights.

Key Features of Neptune Analytics

Understanding the unique capabilities of Neptune Analytics is crucial for recognizing its place in a graph data pipeline. Here are the standout features:

- **In-Memory Graph Processing**
  Neptune Analytics loads entire graph datasets into memory, which drastically reduces query response times and enhances performance for analytic tasks.

- **Built-in Graph Algorithms**
  The service includes a rich library of pre-optimized graph algorithms, including:

  - Pathfinding (BFS, SSSP)

  - Centrality (PageRank, Degree, Closeness)

  - Community detection (Label Propagation, Weakly Connected Components)

  - Similarity (Jaccard, Overlap)

  - Vector-based algorithms for similarity search

- **Low-Latency Queries**
  With support for **openCypher**, a popular query language for property graphs, users can perform complex graph traversals and analytical queries efficiently.

- **Vector Search Capabilities**
  Neptune Analytics supports vector indexing and similarity operations, making it suitable for **hybrid search scenarios**, such as combining semantic vector similarity with graph traversals.

- **Data Integration**
  Load data from:

  - **Amazon S3**

  - **Amazon Neptune Database**

  - **Neptune Snapshots**

○ Other AWS data sources using batch and bulk import operations

- **Flexible Connectivity Options**

  ○ Public or private endpoint configuration

  ○ AWS PrivateLink support for secure, VPC-based access

- **Elastic and Serverless**
  Neptune Analytics provisions resources automatically based on graph size and workload—users don't need to manage clusters or instances manually.

Neptune Analytics vs. Neptune Database

Though they share the "Neptune" name, Neptune Analytics and Neptune Database are built for **distinct purposes**. Understanding their differences will help in choosing the right tool for each task.

Feature	Neptune Database	Neptune Analytics
Primary Use	Online transactional processing (OLTP)	Graph analytics and data science
Data Model	Property graph (PG) and RDF	Property graph
Performance	Optimized for high-throughput queries	Optimized for large-scale analytical queries

9

Scalability	Up to 100,000 queries/sec	Memory-optimized for billions of relationships
Query Language	openCypher, SPARQL, Gremlin	openCypher
Data Storage	Persistent (disk-based)	In-memory
Workload Type	Real-time apps, microservices	Exploration, modeling, analysis, ML preprocessing
Integration	App backend integration	ML/AI, data science pipelines

When to Use Neptune Analytics

Neptune Analytics excels in **exploratory, investigative, and algorithm-heavy graph workflows**, including:

- **Fraud Detection and Investigation**
  Quickly identify anomalies or suspicious connections across vast financial or transaction networks.

- **Recommendation Systems**
  Use similarity algorithms and vector embeddings to power content or product recommendations.

- **Cybersecurity**
  Analyze attack paths, vulnerabilities, and relationships among infrastructure elements.

- **Knowledge Graph Analysis**
  Traverse entity graphs, compute centrality metrics, and enrich metadata with embeddings.

- **Customer 360 and Relationship Mapping**
  Analyze all relationships a customer has across

different channels, improving personalization.

How Neptune Analytics Works

Memory-Optimized Engine

At its core, Neptune Analytics leverages a **memory-optimized architecture**. When data is loaded, it's held in memory to facilitate extremely fast access and processing. This design is ideal for workloads that need high-throughput access to interconnected data structures.

Graph Provisioning

Creating a Neptune Analytics graph involves selecting a name, size (measured in **m-NCUs**, or Neptune Capacity Units), and optionally enabling features like vector search. Graphs can be provisioned in under five minutes and can be either:

- **Empty graphs** – To be loaded with data post-creation.

- **Pre-loaded graphs** – Created by importing from Amazon S3, snapshots, or a Neptune database.

Querying and Algorithm Execution

Once the data is in place, users can:

- Execute queries via **openCypher** syntax.

- Run **graph algorithms** using pre-built function calls (e.g., `.pageRank`, `.labelPropagation`).

- Use **Neptune Notebooks** or the **AWS CLI/SDKs** for interactive analysis or automation.

Integration with Other AWS Services

Neptune Analytics integrates smoothly with:

- **Amazon SageMaker** – For ML pipelines and AI notebooks

- **Amazon EC2** – For hosting applications or notebooks

- **Amazon S3** – For bulk or batch data ingestion

- **IAM** – For fine-grained access control and security

Real-World Use Cases

Case Study: E-commerce Product Recommendations

An e-commerce company uses Neptune Analytics to power its product recommendation engine. The product-customer interaction data is modeled as a graph with nodes representing users and products, and edges denoting interactions like "viewed," "purchased," or "liked." Using **.jaccardSimilarity** and **.pageRank**, they compute product similarity scores and identify influential users for marketing campaigns.

Case Study: Network Threat Detection

A cybersecurity firm loads event logs and system relationships into Neptune Analytics. Using **.wcc (Weakly Connected Components)** and **.closenessCentrality**, the team rapidly identifies isolated or high-risk nodes within their infrastructure graph.

Benefits of Using Neptune Analytics

- **Speed**: Analyze massive graphs in seconds.

- **Scalability**: Designed for billions of relationships.

- **Simplicity**: No need to manage infrastructure or scale manually.

- **Flexibility**: Use a wide array of graph algorithms and vector operations.

- **Security**: Fully integrated with AWS IAM and private network options.

Limitations to Consider

- **Ephemeral Storage**: Because it's memory-based, Neptune Analytics is not a long-term storage solution. Data must be loaded or restored as needed.

- **No Support for RDF/SPARQL**: Unlike Neptune Database, Neptune Analytics is currently focused on **property graph models** and does not support RDF triple stores or SPARQL queries.

- **Write Constraints**: Primarily built for reading and analyzing data. Mutation operations exist but are limited compared to transactional databases.

Tips for Getting Started

Tip 1: Choose the Right Graph Size
Start with a smaller memory size and scale up only if needed. Neptune Analytics supports elastic provisioning.

Tip 2: Use OpenCypher Familiarity
If you're coming from a Neo4j background or familiar with Cypher, you'll find Neptune's openCypher support intuitive.

Tip 3: Take Advantage of Notebooks
Use Neptune's Jupyter-based notebooks to prototype queries, visualize results, and explore datasets interactively.

Tip 4: Preprocess Data
Before importing, clean and structure your data in CSV, Parquet, or RDF formats as needed. Batch loading is faster when your data is well-formed.

Example: A Simple Query in openCypher

```
MATCH (user:Customer)-[:BOUGHT]-
>(product:Item)
RETURN user.name, product.title
LIMIT 10
```

This query returns 10 customer-product purchase relationships. Executed in Neptune Analytics, this type of query benefits from fast in-memory traversal.

Conclusion

Neptune Analytics is a game-changing service for those working with large-scale graph data. With its memory-first design, pre-built analytical algorithms, and seamless AWS integration, it empowers users to derive insights from complex networks with unprecedented speed.

As graph analytics continues to grow in relevance across industries, mastering tools like Neptune Analytics will be essential. In the next chapter, we will explore its **features in depth**, including a breakdown of supported algorithms and how to use them effectively.

Chapter 2: Features

In this chapter, we will explore the key features of **Amazon Neptune Analytics**, a powerful graph analytics engine designed to process and analyze large-scale graph data efficiently. As graph data becomes increasingly vital in areas such as fraud detection, recommendation engines, network analysis, and knowledge graphs, Neptune Analytics offers a suite of capabilities to make working with this data intuitive, fast, and scalable.

Introduction to Neptune Analytics Features

Amazon Neptune Analytics is a **memory-optimized graph database engine** designed for high-performance analytics. Unlike traditional transactional graph databases, Neptune Analytics is engineered to load and operate on **massive datasets entirely in memory**, enabling rapid query execution and the ability to run complex graph algorithms with ease.

Here's an overview of what makes Neptune Analytics stand out:

- **In-memory data processing**

- **Support for property graphs using openCypher**

- **Pre-built graph algorithms**

- **Vector search and similarity capabilities**

- **Flexible data loading from S3 or Neptune Database**

- **Fully managed service with dynamic resource allocation**

Let's explore each of these core features in more detail.

In-Memory Graph Storage and Processing

One of Neptune Analytics' foundational features is its ability to **store graph data entirely in memory**. This architectural choice is critical for performance, especially when dealing with billions of nodes and edges.

Benefits of In-Memory Architecture:

- **Low-latency queries**: Accessing data from memory is significantly faster than disk-based storage.

- **Real-time analytics**: Supports near real-time insights for interactive applications.

- **Efficient algorithm execution**: Graph algorithms like PageRank, shortest path, or centrality measures can run significantly faster.

Example Use Case

Suppose you're building a **cybersecurity investigation tool**. You can ingest threat intelligence data into Neptune Analytics and run path-finding algorithms to detect suspicious relationships in milliseconds—perfect for incident response scenarios.

Graph as a Service

Neptune Analytics is fully managed. This means AWS handles provisioning, patching, scaling, and monitoring, allowing you to focus solely on analyzing data and building graph-powered applications.

Key Managed Features:

- **Auto-provisioned compute**: Resources are allocated based on the size and complexity of your data.

- **No infrastructure management**: No need to manage servers, disk storage, or manual scaling.

- **Pay-as-you-go model**: You're charged based on memory capacity (m-NCUs), not query volume.

Tip:

Start with a smaller graph size and scale up only when needed to optimize costs. You can monitor memory usage to guide scaling decisions.

Flexible Data Ingestion

Neptune Analytics supports data loading from various sources, making it easy to integrate with existing data pipelines.

Supported Data Sources:

1. **Amazon S3** – Bulk or batch loading of CSV, Parquet, or RDF files

2. **Amazon Neptune Database** – Load directly from a live graph or a snapshot

3. **openCypher Queries** – Insert or update data interactively

Ingestion Methods:

- **Bulk Import**: Best for loading large datasets quickly into an empty graph.

- **Batch Load**: Ideal for incremental data updates.

- **openCypher Queries**: Useful for fine-grained inserts and updates based on logic.

Example

To load CSV files from S3:

```
aws neptune-graph create-graph-using-
import-task \
  --graph-name "demo-graph" \
  --format "CSV" \
  --region "us-east-1" \
  --source "s3://my-graph-bucket/data/" \
  --role-arn
"arn:aws:iam::123456789012:role/MyGraphRole
"
```

Rich Query Support with openCypher

Neptune Analytics uses **openCypher**, a popular, SQL-like query language tailored for graph data. This enables users to express complex graph patterns intuitively.

Capabilities:

- **Pattern matching**: Easily find paths, relationships, or subgraphs.

- **Transformations**: Use clauses like MATCH, WHERE, RETURN, WITH, and SET.

- **Aggregations**: Compute group-based metrics.

- **Filtering**: Apply granular criteria to reduce result sets.

Query Example

```
MATCH (p:Person)-[:FRIEND_OF]->(f:Person)
WHERE p.age > 30 AND f.age < 30
RETURN p.name, f.name
```

This query finds people over 30 who are friends with people under 30.

Built-in Graph Algorithms

Neptune Analytics includes a **robust library of optimized graph algorithms**. These are native procedures written for speed and scalability.

Categories of Algorithms:

1. **Path-finding**

   ○ Shortest Path (SSSP)

   ○ Breadth-First Search (BFS)

2. **Centrality**

- Degree Centrality

- PageRank

- Closeness Centrality

3. **Community Detection**

- Weakly Connected Components (WCC)

- Strongly Connected Components (SCC)

- Label Propagation

4. **Similarity Measures**

- Jaccard Similarity

- Overlap Similarity

Example: Running PageRank

```
CALL algo.pageRank()
YIELD nodeId, score
RETURN nodeId, score
ORDER BY score DESC
LIMIT 10
```

This will compute and return the top 10 nodes with the highest PageRank score in the graph.

Vector Search and Similarity

Neptune Analytics supports **vector indexing and vector similarity search**, a critical feature for modern use cases like:

- **Recommendation engines**

- **Semantic search**

- **AI-powered knowledge graphs**

Vector Features:

- **Vector embedding support**

- **Top-K nearest neighbor search**

- **Distance metrics**: Cosine, Euclidean, etc.

Example: Inserting Vectors

```
CALL vectors.upsert([
  { id: "node1", embedding: [0.1, 0.2, 0.3] },
  { id: "node2", embedding: [0.4, 0.5, 0.6] }
])
```

Example: Vector Similarity Search

```
CALL vectors.topKByEmbedding([0.2, 0.3, 0.4], 5)
YIELD nodeId, distance
RETURN nodeId, distance
```

This returns the 5 most similar nodes to a given vector.

Interactive Querying and Visualization with Notebooks

Neptune Analytics integrates with **Amazon SageMaker notebooks** and **local Jupyter environments** for interactive querying and graph visualization.

Notebook Features:

- Magic commands for openCypher queries (%%oc)

- Graph data preview and summaries

- Easy setup with CloudFormation or manual deployment

Common Magics:

- %load – Load data into the graph

- %%oc – Execute openCypher query

- %summary – View high-level graph metadata

Secure and Scalable Access

Security and scalability are built into Neptune Analytics by design.

Security Features:

- **IAM-based access control**

- **VPC isolation**

- **AWS PrivateLink support**

- **Data encryption (AWS KMS)**

Scalability:

- Neptune Analytics auto-scales resources based on memory size.

- You can scale from small (128 m-NCUs) to very large graphs (4096 m-NCUs).

Integration with AWS Ecosystem

Neptune Analytics integrates tightly with other AWS services:

- **Amazon S3** – For data input

- **IAM** – For access control

- **CloudWatch** – For monitoring

- **CloudFormation** – For infrastructure as code

- **SageMaker** – For AI/ML integration

Tip:

You can automate graph creation, data loading, and algorithm execution using AWS Lambda and Step Functions to build scalable pipelines.

Real-World Applications

Let's take a look at some practical use cases where these features are invaluable:

1. **Fraud Detection**
    Use graph algorithms to detect abnormal patterns, communities, and money trails.

2. **Social Network Analysis**
    Leverage centrality metrics and label propagation to identify influencers and communities.

3. **Recommendation Engines**
    Combine graph traversals with vector similarity to build personalized experiences.

4. **IT and Network Monitoring**
    Use path algorithms to trace incidents and root causes across interconnected systems.

5. **Knowledge Graphs**
    Store entities and relationships, enrich with embeddings, and reason using graph algorithms.

Summary of Key Features

Feature	Description
In-memory Processing	High-speed queries and algorithms with memory-resident graphs
openCypher Support	Intuitive and powerful query language for property graphs
Pre-built Graph Algorithms	Native implementations of common graph algorithms
Vector Indexing & Search	Search and match nodes using embeddings
Flexible Data Loading	Load from S3, Neptune DB, or via queries
Notebook Integration	Interact and visualize data using Jupyter environments
Secure & Scalable	IAM, encryption, VPC, PrivateLink, and dynamic scaling
AWS Ecosystem Integration	Works seamlessly with AWS S3, IAM, CloudWatch, CloudFormation, and more

Final Thoughts

Amazon Neptune Analytics bridges the gap between graph storage and advanced analytics. Its combination of **in-memory performance**, **prebuilt algorithms**, and **openCypher support**, along with **modern features like vector search**, makes it a powerful tool for developers, data scientists, and architects alike.

As we move deeper into graph-powered applications and AI-driven knowledge discovery, Neptune Analytics stands out as a flexible, scalable, and high-performance solution ready for enterprise workloads.

Chapter 3: Neptune Analytics vs. Neptune Database

Amazon Neptune offers two powerful but distinct tools for working with graph data in the cloud: **Neptune Database** and **Neptune Analytics**. While they share common ground—both are managed AWS services designed to handle graph workloads—they cater to different use cases, performance characteristics, and analytical needs.

In this chapter, we'll walk through the **key differences**, **architectural philosophies**, **ideal use cases**, and **real-world scenarios** that help you decide when to use Neptune Analytics versus Neptune Database.

Understanding the Graph Paradigm

Before diving into comparisons, it's worth reinforcing the core concept they both support: **graphs**.

Graphs are data structures that represent entities as **nodes (vertices)** and their relationships as **edges**. This structure is ideal for modeling:

- Social networks

- Knowledge graphs

- Fraud detection

- Recommendation engines

- Network topologies

Both Neptune Database and Neptune Analytics leverage this model but are optimized for **different types of graph workloads**.

The Core Philosophy of Each Service

Neptune Database

- **Purpose:** Transactional graph database (OLTP)

- **Engine:** Purpose-built to handle high-throughput, low-latency graph operations

- **Focus:** Operational queries (e.g., "Who are this person's friends?"), real-time applications

- **Languages:** Supports Gremlin, SPARQL, and openCypher

- **Deployment:** Highly available, multi-AZ, supports serverless mode

Neptune Analytics

- **Purpose:** Analytical graph processing (OLAP)

- **Engine:** Memory-optimized analytics engine

- **Focus:** Graph-wide computation (e.g., PageRank, community detection)

- **Languages:** Uses openCypher and built-in graph algorithms

- **Deployment:** Temporary or persistent in-memory graphs for analytics

Key Differences at a Glance

Feature	Neptune Database	Neptune Analytics
Primary Use	Transactional operations	Analytical graph computations
Engine Type	Persistent, storage-backed	In-memory, optimized for speed
Query Support	Gremlin, SPARQL, openCypher	openCypher, graph algorithms
Performance Model	Scales with query volume	Scales with graph size and memory
High Availability	Multi-AZ, failover support	Compute auto-provisioned, but no multi-AZ HA
Vector Search	Limited	Full vector search support
Algorithms	Not built-in	Built-in algorithm library
Latency	Milliseconds	Sub-seconds to seconds (for large-scale analysis)
Data Storage	Durable storage	In-memory (ephemeral)
Integration	Strong with real-time apps	Better suited for batch analysis and data science

When to Use Neptune Database

Neptune Database excels in traditional graph database roles where **transactions, low-latency access, and persistent data** are critical.

Ideal Use Cases

1. **Social Media Applications**

   o   Real-time querying of user connections

   o   "Friends of friends" or mutual connections

2. **Customer 360 Views**

   o   Combine data from CRM, sales, and support into unified graph

   o   Serve real-time dashboards and APIs

3. **Fraud Detection**

   o   Real-time transaction anomaly checking

   o   Relationship pattern detection between entities

4. **Recommendation Systems**

   o   Light personalization based on user paths and relationships

Example

```
MATCH (u:User {id: '123'})-[:FOLLOWS]-
>(f:User)
RETURN f.name
```

This query retrieves all users followed by a given user—ideal for Neptune Database's low-latency response times.

When to Use Neptune Analytics

Neptune Analytics shines when you need to **perform deep analysis on massive graphs**—millions or billions of relationships—where **data science, ML workflows, and trend detection** are key.

Ideal Use Cases

1. **Network Threat Detection**

   - Apply algorithms like connected components to isolate vulnerabilities

2. **Recommendation Engines**

   - Use PageRank, centrality measures, or vector similarity to drive recommendations

3. **Graph Exploration**

   - Explore large-scale enterprise knowledge graphs for hidden patterns

4. **Content Personalization**

   - Combine graph algorithms and vector embeddings for hyper-targeted content

5. **Scientific and Research Graphs**

   - Understand relationships in biological or citation graphs

Example

```
CALL algo.pageRank()
YIELD node, score
RETURN node, score
```

```
ORDER BY score DESC
LIMIT 10
```

This ranks the most important nodes using PageRank—a typical use case for Neptune Analytics.

The Power of Memory: Neptune Analytics' Advantage

A cornerstone of Neptune Analytics is its **in-memory engine**, which allows:

- Massive graph ingestion (tens of billions of relationships)

- Sub-second algorithm execution times

- Efficient vector indexing and similarity search

- Fast iteration for data scientists and analysts

Because it avoids disk I/O and scales memory based on graph size, Neptune Analytics is ideal for **exploratory and batch analytical workloads**.

Memory-Based Execution Example

Let's say you need to compute **closeness centrality** across a graph with 100 million nodes.

In Neptune Database, this would require building your own traversal strategy and likely hit performance bottlenecks.

In Neptune Analytics:

```
CALL algo.closenessCentrality()
```

```
YIELD node, closeness
RETURN node, closeness
ORDER BY closeness DESC
LIMIT 5
```

This would execute in-memory, often within seconds.

Data Movement Between the Two Services

From Neptune Database to Neptune Analytics

Neptune Analytics is designed to work **in tandem** with Neptune Database. You can easily move data from a live Neptune Database or from snapshots.

Options include:

- Export from Neptune Database to Amazon S3 and import into Neptune Analytics

- Directly load from a Neptune snapshot into Neptune Analytics

- Use AWS CLI or SDKs to automate this pipeline

Workflow Example

1. Run your live graph in Neptune Database

2. Periodically snapshot the data

3. Load the snapshot into Neptune Analytics

4. Run batch algorithms or deep analysis

5. Feed results back to production systems

Query Language Support

One of the distinctions is in the **query languages** supported.

Feature	Neptune Database	Neptune Analytics
Gremlin	☑	✘
SPARQL	☑	✘
openCypher	☑	☑ (primary interface)

Neptune Analytics centers on **openCypher** and a rich set of **graph algorithm procedures** such as `.pageRank`, `.degree`, `.scc`, `.labelPropagation`, and more.

Vector Search and Embeddings

One of Neptune Analytics' standout features is **vector similarity search within the graph context**.

Why It Matters

In modern ML and AI systems, entities (like products or people) are often represented as high-dimensional vectors, or **embeddings**. Neptune Analytics allows you to:

- Load these embeddings directly

- Index them using vector indexing

- Run top-K similarity queries

Example

```
CALL algo.vectors.topKByNode({node: 'p123',
k: 5})
YIELD similarNode, score
RETURN similarNode, score
```

This enables hybrid graph + vector search, which is foundational in modern recommender systems and knowledge graphs.

Security, Compliance, and IAM

Both Neptune Database and Neptune Analytics integrate with AWS IAM for authentication and authorization, but there are some differences in connectivity and data exposure.

Security Feature	Neptune Database	Neptune Analytics
IAM support	☑	☑
VPC support	☑	☑
Public endpoints	Optional	Disabled by default
AWS PrivateLink	☑	☑
Encryption at rest	☑ (KMS)	☑ (KMS)

Cost Considerations

Neptune Database

- Charges based on instance size, storage, and I/O

- Serverless mode allows scaling to zero when idle

- Ideal for always-on apps

Neptune Analytics

- Charges based on memory allocation (m-NCUs)

- Costs increase with graph size and vector search configurations

- Optimized for episodic, bursty analytics workloads

A typical pattern is to **spin up Neptune Analytics temporarily** for analysis, then tear it down to control costs.

Real-World Comparison: A Case Study

Use Case: Personalized News Feed

- A social media platform needs to serve real-time news feeds to users and also perform periodic analysis to optimize recommendations.

Solution:

- **Neptune Database** is used to:

- o Store user connections and preferences

- o Serve real-time "friend activity" queries

- **Neptune Analytics** is used to:

  - o Run monthly PageRank and community detection algorithms

  - o Use vector embeddings to recommend articles or groups

Result:

- Combines operational and analytical strengths

- Reduces time-to-insight from hours to minutes

- Keeps real-time latency low while enhancing personalization

Summary of Recommendations

If you need to...	Use this service
Handle real-time user interactions	Neptune Database
Perform graph-wide analysis (e.g., PageRank)	Neptune Analytics
Maintain persistent graph storage	Neptune Database
Load and analyze large graphs episodically	Neptune Analytics
Execute Gremlin or SPARQL queries	Neptune Database

Run vector similarity search	Neptune Analytics
Perform fraud detection in production	Neptune Database
Explore network threats or communities	Neptune Analytics

Final Thoughts

Neptune Database and Neptune Analytics are **complementary services**, not competitors. By understanding their strengths, you can:

- **Optimize performance**

- **Control costs**

- **Unlock advanced analytical capabilities**

Most enterprise graph strategies will benefit from **using both**, orchestrated together in a thoughtful architecture. Neptune Database serves as the operational heart of your graph, while Neptune Analytics becomes the **analytical brain**, uncovering deeper insights.

Getting Started

Chapter 4: Create an Empty Neptune Graph

Creating an empty Neptune Analytics graph is a foundational step when working with Amazon Neptune's in-memory graph analytics engine. This chapter walks you through the process of creating an empty Neptune graph from scratch using multiple methods: the AWS Management Console, the AWS Command Line Interface (CLI), and AWS CloudFormation. It also covers all the configuration options available, including memory settings, networking, vector search, and IAM permissions.

Introduction

Neptune Analytics is designed for lightning-fast analysis of large-scale graph datasets. Whether you're preparing to load data from an external source or testing queries in an empty graph environment, understanding how to create a clean, unpopulated graph is crucial.

There are three primary ways to create an empty Neptune Analytics graph:

- Using the **AWS Management Console**

- Using the **AWS CLI**

- Using **AWS CloudFormation**

Each method offers a different level of automation and control, and you should choose based on your comfort with AWS tools and infrastructure-as-code preferences.

Why Create an Empty Graph?

An empty graph serves several use cases:

- **Prototyping and Testing**: Quickly run queries and algorithms on a new structure before scaling up.

- **Incremental Loading**: Load and test subsets of data progressively.

- **Graph Schema Definition**: Design the vertex and edge types you expect to use.

Pre-Requisites Before Creating a Graph

Before you create a Neptune Analytics graph, make sure you have the following:

- **An active AWS account**

- **Appropriate IAM permissions** (either directly or through an IAM role)

- **A selected AWS region**

- **Understanding of your network requirements** (public vs. private access)

AWS Management Console Method

This is the most user-friendly way to create an empty Neptune Analytics graph. Follow these steps:

Step-by-Step: Using AWS Console

1. **Sign in** to the AWS Management Console and navigate to **Amazon Neptune**:
    https://console.aws.amazon.com/neptune/

2. **Choose Region**: In the top right, select the AWS region where you want to deploy your graph.

3. **Navigate to Graphs**:
    In the left sidebar, under the "Analytics" section, click **Graphs**.

4. **Create New Graph**:
    Click on the **Create Graph** button.

5. **Graph Settings**:

    o   **Graph name**: Choose a unique identifier for your graph.

    o   **Memory**: Choose how much provisioned memory (in m-NCUs) to allocate. A minimum of 128 is recommended.

    o   **Replica count**: Specify the number of replicas (from 0 to 2). Remember, each replica incurs additional charges.

6. **Choose Data Source**:
    Select **Create an empty graph**. This ensures no data is preloaded.

7. **Configure Network Access**:

    o   **Public connectivity**: Allows internet access.

    o   **Private connectivity**: Accessible only within a VPC.

⚠ **Note**: Private connectivity requires extra permissions like `ec2:CreateVpcEndpoint`, `ec2:DescribeVpcs`, etc.

8. **Optional: Vector Search Configuration**
   Enable this if your graph will perform vector search. Set the vector dimension, such as 384, depending on your embedding size.

9. **Click Create**.

Your graph will begin provisioning. Once the status changes to **Available**, it's ready to use.

AWS CLI Method

If you prefer scripting or automating your deployments, the AWS CLI provides full flexibility.

Sample Command for Public Graph Endpoint

```
aws neptune-graph create-graph \
  --graph-name 'my-empty-graph' \
  --region us-east-1 \
  --provisioned-memory 128 \
  --public-connectivity \
  --replica-count 0 \
  --vector-search '{"dimension": 384}'
```

Sample Command for Private Graph Endpoint

```
aws neptune-graph create-private-graph-endpoint \
  --vpc-id vpc-0a9b7a5b15 \
```

```
  --subnet-ids subnet-06a4b41a6221b subnet-
0840a4b327ab77 subnet-0353627ab123 \
  --vpc-security-group-ids sg-0ab7abab56ab
\
  --graph-identifier g-146a51b7a151ba \
  --region us-east-1
```

Monitor Graph Status

```
aws neptune-graph get-graph --graph-
identifier g-146a51b7a151ba
```

List Existing Graphs

```
aws neptune-graph list-graphs
```

> **Tip**: Set environment variables for credentials or use named profiles to simplify CLI usage.

AWS CloudFormation Method

For infrastructure as code and automation, CloudFormation is ideal.

Benefits of Using CloudFormation

- **Repeatable**: Easily recreate environments.

- **Version controlled**: Manage graph infrastructure like code.

- **Integrated**: Combine with CI/CD pipelines.

Sample CloudFormation Template (Public Graph)

```
AWSTemplateFormatVersion: 2010-09-09
Description: NeptuneGraph Graph Create Demo
using CloudFormation
Resources:
  NeptuneGraph:
    Type: AWS::NeptuneGraph::Graph
    DeletionPolicy: Delete
    Properties:
      DeletionProtection: false
      GraphName: neptune-graph-demo
      ProvisionedMemory: 128
      ReplicaCount: 1
      PublicConnectivity: true
      Tags:
        - Key: stage
          Value: test
```

Sample CloudFormation Template (Private Graph)

```
AWSTemplateFormatVersion: 2010-09-09
Resources:
  NeptuneGraph:
    Type: AWS::NeptuneGraph::Graph
    DeletionPolicy: Delete
    Properties:
      GraphName: neptune-graph-private
      ProvisionedMemory: 128
      ReplicaCount: 1
      PublicConnectivity: false
      Tags:
        - Key: stage
          Value: dev
  NeptuneGraphPrivateEndpoint:
```

```
    Type:
AWS::NeptuneGraph::PrivateGraphEndpoint
    DeletionPolicy: Delete
    Properties:
      GraphIdentifier: !Ref NeptuneGraph
      VpcId: myVpc
```

Launching the Stack

You can use the CloudFormation console or CLI to deploy the template.

```
aws cloudformation create-stack \
  --stack-name NeptuneGraphStack \
  --template-body file://neptune-graph-
template.yaml \
  --capabilities CAPABILITY_NAMED_IAM
```

> ☑ **Best Practice**: Enable deletion protection only after initial testing to prevent accidental removal.

Key Configuration Options

Graph Name

- Must be unique within your AWS account and region.

- Cannot be changed after graph creation.

Memory (ProvisionedMemory)

- m-NCU (Neptune Capacity Unit) ranges from 128 to 1024.

- Each unit provides ~1 GiB of memory.

- More memory = higher cost but better performance.

Replicas

- Optional failover replicas for high availability.

- Default: 1 replica. Maximum: 2.

Connectivity

- **Public**: Accessible from the internet.

- **Private**: Restricted to a specific VPC and subnet(s).

Vector Search

If you're using embeddings (e.g., for recommendation engines or semantic search):

```
"vector-search": {
  "dimension": 384
}
```

🔍 **Use case**: Graph + vector search = powerful hybrid for advanced analytics.

IAM Permissions

Creating graphs (especially private ones) may require the following permissions:

- `neptune-graph:CreateGraph`

- `ec2:CreateVpcEndpoint`

- `ec2:Describe*`

- `route53:AssociateVPCWithHostedZone` (for custom DNS)

- `iam:PassRole` (when specifying IAM roles)

Ensure your IAM user or role includes these permissions, or graph creation will fail.

Common Issues and Troubleshooting

Issue	Cause	Solution
Graph stuck in "Creating"	Insufficient permissions or networking misconfiguration	Check IAM roles and VPC/subnet settings
Cannot connect to graph	Public endpoint not enabled or security group blocks traffic	Verify connectivity settings and port access (443, 8182)
Vector configuration invalid	Dimension not specified or incorrect	Check vector settings; valid range is 1–2048

Example Use Case: Testing Graph Algorithms

Let's say you want to test the `.pageRank` algorithm on synthetic data.

1. Create an empty graph.

2. Load sample nodes and edges using openCypher.

3. Run the `.pageRank` algorithm.

4. Analyze results using Jupyter notebook or CLI.

This workflow is ideal for development and learning.

Tips for Working with Empty Graphs

- **Use notebooks** to visually validate graph structure.

- **Batch load small datasets** to test schema and queries.

- **Version your CloudFormation templates** for rollback.

Summary

Creating an empty Neptune Analytics graph is the first step toward building scalable, high-performance graph solutions. Whether you use the console for simplicity, CLI for scripting, or CloudFormation for automation, AWS gives you flexible tools to get started.

A well-configured graph lays the groundwork for success in all your analytical workloads — from basic queries to full-blown vector-powered recommendations.

Chapter 5: Create a Neptune Graph from Existing Sources

Creating a Neptune Analytics graph from existing data sources is one of the most powerful ways to accelerate your journey into graph analytics. Instead of starting from scratch, you can bring in rich, connected data from Amazon S3, Neptune databases, or snapshots, allowing you to instantly leverage Neptune Analytics' high-performance, in-memory graph processing engine. In this chapter, we will explore the various methods, options, and best practices for creating a Neptune Analytics graph using existing data.

Overview

Neptune Analytics supports seamless ingestion from multiple sources:

- **Amazon S3**: Supports Parquet, CSV, and RDF data formats.

- **Amazon Neptune Database**: You can import live data directly from a Neptune cluster.

- **Neptune Cluster Snapshots**: Restore data from a previously saved point-in-time state of a graph.

This chapter covers the entire lifecycle of creating a graph from existing sources, including:

- Requirements and prerequisites

- Source types and format expectations

- Step-by-step instructions using the AWS Console, CLI, and API

- IAM roles and permission setup

- Tips and troubleshooting

Prerequisites

Before creating a Neptune Analytics graph from existing data, ensure the following prerequisites are met:

- **IAM Role with Appropriate Permissions**: You need an IAM role with access to the data source (e.g., S3 buckets) and Neptune Analytics service permissions.

- **Data Format Compatibility**: Your data must conform to one of the supported formats: CSV, Parquet, or RDF.

- **Amazon S3 Bucket Access**: If using S3, ensure your bucket is accessible from the Neptune Analytics service and contains properly formatted files.

- **Neptune Snapshot or Cluster Availability**: If importing from a Neptune source, ensure the target database or snapshot is in a usable state and accessible.

Supported Data Sources

Amazon S3

S3 is the most flexible option for bulk data ingestion. Neptune Analytics supports the following formats:

- **CSV**: Column-based files, often used for node and edge representations.

- **Parquet**: A compressed columnar storage format ideal for large-scale data.

- **RDF**: A W3C standard format used in semantic graphs.

Neptune Database

You can load live data directly from a running Neptune database, which is useful for creating analytics snapshots without interrupting production workloads.

Neptune Snapshots

Snapshots offer a consistent point-in-time image of your graph data, allowing for reproducible analytics or recovery from a known good state.

Using the AWS Console

Step-by-Step: Importing from Existing Sources via Console

1. **Navigate to the Neptune Console**
   Open the Neptune Console, and under the **Analytics** section, select **Graphs**.

2. **Click 'Create Graph'**
   Choose **Create Graph** to initiate the graph provisioning wizard.

3. **Name and Configure Graph**

   o Enter a graph name.

   o Specify minimum and maximum memory (m-NCUs).

   o Choose public or private connectivity.

4. **Choose Data Source** Select **Create Graph from Existing Source**.

5. **Select Data Source Type**

   o Choose from **Amazon S3**, **Neptune DB Snapshot**, or **Neptune Database**.

6. **Provide Source Details**

   o For **S3**:

      ■ Enter the S3 URI (must end with a slash).

      ■ Choose data format (CSV, Parquet, RDF).

      ■ Provide an IAM role with read permissions.

   o For **Snapshots**:

      ■ Select the snapshot from the dropdown.

- Provide an IAM role if required.

   - For **Live Database**:

      - Choose the source cluster.

      - Assign IAM role with appropriate permissions.

7. **Select Vector Search Settings (Optional)**

   - Enable vector search and specify the dimension, if you plan to use vector algorithms.

8. **Add Tags (Optional)**

   - Add metadata tags for cost management or resource grouping.

9. **Review and Create**

   - Review your configuration and click **Create Graph**.

Using the AWS CLI

Creating a Neptune Analytics graph from S3 via the CLI is efficient for automation and repeatable deployments.

Sample CLI Command: Load from S3

```
aws neptune-graph create-graph-using-
import-task \
  --graph-name "neptune-graph-from-s3-
source" \
  --region "us-east-1" \
```

```
  --format "CSV" \
  --role-arn
"arn:aws:iam::123456789012:role/GraphExecut
ionRole" \
  --source "s3://neptune-demo-test-us-east-
1/test-data-csv/" \
  --public-connectivity \
  --min-provisioned-memory 256 \
  --max-provisioned-memory 256
```

Key CLI Options

- `--format`: Choose from CSV, Parquet, RDF

- `--role-arn`: IAM role with appropriate permissions

- `--source`: Full path to the S3 bucket

- `--min-provisioned-memory` and `--max-provisioned-memory`: Graph capacity settings

IAM Role Requirements

To import data securely, Neptune Analytics uses IAM roles with specific permissions.

Required Permissions for S3 Import

```
{
  "Version": "2012-10-17",
  "Statement": [
    {
      "Effect": "Allow",
```

```
     "Action": ["s3:GetObject",
"s3:ListBucket"],
     "Resource": [
       "arn:aws:s3:::your-bucket-name",
       "arn:aws:s3:::your-bucket-name/*"
     ]
   },
   {
     "Effect": "Allow",
     "Action": "neptune-graph:*",
     "Resource": "*"
   }
  ]
}
```

> **Tip:** Always follow the principle of least privilege. Grant access only to the specific S3 buckets and Neptune graphs needed for the task.

Monitoring Import Progress

Once the graph creation process begins, Neptune Analytics runs an internal import task.

CLI: Check Import Task Status

```
aws neptune-graph get-graph --graph-
identifier <graph-id>
```

Look for status: AVAILABLE to confirm successful graph provisioning.

Console

In the Neptune console, each graph displays a status indicator. During import, it may show:

- **CREATING**: Graph is being provisioned.

- **IMPORTING**: Data is being loaded.

- **AVAILABLE**: Graph is ready for querying.

Error Handling and Troubleshooting

Common Issues

- **Access Denied (403)**: Ensure IAM role has the required permissions.

- **Data Format Errors**: Validate data structure matches format requirements.

- **S3 Path Issues**: Double-check S3 path ends in `/` and points to the correct folder.

Debugging Tips

- Use CloudWatch logs for detailed errors during import.

- Check AWS CLI return messages for stack traces.

- Use `describe-import-task` if using advanced SDK methods.

Example Use Cases

Use Case 1: Customer 360 from S3 CSVs

Your marketing team maintains customer profiles and transaction data in flat CSV files. Load this data into Neptune Analytics to run algorithms like:

- **PageRank** for customer influence

- **Closeness Centrality** to find central customers in purchase networks

Use Case 2: Security Analysis from Snapshot

Load a production snapshot of your Neptune database graph to Neptune Analytics and run:

- **Shortest Path** algorithms to trace breach vectors

- **Label Propagation** to detect network communities

Use Case 3: Knowledge Graph from RDF in S3

Academic or semantic data in RDF format can be ingested directly from S3 to support:

- Ontological analysis

- Entity linking using similarity algorithms

Best Practices

- **Pre-validate Data**: Use lightweight data profiling tools before import.

- **Use Parquet for Scale**: Prefer Parquet for large datasets due to compression and I/O benefits.

- **Tag Your Graphs**: Use AWS tags to manage costs and ownership.

- **Snapshot Frequently**: After a successful import, snapshot the graph for reuse.

- **Secure Your IAM Roles**: Rotate credentials and apply fine-grained policies.

Summary

Creating a Neptune Analytics graph from existing sources streamlines the setup of advanced graph analytics environments. Whether you're using files stored in Amazon S3, snapshots from Neptune, or live database clusters, Neptune Analytics empowers you to bring data closer to analysis.

By understanding the required IAM roles, data format expectations, and import workflows, you can confidently provision graphs at scale and drive insights using Neptune's powerful graph engine.

Key Takeaways

- Use **Amazon S3** for flexible, scalable imports with support for CSV, RDF, and Parquet.

- Load from **Neptune Snapshots** or **live Neptune Databases** for real-time or point-in-time data analysis.

- Assign IAM roles with the least privilege required to perform the import.

- Monitor progress via the AWS Console or CLI.

- Apply graph algorithms post-import to extract value from your data immediately.

Chapter 6: Connecting to a Graph

Introduction

Once you've created a Neptune Analytics graph—whether empty or preloaded with data—the next critical step is connecting to it. Neptune Analytics provides flexible and secure ways to connect depending on your application architecture, data sensitivity, and network topology. This chapter explores all available connection methods to a Neptune Analytics graph, including public and private endpoints, VPC configurations, AWS PrivateLink, cross-VPC and cross-account access, and SDK/CLI integration.

By the end of this chapter, you'll be equipped with the knowledge to establish reliable, secure, and performant connections to your Neptune Analytics graph, no matter where your applications live.

Types of Connectivity in Neptune Analytics

Neptune Analytics supports two primary types of connectivity:

- **Public Endpoint**
  Allows access over the internet or from any AWS resource with internet access.

- **Private Endpoint**
  Limits access to resources within a specified Amazon Virtual Private Cloud (VPC).

Each method comes with its own trade-offs between **security**, **performance**, and **accessibility**, so choosing the right option depends on your use case.

Connecting Using a Public Endpoint

A **public endpoint** enables you to connect to your Neptune Analytics graph from any location with internet access. This is ideal for:

- Quick starts and tutorials

- Low-sensitivity data exploration

- Testing or prototyping

Steps to Enable Public Connectivity

1. **During Graph Creation**
   When provisioning the graph in the AWS Console, select the **Allow from public** checkbox under the **Network and Security** section.

2. **After Graph Creation**
   You can update the graph configuration using the AWS CLI or SDKs to enable public connectivity.

Example: Enabling Public Access via AWS CLI

```
aws neptune-graph update-graph \
  --graph-identifier g-0123456789 \
  --public-connectivity
```

Security Considerations

Even when public connectivity is enabled:

- **All requests require AWS Signature Version 4 (SigV4)** for authentication.

- IAM roles and policies strictly control access.

- Best practices include whitelisting IPs via security groups and avoiding public endpoints for production use.

Connecting Using a Private Endpoint (VPC)

For higher security and compliance, Neptune Analytics supports private connectivity through VPCs.

When to Use

- Access from EC2, SageMaker, or Lambda within the same VPC

- Sensitive or regulated data

- Production systems with restricted access

How Private Endpoints Work

A **private graph endpoint** is provisioned within your VPC and is accessible only to resources in:

- The same **VPC**

- The same **subnets**

- With compatible **security groups**

Required IAM Permissions

To create a private graph endpoint, ensure the following permissions are included in your IAM policy:

- `ec2:CreateVpcEndpoint`

- `ec2:Describe*`

- `route53:AssociateVPCWithHostedZone`

CLI Example: Create a Private Endpoint

```
aws neptune-graph create-private-graph-
endpoint \
  --vpc-id vpc-1234abcd \
  --subnet-ids subnet-1111 subnet-2222
subnet-3333 \
  --vpc-security-group-ids sg-9876abcd \
  --graph-identifier g-0123456789 \
  --region us-east-1
```

DNS and Access

Private endpoints use internal DNS names like:

```
g-0123456789.us-east-1.neptune-
graph.amazonaws.com
```

Your application must reside in the same network and subnet space to resolve and connect to this DNS address.

AWS PrivateLink Integration

AWS PrivateLink provides secure, scalable access to Neptune Analytics services from other VPCs, accounts, or even on-premises environments.

Services Supported

- `neptune-graph`: Control plane (e.g., create, modify graphs)

- `neptune-graph-data`: Data plane (e.g., run queries)

Why Use PrivateLink?

- **Cross-VPC or cross-account access** to Neptune Analytics

- **Private connectivity** without exposing data to the public internet

- **Secure DNS routing** inside VPC

Creating an Interface Endpoint via CLI

```
aws ec2 create-vpc-endpoint \
  --vpc-id vpc-abc123 \
  --subnet-ids subnet-aaa subnet-bbb \
  --vpc-endpoint-type Interface \
  --service-name com.amazonaws.us-east-
1.neptune-graph-data \
  --security-group-ids sg-00001111
```

Enabling Private DNS

```
aws ec2 modify-vpc-endpoint \
  --vpc-endpoint-id vpce-abc123 \
  --private-dns-enabled
```

Ensure `enableDnsSupport` and `enableDnsHostnames` are set to `true` in your VPC configuration.

Connecting from the Same VPC

This is the **most straightforward** and **secure** setup.

Requirements

- Your resource (e.g., EC2, Lambda, SageMaker notebook) is in the **same VPC and subnet** as your graph.

- The **security group** allows inbound access on port 443 (HTTPS) or optionally 8182 (for openCypher).

Sample Use Case

Connecting from a Jupyter notebook hosted in a SageMaker instance located within the same VPC as the graph.

Troubleshooting Tip

If your VPC uses the CIDR block $172.17.0.0/16$, it may conflict with Docker internal routing and cause connectivity issues. Use the **Reachability Analyzer** to diagnose such issues.

Connecting from a Different VPC (or Account)

In more complex architectures, applications may reside in **separate VPCs or even AWS accounts**. This is common in microservice environments or multi-account setups.

Step-by-Step Setup

1. **Establish VPC Connectivity**

   o Use **VPC Peering**, **Transit Gateway**, or **VPN** to link networks.

   o Update security groups and network ACLs.

2. **Create Private Endpoint in VPC A**

   o Use `create-private-graph-endpoint` API.

3. **Configure DNS in VPC B Using Route 53**

   o Create a **private hosted zone** with the domain matching the graph endpoint.

   o Add **A-record** pointing to the endpoint DNS.

4. **Associate Hosted Zone with VPC B**

   o Ensure both VPCs have DNS hostnames and support enabled.

5. **IAM Cross-Account Role Setup (If Needed)**

   o Create an IAM role in Account A with access to the graph.

   o Allow Account B's role to assume it using `sts:AssumeRole`.

Accessing the Graph via Different Interfaces

Once connectivity is established, Neptune Analytics offers multiple interfaces for querying and managing the graph.

AWS CLI

```
aws neptune-graph execute-query \
  --graph-identifier g-0123456789 \
  --region us-east-1 \
  --query-string "MATCH (n) RETURN n LIMIT 5" \
  --language open_cypher \
  out.txt
```

Python (Boto3)

```
import boto3

client = boto3.client('neptune-graph',
region_name='us-east-1')

response = client.execute_query(
    graphIdentifier='g-0123456789',
    queryString='MATCH (n) RETURN n LIMIT 5',
    language='open_cypher'
)

print(response['payload'].read().decode('utf-8'))
```

Jupyter Notebooks with `%graph_notebook_host`

```
%graph_notebook_host https://g-0123456789.us-east-1.neptune-graph.amazonaws.com
```

```
%%oc
MATCH (n) RETURN n LIMIT 10
```

AWSCurl

For direct signed HTTP requests:

```
awscurl -X POST "https://g-0123456789.us-
east-1.neptune-graph.amazonaws.com/queries"
\
  -H "Content-Type: application/x-www-form-
urlencoded" \
  --region us-east-1 \
  --service neptune-graph \
  -d "query=MATCH (n) RETURN n LIMIT 1"
```

Best Practices for Secure and Stable Connections

- **Always sign your requests with SigV4** (automatically handled by AWS SDKs/CLI).

- **Avoid public endpoints for production systems.**

- **Use IAM roles and policies** for access control.

- **Enable Private DNS** when using PrivateLink.

- **Monitor traffic** using VPC flow logs or AWS CloudTrail.

Troubleshooting Connectivity

- Use the **Reachability Analyzer** to check network paths.

- Confirm **port 443** is open in your security group.

- Verify **IAM permissions** for the calling role or user.

- Ensure your application is in the **correct subnet and AZ**.

- If using Route 53 private zones, validate DNS resolution with tools like `dig` or `nslookup`.

Summary

Neptune Analytics offers flexible and secure connectivity options that fit a wide range of network topologies. Whether you're building data science notebooks in SageMaker, deploying microservices in containers, or running ML pipelines across accounts, there's a robust method to connect to your graph.

In this chapter, you learned:

- How to configure and connect using public or private endpoints

- How to work across VPCs and AWS accounts

- How to use AWS CLI, SDKs, and Jupyter to access Neptune Analytics

- Best practices and troubleshooting tips for network setup

Chapter 7: AWS PrivateLink

In this chapter, we explore **AWS PrivateLink** in the context of **Amazon Neptune Analytics**. PrivateLink provides secure, scalable, and private connectivity between your Virtual Private Cloud (VPC) and AWS services without exposing traffic to the public internet. When it comes to Neptune Analytics—where data privacy, performance, and control are crucial—PrivateLink plays a pivotal role in enabling **private access to Neptune's control and data plane APIs**.

We will cover:

- What AWS PrivateLink is and why it's important

- How Neptune Analytics uses AWS PrivateLink

- Types of interface endpoints for Neptune Analytics

- Setup instructions and considerations

- Use cases for PrivateLink with Neptune Analytics

- Best practices for implementing PrivateLink

What is AWS PrivateLink?

AWS PrivateLink is a networking service designed to keep traffic between your VPC and AWS services on the **Amazon internal network**. Rather than routing data over the internet, PrivateLink allows you to expose or consume services via **private IPs** within your VPC.

Key Benefits:

- **Enhanced Security**: Traffic never leaves the AWS network, reducing exposure to threats.

- **Simplified Network Architecture**: No need for NAT, VPN, or firewalls.

- **Private DNS Integration**: Enables seamless connectivity via DNS names that resolve to private IPs.

- **Support for VPC Peering and Direct Connect**: Extend access to on-prem or cross-region applications securely.

How Neptune Analytics Uses PrivateLink

Amazon Neptune Analytics supports AWS PrivateLink to expose two distinct services via **Interface VPC Endpoints (powered by Elastic Network Interfaces, or ENIs)**:

1. **Control Plane Service:** `neptune-graph`

   - Used for operations like creating, listing, or deleting Neptune Analytics graphs.

2. **Data Plane Service:** `neptune-graph-data`

   - Used for query execution and data retrieval operations.

These endpoints allow applications within your VPC (or connected environments) to interact with Neptune

Analytics **without relying on public connectivity**, creating a secure and isolated architecture.

Interface Endpoints in Neptune Analytics

AWS PrivateLink works through **interface VPC endpoints**, which are ENIs that provide entry points to supported services. In Neptune Analytics, two types of endpoints can be created:

Endpoint Type	Service Name	Used For	Supports VPC Endpoint Policies
Control Plane	neptune-graph	Graph creation, deletion, etc.	✘ No
Data Plane	neptune-graph-data	Query execution, data access	☑ Yes

Important Notes:

- You must create separate interface endpoints for control and data operations.

- **VPC endpoint policies** can be applied **only** to the data plane endpoints.

When to Use PrivateLink with Neptune Analytics

While Neptune Analytics graphs can be configured for **public or private connectivity**, enabling AWS PrivateLink provides a **controlled and highly secure environment**, which is essential for production workloads or regulatory requirements.

Use PrivateLink If:

- You want to **restrict internet access** to graph endpoints.

- Your application runs in **private subnets** with no NAT gateways.

- You're accessing Neptune Analytics from **on-premises via Direct Connect or VPN**.

- You require **fine-grained control** using endpoint policies (on the data plane).

- You plan to use **cross-VPC connectivity** for graph access.

Creating Private VPC Endpoints for Neptune Analytics

To use PrivateLink, you'll create **interface VPC endpoints** in your VPC. Below is a step-by-step walkthrough.

Step 1: Create Interface Endpoint via AWS CLI

For Control Plane:

```
aws ec2 create-vpc-endpoint \
  --vpc-id vpc-0123456789abcdef0 \
  --service-name com.amazonaws.us-east-
1.neptune-graph \
  --vpc-endpoint-type Interface \
  --subnet-ids subnet-abc123 subnet-def456
\
```

74

```
--security-group-ids sg-0123abcd
```

For Data Plane:

```
aws ec2 create-vpc-endpoint \
  --vpc-id vpc-0123456789abcdef0 \
  --service-name com.amazonaws.us-east-
1.neptune-graph-data \
  --vpc-endpoint-type Interface \
  --subnet-ids subnet-abc123 subnet-def456
\
  --security-group-ids sg-0123abcd
```

Step 2: Enable Private DNS (Recommended)

Enable private DNS to resolve the default Neptune Analytics endpoint names to your VPC endpoints:

```
aws ec2 modify-vpc-endpoint \
  --vpc-endpoint-id vpce-abc12345 \
  --private-dns-enabled
```

Step 3: Verify Connectivity

- Use dig, nslookup, or curl to confirm resolution to private IPs.

- You can now call the Neptune Analytics APIs using the same SDKs or CLI as before, and your traffic stays within the AWS network.

VPC Endpoint DNS Names

Each interface endpoint comes with **regional and zonal DNS names**:

- **Regional**:
  ```
  vpce-<id>.neptune-
  graph.<region>.vpce.amazonaws.com
  ```

- **Zonal**:
  ```
  vpce-<id>-<az>.neptune-
  graph.<region>.vpce.amazonaws.com
  ```

Use Case:

If you're building **zone-isolated architectures**, use zonal endpoints to ensure that requests stay within specific availability zones.

Example: Executing a Query via PrivateLink

Assuming you've set up a private endpoint for the data plane and enabled DNS, here's how to run a query:

```
aws neptune-graph execute-query \
  --graph-identifier g-0123456789 \
  --region us-east-1 \
  --query-string "MATCH (n) RETURN n LIMIT
1" \
  --language open_cypher \
  out.txt
```

This command will use the VPC endpoint automatically (if DNS is correctly resolved).

IAM and Endpoint Policies

While the control plane endpoint does **not support endpoint policies**, the **data plane does**.

Example Endpoint Policy (Data Plane):

Allow only GetGraphSummary for a specific graph:

```
{
  "Version": "2012-10-17",
  "Statement": [
    {
      "Sid": "AccessToSpecificGraphOnly",
      "Principal": "*",
      "Action": [
        "neptune-graph:GetGraphSummary"
      ],
      "Effect": "Allow",
      "Resource": [
        "arn:aws:neptune-graph:us-east-
1:123456789012:graph/g-0123456789"
      ]
    }
  ]
}
```

Cross-VPC and Cross-Account Access

Sometimes, you may need to access a Neptune Analytics graph from **another VPC** or even **another AWS account**. PrivateLink supports this, but it requires:

1. **VPC Peering or Transit Gateway** between the source and target VPCs.

2. **DNS routing** via **Amazon Route 53 Private Hosted Zones**.

3. **IAM cross-account roles** for authenticated access.

Example Workflow:

- VPC A has the Neptune Analytics graph and the private endpoint.

- VPC B wants to access that graph.

- You configure VPC peering and Route 53 to forward DNS to the graph endpoint.

- IAM Role B assumes IAM Role A via `sts:AssumeRole`.

Key Considerations and Limitations

Here are some critical aspects to keep in mind when using AWS PrivateLink with Neptune Analytics:

Consideration	Details
Control Plane Policy Support	✗ No support for endpoint policies
Data Plane Policy Support	☑ Supported
TLS Versions Supported	☑ TLS 1.2 only (TLS 1.1 and below not supported)
Private & Hybrid DNS	✗ Not supported out of the box
FIPS Endpoints	☑ Supported for control plane in specific regions (e.g., us-east-1)
IPv6	Not currently supported
Network Access	Only from within VPC or connected environments

Best Practices for Using PrivateLink

To get the most out of PrivateLink in Neptune Analytics:

- **Enable Private DNS**: Ensures applications don't need to change hardcoded URLs.

- **Use Endpoint Policies**: Restrict actions and resources at the endpoint level.

- **Monitor via CloudWatch**: Keep an eye on traffic, failures, and usage metrics.

- **Keep Control and Data Plane Separate**: Assign distinct security groups and rules.

- **Automate Setup with CloudFormation**: Use templates for consistent deployment across environments.

Use Case Spotlight: Private Analytics for Sensitive Graphs

Scenario: A healthcare analytics provider wants to analyze patient care graphs without any data leaving the VPC.

Solution:

- Set up Neptune Analytics with **private connectivity only**

- Create **PrivateLink endpoints** for both control and data plane

- Use **IAM policies** and **endpoint policies** to restrict graph access to authorized roles

- Set up SageMaker notebooks within the same VPC to run graph analytics securely

Summary

AWS PrivateLink is an essential feature for deploying Neptune Analytics in **secure, compliant, and enterprise-grade environments**. It allows you to:

- Privately access both control and data APIs of Neptune Analytics

- Integrate securely with other VPCs or on-prem environments

- Use IAM and endpoint policies to fine-tune access control

- Ensure that no traffic traverses the public internet

With proper setup, PrivateLink provides a robust foundation for running Neptune Analytics workloads in production—safely, scalably, and efficiently.

Chapter 8: Accessing the Graph

Once you've created a graph in Neptune Analytics, the next step is to access it—whether to run queries, load data, explore relationships, or perform analytics. This chapter walks through the various ways you can interact with a Neptune Analytics graph, from using SDKs and CLI tools to setting up secure network access. We'll also explore best practices, tips for configuring your environment, and example queries to get you started.

Understanding Graph Access in Neptune Analytics

Accessing a Neptune Analytics graph involves three key components:

1. **Graph Endpoint** – The network address used to send requests to your graph.

2. **Authentication** – Using AWS Identity and Access Management (IAM) for secure access.

3. **Client Interface** – The tool or SDK you use to connect (e.g., AWS CLI, Python SDK, Jupyter notebook).

Neptune Analytics supports **both public and private connectivity**, and all interactions must be **authenticated using IAM credentials**.

Types of Graph Endpoints

There are two main types of endpoints in Neptune Analytics:

- **Public Endpoint**: Accessible over the internet (if enabled during graph creation).

- **Private Endpoint**: Accessible only within the same Amazon Virtual Private Cloud (VPC).

When creating a Neptune Analytics graph, public connectivity is **disabled by default** for security reasons. However, you can enable or configure it during or after graph creation.

Authentication and IAM Integration

Neptune Analytics uses **AWS Signature Version 4 (SigV4)** to authenticate requests. This means all API requests must be signed using valid AWS credentials. You can authenticate using:

- AWS CLI with IAM credentials

- AWS SDKs with credential profiles

- AWSCurl (a curl-like tool for signed requests)

- SageMaker notebooks with IAM roles

- EC2 instances in a configured VPC

Tip: IAM Permissions

To access a Neptune Analytics graph, your IAM role or user must have permissions such as:

```
{
  "Effect": "Allow",
  "Action": "neptune-graph:ExecuteQuery",
  "Resource": "arn:aws:neptune-
graph:<region>:<account>:graph/<graph-id>"
}
```

Accessing the Graph from a Public Endpoint

If your Neptune Analytics graph was configured with
public connectivity enabled, you can access it from any
device or service with internet access and proper
credentials.

Benefits:

- Easy setup

- Useful for development and testing

- No need for additional network configuration

Example CLI Command
```
aws neptune-graph execute-query \
--graph-identifier g-0123456789 \
--region us-east-1 \
--query-string "MATCH (n) RETURN n LIMIT 1"
\
--language open_cypher out.txt
```

Python Example Using Boto3

```python
import boto3

client = boto3.client('neptune-graph')

response = client.execute_query(
    graphIdentifier='g-0123456789',
    queryString='MATCH (n) RETURN n LIMIT 1',
    language='OPEN_CYPHER'
)

print(response['payload'].read().decode('utf-8'))
```

Accessing the Graph from a Private Endpoint

Private connectivity ensures that your graph is **only accessible within a specific VPC**, increasing security for production workloads.

Accessing from Within the Same VPC

You can connect to the graph from:

- EC2 instances

- AWS Lambda functions

- SageMaker notebooks

Ensure that:

- The resource is in the same **VPC and subnet** as the graph's private endpoint.

- The **security group** allows inbound/outbound traffic on **port 443** (HTTPS).

- IAM permissions are correctly configured.

Accessing from a Different VPC (or Cross-Account)

To connect to a graph in **VPC A** from **VPC B**:

1. **Establish network connectivity** between VPCs (VPC peering or Transit Gateway).

2. **Use Route 53 Private Hosted Zones** to route DNS traffic to the private endpoint.

3. **Create IAM roles** to allow cross-account access if needed.

4. **Update DNS records** to route graph DNS to VPC endpoint DNS.

Using AWS PrivateLink

AWS PrivateLink enables **secure, private connectivity** between VPCs using **interface endpoints**.

Neptune Analytics supports two PrivateLink services:

- `neptune-graph`: Control plane (graph creation, deletion)

- `neptune-graph-data`: Data plane (query execution)

Example: Creating a VPC Endpoint for Data Plane

```
aws ec2 create-vpc-endpoint \
--region us-east-1 \
--service-name com.amazonaws.us-east-
1.neptune-graph-data \
--vpc-id vpc-0a1b2c3d4e \
--subnet-ids subnet-01234 \
--vpc-endpoint-type Interface \
--security-group-ids sg-0123456789abcdef
```

Be sure to **enable private DNS resolution** for the endpoint so it maps correctly to your graph's DNS.

Using Notebooks for Graph Access

Neptune Analytics integrates seamlessly with **graph-notebook**, a Jupyter-based toolkit that provides:

- Visual query results

- Graph visualization

- Magic commands to simplify operations

Supported Magic Commands

- `%%oc`: Run openCypher queries

- `%summary`: Get graph metadata

- `%load`: Load data into the graph

- `%status`: Monitor query status

- `%graph_notebook_host`: Set endpoint

Example Query
```
%%oc
MATCH (p:Person)-[:KNOWS]->(friend)
RETURN p.name, friend.name
```

Example Notebook Setup
```
export GRAPH_NOTEBOOK_HOST="g-
0123456789.us-east-1.neptune-
graph.amazonaws.com"
export GRAPH_NOTEBOOK_AUTH_MODE="IAM"
```

You can also launch a **SageMaker notebook** with built-in Neptune Analytics configuration using AWS CloudFormation.

Using SDKs to Access Neptune Analytics

Python (Boto3)

See earlier example. You can also customize timeouts:

```
from botocore.config import Config

client = boto3.client('neptune-graph',

config=Config(retries={"total_max_attempts"
: 1}, read_timeout=None))
```

JavaScript (Node.js)

```javascript
import { NeptuneGraphClient,
ExecuteQueryCommand } from "@aws-
sdk/client-neptune-graph";

const client = new NeptuneGraphClient({});
const command = new ExecuteQueryCommand({
    graphIdentifier: "g-0123456789",
    queryString: "MATCH (n) RETURN n LIMIT
1",
    language: "OPEN_CYPHER"
});

const result = await client.send(command);
console.log(await
result.payload.transformToString('utf-8'));
```

Java (SDK v2)

```java
NeptuneGraphClient client =
NeptuneGraphClient.builder()
    .region(Region.US_EAST_1)
    .build();

ExecuteQueryRequest request =
ExecuteQueryRequest.builder()
    .graphIdentifier("g-0123456789")
    .queryString("MATCH (n) RETURN n LIMIT
1")
    .language(QueryLanguage.OPEN_CYPHER)
    .build();
```

```
ExecuteQueryResponse response =
client.executeQuery(request);
System.out.println(response.payload().asUtf
8String());
```

Using AWSCurl to Access Neptune Graphs

AWSCurl is useful when you want to interact with Neptune Analytics directly over HTTP, especially for debugging.

Sample Command
```
awscurl -X POST "https://g-0123456789.us-
east-1.neptune-graph.amazonaws.com/queries"
\
-H "Content-Type: application/x-www-form-
urlencoded" \
--region us-east-1 \
--service neptune-graph \
-d "query=MATCH (n) RETURN n LIMIT 1"
```

AWSCurl automatically signs requests using your AWS credentials.

Best Practices for Secure and Reliable Access

1. **Always use IAM-authenticated access**

   o Avoid hardcoding credentials

   o Use roles with least privilege

2. **Enable logging**

o Use AWS CloudTrail to audit API calls

3. **Avoid timeouts**

    o For long-running queries, set timeouts to 0 or large values

4. **Close input streams in SDK clients**

    o Prevents memory leaks and client reuse issues

5. **Limit retries on large queries**

    o Set `MAX_ATTEMPTS=1` in CLI or SDK to prevent double execution

Python Boto3 Retry Settings

```
client = boto3.client('neptune-graph',

config=Config(retries={"total_max_attempts"
: 1}, read_timeout=None))
```

CLI Settings

```
export AWS_MAX_ATTEMPTS=1
aws neptune-graph execute-query \
--cli-read-timeout 0 \
--graph-identifier g-0123456789 \
--query-string "MATCH (n) RETURN n LIMIT 1"
\
--region us-east-1 \
--language open_cypher out.txt
```

Troubleshooting Access Issues

- **"Permission denied" errors?**

  - Check IAM policies and graph ARN syntax

- **Timeouts?**

  - Increase read timeout or verify connectivity

- **Unable to resolve endpoint?**

  - Check VPC DNS settings and PrivateLink configuration

- **Query failing intermittently?**

  - Ensure `MAX_ATTEMPTS=1` and verify query syntax

Use **Reachability Analyzer** and `GetPrivateGraphEndpoint` API to help debug private access paths.

Summary

Neptune Analytics offers multiple flexible methods to access and interact with your graph:

- Public or private endpoints

- AWS SDKs in nearly all major languages

- Jupyter notebooks with built-in graph magics

- CLI and AWSCurl for command-line access

By leveraging IAM security, PrivateLink networking, and the AWS SDK ecosystem, you can build scalable, secure, and powerful graph applications.

Chapter 9: Best Practices

When working with Amazon Neptune Analytics, following best practices ensures your graph workloads are performant, secure, scalable, and cost-effective. Whether you're designing your graph data model, writing openCypher queries, or managing vector search, small improvements can have a significant impact when operating at scale.

This chapter covers best practices across several domains of Neptune Analytics, including query optimization, data modeling, performance tuning, security, and general operations.

Why Best Practices Matter

Neptune Analytics is designed for high-throughput, in-memory graph processing. However, poor choices in data design or query structure can lead to inefficient memory usage, long-running queries, or even failed executions.

Key benefits of following best practices:

- **Reduced query latency**

- **Lower compute cost (m-NCUs)**

- **Improved graph traversal efficiency**

- **Simplified troubleshooting**

- **Better overall maintainability**

Query Optimization Best Practices

Writing efficient queries in openCypher is essential for Neptune Analytics performance.

Use the SET Clause to Remove or Update Multiple Properties

Instead of writing multiple lines to set or remove properties, use a single SET statement.

☑ **Recommended**:

```
MATCH (n:Person)
SET n.name = "Alice", n.age = 30
```

✕ **Avoid**:

```
MATCH (n:Person)
SET n.name = "Alice"
SET n.age = 30
```

Use Parameterized Queries

Avoid hardcoding values. Parameterized queries help with performance and are easier to cache and reuse.

☑ **Recommended**:

```
MATCH (p:Product) WHERE p.id = $productId
RETURN p
```

✕ Avoid:

```
MATCH (p:Product) WHERE p.id = "1234"
RETURN p
```

Use Flattened Maps Instead of Nested Maps in UNWIND

Nested maps in UNWIND are currently limited and error-prone.

☑ Use:

```
UNWIND [{id:1, name:"A"}, {id:2, name:"B"}]
AS row
CREATE (n:Node {id: row.id, name:
row.name})
```

✕ Avoid:

```
UNWIND [{person: {id:1, name:"A"}}] AS row
CREATE (n:Node {id: row.person.id, name:
row.person.name})
```

Optimize Variable-Length Path (VLP) Queries

Place the more **restrictive node patterns** on the **left side** of VLPs to reduce traversal size.

☑ Example:

```
MATCH (a:Start {id: $id})-[*1..5]->(b:End)
RETURN b
```

This ensures filtering is done before traversing.

Avoid Redundant Node Label Checks

If you're using highly specific relationship types, checking node labels might be unnecessary.

☑ **Use**:

```
MATCH (:Person)-[:EMPLOYED_BY]->(:Company)
```

✗ **Avoid**:

```
MATCH (p:Person)-[:EMPLOYED_BY]-
>(c:Company)
```

Unless you need to return or filter by properties on p or c, labels aren't needed.

Use Specific Edge Labels

Generalized relationship types (e.g., [:RELATED_TO]) make queries less efficient.

☑ **Define clear edge labels**:

- :FRIENDS_WITH

- :WORKS_AT

- :BOUGHT

This helps both humans and the query planner.

Avoid Using `WITH` When Unnecessary

The `WITH` clause breaks the query into multiple logical parts, which may affect optimization.

Use it only when:

- You need aggregation

- You're limiting result scope

- You want to rename or filter fields

Apply Filters Early

Move restrictive `WHERE` clauses as early in the query as possible to minimize intermediate results.

☑ **Recommended**:

```
MATCH (p:Person) WHERE p.age > 30
RETURN p.name
```

✖ **Avoid**:

```
MATCH (p:Person)
RETURN p.name
WHERE p.age > 30
```

Explicitly Check for Property Existence

Use `exists()` to ensure a property exists before accessing it.

```
MATCH (n)
WHERE exists(n.email)
RETURN n.email
```

This prevents null access errors and improves predictability.

Avoid Named Paths Unless Needed

While named paths (`p = (a)-[:REL]->(b)`) are useful, they increase memory use.

Use only when:

- You're returning or analyzing the full path

- You're passing the path into an algorithm

Graph Data Modeling Best Practices

The way you design your graph model significantly affects performance.

Prefer Custom IDs Over Auto-Generated IDs

Use a property like `id`, `userId`, or `productId` to uniquely identify nodes.

Avoid querying based on Neptune's internal `~id` unless necessary.

Avoid Computations on `~id`

Avoid expressions like:

```
MATCH (n) WHERE n.`~id` = "123"
```

Instead, design your graph so each node has a queryable ID property.

Use Labels Wisely

Overusing labels can increase memory footprint. Choose one or two meaningful labels per node.

☑ `(:Customer)` ☑ `(:Transaction:Online)`

✕ `(:A:B:C:D:E)`

Normalize Graph Structure for Large Datasets

For extremely large graphs:

- Split dense nodes (e.g., use intermediate nodes for many-to-many)

- Use lightweight edge properties

- Avoid deep chains unless necessary

Data Ingestion and Loading

Neptune supports three ways to load data:

- **Bulk import**

- **Batch load**

- **openCypher queries**

Tips for Efficient Data Loading

- Use **bulk import** for large initial datasets (e.g., >10GB).

- Use **batch load** for incremental updates.

- Avoid **reloading the same edge file** twice — it can cause duplicates.

- Validate data format (CSV, Parquet, RDF) before import.

Vector Search Best Practices

If your graph uses vector similarity (e.g., for recommendations), follow these guidelines.

Define Proper Vector Dimensions

Your vector embeddings should have a consistent, known dimension (e.g., 384, 768).

```
"vector-search": {
  "dimension": 384
}
```

Use `vectors.upsert()` Efficiently

- Upsert in **batches**

- Avoid overly large float arrays in a single request

- Validate embeddings before upserting

Optimize `topKByEmbedding` Calls

- Use meaningful filters (`WHERE` clauses) to narrow the search space

- Only retrieve required fields

Monitor Vector Load Errors

Use the loading logs or API response details to debug dimension mismatches, format errors, or invalid embeddings.

Performance Tuning

Neptune Analytics offers fine-grained memory and compute scaling.

Provision Only What You Need

- Start with **128 m-NCUs** for small to medium datasets

- Increase memory if queries timeout or fail

- Monitor usage via **CloudWatch metrics**

Optimize Query Timeouts and Retries

For long-running queries:

- Set SDK/CLI timeouts to a larger value or 0 (no timeout)

- Limit retries to **1** for non-idempotent queries

Python Example:

```python
from botocore.config import Config
boto3.client('neptune-graph',
config=Config(read_timeout=None,
retries={"total_max_attempts": 1}))
```

CLI Example:

```bash
export AWS_MAX_ATTEMPTS=1
aws neptune-graph execute-query \
  --cli-read-timeout 0 \
  --query-string "MATCH (n) RETURN n LIMIT
1"
```

Stream Management

Ensure you **consume and close streams** after reading query responses to allow connection reuse.

Notebook and Visualization Best Practices

When using graph notebooks:

- Use %summary and %%opencypher for interactive exploration.

- Visualize limited results (e.g., LIMIT 50) to avoid browser overload.

- Use %graph_notebook_config to verify your endpoint and service name.

◎ **Pro Tip**: Customize visualization using
`%%graph_notebook_vis_options`.

Security and Access Best Practices

Use IAM Roles and Policies

- Grant only the permissions required (`neptune-graph:*`, `s3:GetObject`, etc.)

- Avoid broad `*` actions in production

- Enable CloudTrail for audit logging

Secure Private Endpoints

- Use **security groups** to restrict access to ports 443/8182

- Use **AWS PrivateLink** and **VPC endpoint policies** to restrict graph access

- For cross-account access, use IAM role assumption

Encrypt Your Graph

- Use a **customer-managed KMS key** for data at rest encryption

- Enable encryption during graph creation

Monitoring and Maintenance

Neptune Analytics provides monitoring hooks and event tracking.

Use CloudWatch Metrics

Track:

- Query counts and latency

- Memory utilization

- Error counts

Track Control and Data Plane Events

Use **AWS CloudTrail** to log:

- `CreateGraph`

- `ExecuteQuery`

- `GetGraphSummary`

- and more

Implement Alerting

Set CloudWatch alarms for:

- High memory usage

- High query latency

- Failed query counts

Cost Management Tips

- Decrease memory size or replicas during off-peak periods

- Delete unused graphs (disable deletion protection first)

- Use **tagging** to track cost allocation per project or environment

Summary

By adopting best practices across graph modeling, query writing, performance optimization, and operational security, you'll be well-positioned to get the most value out of Neptune Analytics. While Neptune Analytics handles much of the infrastructure, it's your attention to detail in graph design and query structure that determines the effectiveness of your analytics workflow.

Using Notebooks

Chapter 10: Sample Notebooks

Amazon Neptune Analytics provides a powerful, scalable environment for performing graph-based analytics. But getting started with graph data science can feel daunting, especially when working with new query languages like openCypher or integrating graph-specific algorithms. That's where **sample notebooks** come in.

This chapter is your comprehensive guide to the sample notebooks provided for Neptune Analytics. These ready-to-use, interactive environments showcase real-world scenarios, help you learn syntax and best practices, and let you immediately test and visualize graph queries and algorithms.

Why Use Sample Notebooks?

Sample notebooks offer significant value for both newcomers and experienced developers:

- **Hands-on learning**: Explore and experiment with queries, algorithms, and visualization in a live environment.

- **Best practices**: Learn idiomatic openCypher patterns and optimal ways to load or query data.

- **Algorithm demos**: See how graph algorithms like PageRank or community detection are applied in realistic use cases.

- **Quick-start data**: Built-in sample datasets remove the friction of sourcing and formatting data.

- **Visualization tools**: See your graph data rendered visually to make patterns and relationships clearer.

Getting Started with Neptune Analytics Notebooks

To use the sample notebooks, you first need a **notebook environment** configured to communicate with your Neptune Analytics graph. There are two main deployment paths:

- **Using SageMaker with a Neptune-provided CloudFormation template**

- **Running locally with Jupyter and the Neptune graph-notebook package**

Each setup automatically integrates with Neptune Analytics APIs and provides magic commands that simplify authentication and querying.

The Graph Notebook Project

All Neptune sample notebooks are part of the open-source AWS Graph Notebook project. This toolkit enhances the Jupyter experience for working with Amazon Neptune by adding:

- Magic commands for openCypher and Gremlin

- Visualization utilities for graph queries

- Preloaded examples and datasets

Note: For Neptune Analytics, only a subset of magic commands is currently supported. These are specifically designed to work with the new Neptune Analytics data plane.

Supported Magic Commands for Neptune Analytics

Here are the Jupyter magic commands compatible with Neptune Analytics graphs:

- `%%oc` or `%%opencypher` — Run an openCypher query

- `%load` — Load data into the graph using the `neptune-load()` integration

- `%seed` — Insert sample data into your graph

- `%summary` — Retrieve high-level graph summary

- `%status` or `%get_graph` — Get the status of the connected graph

- `%graph_notebook_config` — Display the current notebook configuration

- `%graph_notebook_host` — Set the graph endpoint

- `%graph_notebook_service` — Set the Neptune service type (must be `neptune-graph`)

- `%oc_status` — Get query status or cancel queries

- `%%graph_notebook_vis_options` — Customize graph visualization settings

- `%graph_reset` — Clear all data from the current graph

Sample Notebook Categories

The Neptune graph-notebook repository includes various categories of notebooks, many of which are compatible with Neptune Analytics. Here's an overview of some key types:

1. Getting Started

These notebooks help you connect to your Neptune Analytics graph and run your first openCypher queries.

Example contents:

- How to set up `%graph_notebook_host` and `%graph_notebook_service`

- Basic `MATCH`, `RETURN`, and `WHERE` queries

- Visualizing simple graphs

2. Loading Data

Learn how to load graph data using `%load` and `%seed`. These notebooks cover:

- Batch loading small datasets via Cypher

- Loading from S3 using IAM roles

- Example graphs (e.g., social networks or citation networks)

3. Query Patterns

These notebooks focus on Cypher syntax and query composition:

- Filtering with `WHERE`

- Using `UNWIND` and `WITH`

- Aggregation and grouping

- Optional patterns and variable-length paths

4. Graph Algorithms

Some of the most powerful samples demonstrate Neptune Analytics' built-in graph algorithms:

- **PageRank**

- **Closeness Centrality**

- **Jaccard Similarity**

- **Weakly Connected Components (WCC)**

- **Label Propagation**

These notebooks often include:

- A small dataset loaded with `%seed`

- Calls to algorithm procedures (e.g., `.pageRank.mutate`)

- Querying and visualizing the results

5. Use-Case Driven

These are specialized notebooks tailored for real-world applications:

- **Cybersecurity graphs**: Track threats or breaches across a network

- **Recommendation engines**: Use similarity and neighborhood analysis

- **Fraud detection**: Detect suspicious behavior through graph topology

- **Knowledge graphs**: Model entities and relationships for search or inference

---

Example: First Notebook Walkthrough

Let's walk through a simplified example of what a beginner-friendly sample notebook might include.

Step 1: Configure the Notebook

```
%graph_notebook_host g-1234567890.us-east-1.neptune-graph.amazonaws.com
%graph_notebook_service neptune-graph
%graph_notebook_config
```

Step 2: Load Sample Data

```
%seed
```

This loads a toy dataset, such as a mini social network of people who "KNOW" each other.

Step 3: Query the Graph

```
%%oc
MATCH (p:Person)-[:KNOWS]->(friend)
RETURN p.name AS person, friend.name AS
friend
```

Step 4: Visualize the Output

Use the visual graph output to see how people are connected, identify hubs, and intuitively spot relationships.

Installing the Notebooks

You can access sample notebooks in one of two primary ways:

Option 1: Use a SageMaker Notebook Instance

Neptune provides AWS CloudFormation templates that spin up SageMaker notebooks pre-installed with the graph-notebook environment. This is the easiest way to get started with zero setup.

Steps:

1. Launch the Neptune Analytics SageMaker Notebook Stack

2. Specify your Neptune Analytics graph endpoint and VPC info

3. Wait for the stack to deploy (~5 minutes)

4. Open the SageMaker notebook and explore the `/notebooks/Neptune/02-Neptune-Analytics/` directory

Option 2: Run Locally on Jupyter

To run the notebooks locally:

1. Install prerequisites (Python, Jupyter, virtualenv)

Clone the graph-notebook repo

```
git clone https://github.com/aws/graph-notebook.git
cd graph-notebook
pip install -r requirements.txt
```

2.

Install the graph-notebook extensions

```
python3 -m graph_notebook.install --quiet
```

3.

Launch Jupyter

4.

> **Tip:** If your Neptune Analytics graph uses a private VPC, set up a secure tunnel or use a proxy EC2 instance in the same VPC.

Best Practices When Using Notebooks

- **Use IAM roles securely**: Notebooks inherit credentials from the environment, so make sure roles have least-privilege access.

- **Avoid excessive mutations**: For large graphs, avoid running `.mutate` procedures repeatedly in exploration phases.

- **Use `%graph_reset` sparingly**: This clears your graph! Use it when starting fresh, but with caution.

- **Watch for limits**: While notebooks are great for interactive work, long-running or memory-intensive tasks should be batched using APIs or jobs.

- **Use `%summary` often**: Get a snapshot of your graph's size, properties, and labels—it's a handy health check.

Tips for Customizing Sample Notebooks

Want to tweak the sample notebooks for your own data? Here's how:

- **Replace the** %%oc **queries** with your own openCypher queries based on your domain model.

- **Edit** %seed **cells** to use your sample nodes and edges.

- **Visualize subsets of your graph** by filtering on labels or properties (e.g., only show nodes with score > 0.5).

- **Integrate vector search queries** to combine graph traversal with embedding similarity.

What Makes a Good Notebook?

The best notebooks follow a clear structure:

1. **Setup**: Import libraries, set graph host and service.

2. **Data loading**: Seed or import a dataset.

3. **Exploration**: Run some exploratory queries and visualizations.

4. **Analysis**: Apply algorithms or scoring functions.

5. **Interpretation**: Visualize results and discuss patterns.

6. **Cleanup**: Optionally clear the graph or export results.

Summary

Sample notebooks are an essential tool in your Neptune Analytics toolkit. Whether you're testing a new algorithm, learning openCypher, or showcasing a graph to stakeholders, these notebooks make your graph analytics journey smoother and more interactive.

They offer:

- A fast path to hands-on learning

- Practical use-case demonstrations

- Ready-to-run environments with minimal setup

By working through the provided examples and customizing them to your own data, you'll unlock the full potential of Neptune Analytics and accelerate insight discovery from your graph data.

Chapter 11: Create a Notebook with CloudFormation

Introduction

Amazon Neptune Analytics integrates seamlessly with Amazon SageMaker notebooks, giving you a powerful, fully managed environment to explore and visualize graph data. While you can create notebooks manually via the AWS Management Console, using **AWS CloudFormation** to create a notebook brings significant advantages:

- **Infrastructure as Code (IaC)**: Version, repeat, and automate notebook creation.

- **Consistency**: Reuse templates across teams and environments.

- **Speed**: Provision pre-configured environments in minutes.

In this chapter, we'll walk through the process of creating a Neptune Analytics notebook using AWS CloudFormation. You'll learn how to set up the CloudFormation template, configure network and IAM settings, and launch the notebook. We'll also explore best practices for deploying notebooks securely and efficiently.

What is AWS CloudFormation?

AWS CloudFormation is an IaC (Infrastructure as Code) service that lets you **define AWS infrastructure using JSON or YAML templates**. These templates describe the resources you want to provision—such as VPCs, IAM roles, Neptune graphs, and SageMaker notebooks—and

CloudFormation automates the creation and configuration of those resources.

By defining your Neptune Analytics notebook as a CloudFormation stack, you can:

- Automate complex deployments

- Use the same setup across development, staging, and production

- Ensure configuration accuracy

Overview of the Neptune Analytics Notebook Architecture

A Neptune Analytics notebook created with CloudFormation includes several components:

1. **Amazon SageMaker Notebook Instance**
   The compute environment that hosts the Jupyter-based notebook.

2. **IAM Role with Custom Policies**
   Grants the notebook permission to access:

   - Neptune Analytics API operations

   - Amazon S3 (for sample data or loading scripts)

   - Amazon CloudWatch (for logging)

3. **Notebook Lifecycle Configuration (optional)**
   Bootstrap script to install the **Neptune Graph Notebook extension** and auto-configure the

environment.

4. **Networking Settings**
   If you're using a **private Neptune Analytics endpoint**, the notebook must be provisioned in the same VPC and subnet as the graph.

Step-by-Step: Creating the Notebook with CloudFormation

You can launch a Neptune Analytics notebook using either:

- An **official AWS-provided CloudFormation template**

- A **custom template** tailored to your environment

Let's start with the AWS-managed approach.

Using AWS-Provided CloudFormation Templates

AWS provides prebuilt CloudFormation templates for Neptune Analytics notebooks. These templates automatically:

- Create a SageMaker notebook

- Assign the necessary IAM role and permissions

- Configure notebook lifecycle scripts

- Set up VPC/subnet integration if needed

Supported Regions (as of 2025)

- US East (N. Virginia)

- US East (Ohio)

- US West (Oregon)

- Europe (Ireland)

- Europe (Frankfurt)

- Asia Pacific (Singapore, Tokyo)

Quick Launch Links

Each region has a direct **Launch Stack** link. For example:

```
https://console.aws.amazon.com/cloudformati
on/home?region=us-east-
1#/stacks/new?stackName=NeptuneQuickStart&t
emplateURL=https://aws-neptune-customer-
samples.s3.amazonaws.com/v2/cloudformation-
templates/neptune-analytics-sagemaker-
notebook-stack.json
```

Steps

1. **Open the Template Link in the CloudFormation Console**
   Use one of the links above for your region.

2. **Specify Stack Name**
   Example: `NeptuneNotebookStack`

3. **Enter Parameters**

- ○ **GraphEndpoint**: Your Neptune Analytics graph endpoint URL

- ○ **NotebookName**: Unique name for your SageMaker notebook

- ○ **GraphVPC (Optional)**: VPC ID for private endpoint usage

- ○ **GraphSubnetId (Optional)**: Subnet ID for private endpoint

- ○ **GraphSecurityGroup (Optional)**: SG ID associated with Neptune Analytics endpoint

4. **Review and Launch**
   Confirm permissions, then click **Create Stack**.

5. **Wait for Stack Creation**
   It typically takes 5–10 minutes. When complete, the notebook appears in the SageMaker console.

Creating a Custom CloudFormation Template

If you need more control over the notebook environment or want to automate deployment as part of a CI/CD pipeline, you can write your own CloudFormation YAML template.

Basic Template Example

```
AWSTemplateFormatVersion: 2010-09-09
Description: Neptune Analytics Notebook
Stack

Resources:
  NotebookRole:
```

```yaml
    Type: AWS::IAM::Role
    Properties:
      AssumeRolePolicyDocument:
        Version: "2012-10-17"
        Statement:
          - Effect: Allow
            Principal:
              Service:
sagemaker.amazonaws.com
            Action: sts:AssumeRole
      Policies:
        - PolicyName: NeptuneNotebookPolicy
          PolicyDocument:
            Version: "2012-10-17"
            Statement:
              - Effect: Allow
                Action:
                  - s3:GetObject
                  - s3:ListBucket
                Resource: "*"
              - Effect: Allow
                Action: "neptune-graph:*"
                Resource: "*"
              - Effect: Allow
                Action:
                  - logs:CreateLogGroup
                  - logs:CreateLogStream
                  - logs:PutLogEvents
                Resource: "*"

  NeptuneNotebook:
    Type: AWS::SageMaker::NotebookInstance
    Properties:
```

```yaml
      NotebookInstanceName: "neptune-
analytics-notebook"
      InstanceType: ml.t3.medium
      RoleArn: !GetAtt NotebookRole.Arn
      PlatformIdentifier: "notebook-al2-v1"
      LifecycleConfigName: !Ref
NotebookLifecycleConfig

  NotebookLifecycleConfig:
    Type:
AWS::SageMaker::NotebookInstanceLifecycleCo
nfig
    Properties:
      NotebookInstanceLifecycleConfigName:
"NeptuneLifecycle"
      OnStart:
        - Content:
            Fn::Base64: !Sub |
              #!/bin/bash
              sudo -u ec2-user -i <<'EOF'
              echo "export
GRAPH_NOTEBOOK_AUTH_MODE=IAM" >> ~/.bashrc
              echo "export
GRAPH_NOTEBOOK_SERVICE=neptune-graph" >>
~/.bashrc
              echo "export
GRAPH_NOTEBOOK_HOST=${GraphEndpoint}" >>
~/.bashrc
              echo "export
GRAPH_NOTEBOOK_PORT=8182" >> ~/.bashrc
              echo "export
AWS_REGION=${AWS::Region}" >> ~/.bashrc
```

```
                aws s3 cp s3://aws-neptune-
notebook-
${AWS::Region}/graph_notebook.tar.gz /tmp/
                tar -xvzf
/tmp/graph_notebook.tar.gz -C /tmp/

/tmp/graph_notebook/install.sh
                EOF
```

Parameters You Might Add

```
Parameters:
  GraphEndpoint:
    Type: String
    Description: The public or private
endpoint of your Neptune Analytics graph
```

Lifecycle Configuration Script Breakdown

The lifecycle configuration:

- **Sets environment variables** like
  GRAPH_NOTEBOOK_HOST and
  GRAPH_NOTEBOOK_SERVICE

- **Downloads Neptune Graph Notebook extension**
  from S3

- **Runs an install script** to enable visualization,
  magics, and OpenCypher support

This makes your notebook ready to run `%oc` queries and
visualize graph data right away.

After the Stack is Created

1. Go to the SageMaker Console

2. Find your notebook instance (e.g., `neptune-analytics-notebook`)

3. Wait for the status to change to **Ready**

4. Click **Open JupyterLab** or **Open Jupyter** to launch

You should see:

- A pre-installed Neptune notebook extension

- Sample notebooks (if you installed them)

- A working environment to run `%oc` (OpenCypher) queries

Security Best Practices

- **Restrict IAM role permissions**: Grant access only to required graphs and S3 buckets.

- **Encrypt notebooks**: Use KMS keys for notebook encryption.

- **Enable logging**: Capture logs to CloudWatch for monitoring and auditing.

- **Use VPC-bound notebooks**: Especially for production environments using private graph endpoints.

Example Use Case: Data Scientist Workspace

A data scientist needs to analyze customer behavior using Neptune Analytics. Using CloudFormation:

- Their team provisions a notebook with read-only access to customer graph data.

- The notebook is configured to connect to a **private endpoint** within a secure VPC.

- A custom CloudFormation parameter sets the target graph endpoint.

- The lifecycle config installs graph-notebook tools automatically.

This setup eliminates manual provisioning, ensures consistency, and aligns with security policies.

Troubleshooting Deployment Issues

- **Notebook stuck in Pending**: Check IAM role permissions and lifecycle script errors.

- **Lifecycle script fails**: Open logs in `/var/log` inside the notebook or use CloudWatch.

- **Graph not reachable**: Verify VPC/subnet alignment and security group rules.

- **Missing extensions**: Confirm the `graph_notebook.tar.gz` download from S3 was successful.

Summary

Using AWS CloudFormation to create Neptune Analytics notebooks offers automation, repeatability, and consistency. Whether using an AWS-provided stack or building your own, you can rapidly provision environments that are ready to query, visualize, and analyze graph data.

In this chapter, we explored:

- The benefits of using CloudFormation for Neptune notebooks

- How to use AWS-provided templates

- How to write your own custom template

- How to handle VPC, IAM, and lifecycle setup

Chapter 12: Local Hosting

In this chapter, we'll explore how to set up and run **Amazon Neptune Analytics graph notebooks** on your **local machine**. While AWS provides managed environments like **SageMaker AI notebooks**, local hosting is ideal for:

- Developers who prefer working offline or outside AWS-managed tools

- Custom integrations in enterprise dev environments

- Education, training, or evaluation without incurring AWS costs

- Fine-grained control over notebook dependencies and tooling

We'll walk through the complete setup process, necessary tools, configurations, and best practices for connecting your local notebook to a Neptune Analytics graph— whether it uses **public** or **private connectivity**.

Why Host Locally?

There are several benefits to running your Neptune graph notebooks locally:

- **Cost Efficiency**: Avoid SageMaker charges for hosted notebooks

- **Flexibility**: Use your own Jupyter environment, plugins, and packages

- **Offline Development**: Build and test logic without requiring AWS runtime environments

- **CI/CD Integration**: Automate testing of queries and algorithms in development pipelines

- **Advanced Customization**: Modify notebooks, magic commands, or client logic

Tip: You can connect to both **public** and **private** Neptune Analytics endpoints from a local notebook. However, private endpoints require more setup.

Prerequisites

Before hosting a Neptune Analytics notebook locally, ensure the following are installed and configured:

Required Software:

- Python 3.8 or higher

- Jupyter Notebook or JupyterLab

- Git

- pip

Required Python Packages:

- graph-notebook

- boto3

- requests

- awscli

- ipywidgets

- matplotlib (optional for graph visualizations)

Optional but Recommended:

- Docker (for isolated environments)

- Virtualenv (to manage dependencies)

Installing the Graph Notebook Locally

Amazon provides a ready-to-install open-source project for Neptune-compatible Jupyter notebooks.

Step 1: Clone the Repository

```
git clone https://github.com/aws/graph-notebook.git
cd graph-notebook
```

Step 2: Set Up a Python Virtual Environment (Optional but Recommended)

```
python3 -m venv venv
source venv/bin/activate
```

Step 3: Install the Package

```
pip install .
```

This installs the notebook extensions, magic commands, and dependencies required to work with Neptune Analytics.

Step 4: Start the Notebook Server

```
jupyter notebook
```

or for JupyterLab:

```
jupyter lab
```

Connecting to Neptune Analytics

Once the notebook environment is up, you need to configure it to connect to your Neptune Analytics graph.

Use the `%%graph_notebook_config` **Magic**

Run the following in a new Jupyter cell:

```
%%graph_notebook_config

{
  "host": "g-0123456789.us-east-1.neptune-graph.amazonaws.com",
  "port": 8182,
  "auth_mode": "IAM",
  "load_from_s3_role_arn": "",
  "aws_region": "us-east-1",
  "neptune_service": "neptune-graph",
  "ssl": true
}
```

Field Descriptions:

- `host`: The endpoint of your Neptune Analytics graph

- `auth_mode`: Should always be `"IAM"` for Neptune Analytics

- `neptune_service`: Must be set to `"neptune-graph"`

- `port`: Usually 8182 for Neptune Analytics

- `ssl`: Should be `true` (required for HTTPS)

- `aws_region`: Region where your Neptune Analytics graph is hosted

  ⓘ Make sure your AWS CLI is authenticated with an IAM user or role that has access to Neptune Analytics APIs.

Connecting to a Public Graph Endpoint

This is the simplest setup. If your graph was provisioned with **public connectivity enabled**, you can access it directly using the DNS endpoint (e.g., `g-xxxxxx.us-east-1.neptune-graph.amazonaws.com`).

Key Points:

- No extra networking configuration needed

- Must still sign requests using AWS Signature Version 4 (handled by `graph-notebook` magics)

- AWS credentials must be available via `~/.aws/credentials`, environment variables, or an IAM role assumed via `aws sts assume-role`

Sample Query:

```
%%oc
MATCH (n) RETURN n LIMIT 5
```

Connecting to a Private Graph Endpoint

If your Neptune Analytics graph uses **private connectivity only**, you'll need a workaround to route local traffic into your VPC. There are two main approaches:

Option 1: SSH Tunnel via Bastion Host or EC2 Proxy

1. **Launch a Bastion EC2 Instance** in the same VPC/subnet as the private graph endpoint.

2. Set up an **SSH tunnel** from your local machine to the EC2 instance:

```
ssh -i my-key.pem -N -L 8182:g-xxxxxxx.us-
east-1.neptune-graph.amazonaws.com:8182
ec2-user@<ec2-public-ip>
```

This tunnels your local port 8182 to the graph endpoint securely.

3. Modify your notebook config:

```
%%graph_notebook_config

{
  "host": "localhost",
  "port": 8182,
  "auth_mode": "IAM",
  "aws_region": "us-east-1",
  "neptune_service": "neptune-graph",
  "ssl": true
}
```

Option 2: AWS Client VPN or Direct Connect

If your company or organization uses AWS **Client VPN**, **Site-to-Site VPN**, or **Direct Connect**, you can connect to the VPC hosting Neptune Analytics without using a bastion host. Once connected, your private endpoint will resolve internally via DNS.

> 🧠 Be sure to set `enableDnsSupport` and `enableDnsHostnames` to `true` in your VPC to ensure proper resolution of Neptune DNS names.

Running Queries from Local Notebook

Once the notebook is connected, you can use magic commands to run queries:

```
%%oc
MATCH (p:Person)-[:KNOWS]->(f:Person)
RETURN p.name, f.name
```

Or run status checks:

```
%get_graph
```

You can even reset your graph during testing:

```
%graph_reset
```

Loading Data Locally

You can load sample data from CSV or write `openCypher` queries manually. For small datasets, using the `%load` magic is ideal:

```
%load --label Movie --input-file movies.csv
--format csv
```

Alternatively, insert nodes directly:

```
%%oc
CREATE (:Movie {title: "Inception", year:
2010})
```

> ⚠ Loading large data volumes should still be done through S3 batch/bulk loading via the API.

Troubleshooting Tips

Issue	Solution
Graph not reachable	Check networking, VPC routing, SSH tunnel, security groups
"Access Denied" error	Validate IAM permissions and signature configuration
%%oc not recognized	Ensure graph-notebook is installed and kernel restarted
DNS resolution failure	If using private endpoint, use Route 53 private hosted zone or SSH tunnel
Missing AWS credentials	Configure via aws configure or environment variables

Best Practices

- Use **virtual environments** to isolate dependencies

- For frequent access to private graphs, consider **VPN** over SSH tunneling

- Store multiple graph configurations in JSON files for quick switching

- Keep your **graph-notebook** project up to date (git pull && pip install .)

- Use %%graph_notebook_vis_options to customize how returned data is visualized

Summary

Local hosting of Neptune Analytics notebooks is an excellent option for developers who need flexibility, control, and local testing capabilities. Whether you're accessing graphs over public endpoints or securely tunneling into a private VPC, the setup is straightforward with the right tools.

By installing the `graph-notebook` package and configuring your environment properly, you can enjoy the full power of Neptune Analytics—locally.

Create and Load Graph Data

Chapter 13: Create a Graph

Creating a graph is the foundational step in using Neptune Analytics. Whether you're setting up a fresh analytics environment, migrating data from an existing Neptune database, or importing from Amazon S3, Neptune Analytics offers a flexible and efficient path to get your graph up and running.

In this chapter, we'll walk through the various methods you can use to create a graph, explain the available configuration options, and provide step-by-step instructions using the AWS Management Console, AWS CLI, and AWS CloudFormation. You'll also learn about key concepts like public vs. private connectivity, vector search settings, and best practices for provisioning.

Understanding the Neptune Analytics Graph

A **Neptune Analytics graph** is a managed, memory-optimized, in-memory representation of graph data. When you create a graph, Neptune automatically provisions compute and memory based on the graph size and your configuration.

Each graph has:

- A **unique identifier**

- A set amount of **memory (measured in Neptune Capacity Units - m-NCUs)**

- **Optional replica(s)** for high availability

- **Vector indexing** settings (if needed)

- **Connectivity options** (public or private)

There are two primary ways to create a Neptune Analytics graph:

1. **Create an empty graph** and load data later

2. **Create a graph with data** loaded during creation (from Amazon S3, a Neptune cluster, or a snapshot)

Graph Creation Options

Option	Description
Empty graph	Starts with no data. Ideal for dynamic loading or building from scratch.
Graph from source	Loads data during creation from S3, Neptune DB, or snapshot. Best for large imports.
Public endpoint	Accessible over the internet (if enabled).
Private endpoint	Accessible only within a designated VPC.
Vector indexing	Enables vector search. Requires specifying vector dimension at graph creation.

Creating an Empty Graph via AWS Console

Let's begin with the most visual and user-friendly method.

Step-by-Step: AWS Management Console

1. **Sign in** to the AWS Management Console

2. In the **left navigation panel**, click **"Graphs"** under the *Analytics* section

3. Click **"Create graph"**

4. Enter a **graph name** (must be unique within your AWS account and region)

5. Under **Data source**, select **"Empty graph"**

6. Choose the **provisioned memory** (m-NCUs)

   ○ Each m-NCU provides ~1 GiB of memory and associated compute

   ○ Range: 128–4096 m-NCUs

7. Select **replica count** (optional)

   ○ Each replica incurs additional charges

8. Choose **connectivity options**:

   ○ **Public**: enables access over the internet

   ○ **Private**: limits access to your VPC (requires additional permissions)

9. (Optional) Enable **vector search**

   ○ Specify vector dimension (e.g., 384)

10. Click **Create graph**

Notes:

- Graph status will be `Creating` initially.

- Once the status becomes `Available`, the graph is ready for queries and data loading.

Creating an Empty Graph via AWS CLI

For automation or scripting, the AWS CLI offers a quick way to create a graph.

Public Endpoint Example

```
aws neptune-graph create-graph \
  --graph-name "test-analytics-graph" \
  --region us-east-1 \
  --provisioned-memory 128 \
  --public-connectivity \
  --replica-count 0 \
  --vector-search '{"dimension": 384}'
```

Private Endpoint Example

```
aws neptune-graph create-private-graph-
endpoint \
  --vpc-id vpc-0a9b7a5b15 \
  --subnet-ids subnet-06a4b41a6221b subnet-
0840a4b327ab77 subnet-0353627ab123 \
  --vpc-security-group-ids sg-0ab7abab56ab
\
  --graph-identifier g-146a51b7a151ba \
  --region us-east-1
```

Monitoring Graph Creation

```
aws neptune-graph get-graph \
  --graph-identifier g-146a51b7a151ba
```

List All Graphs

```
aws neptune-graph list-graphs
```

Creating a Graph Using AWS CloudFormation

To treat your infrastructure as code, you can use AWS
CloudFormation templates to automate graph creation.

Sample CloudFormation Template (Public Endpoint)

```
AWSTemplateFormatVersion: 2010-09-09
Description: NeptuneAnalytics Graph with
Public Endpoint
Resources:
  NeptuneGraph:
    Type: AWS::NeptuneGraph::Graph
    DeletionPolicy: Delete
    Properties:
      GraphName: neptune-graph-demo
      ProvisionedMemory: 128
      ReplicaCount: 1
      PublicConnectivity: true
      Tags:
        - Key: stage
          Value: test
```

Sample CloudFormation Template (Private Endpoint)

```
AWSTemplateFormatVersion: 2010-09-09
Description: NeptuneAnalytics Graph with
Private Endpoint
Resources:
  NeptuneGraph:
    Type: AWS::NeptuneGraph::Graph
    DeletionPolicy: Delete
    Properties:
      GraphName: neptune-graph-demo
      ProvisionedMemory: 128
      ReplicaCount: 1
      PublicConnectivity: false
      Tags:
        - Key: stage
          Value: test
  NeptuneGraphPrivateEndpoint:
    Type:
AWS::NeptuneGraph::PrivateGraphEndpoint
    DeletionPolicy: Delete
    Properties:
      GraphIdentifier: !Ref NeptuneGraph
      VpcId: myVpc
```

Deployment Tips

- Use **nested stacks** to manage resources modularly

- Remember: **graph name, VPC, subnet IDs, and vector search settings cannot be changed after creation**

Vector Search Configuration

If you plan to use **vector similarity search**, you must enable vector indexing **during graph creation**.

Configuration Fields

- **dimension**: Integer representing the dimensionality of your vectors

  - Common values: 128, 256, 384, 768

- Vector search is ideal for use cases involving:

  - Recommendation systems

  - Semantic search

  - Machine learning embeddings

Choosing Between Public and Private Endpoints

Feature	Public Endpoint	Private Endpoint
Setup	Simple	Requires VPC, subnet, security groups
Access	Global (if IAM allows)	VPC-only (or peered)
Security	Good (with IAM)	Best
Use case	Development, testing	Production workloads

Best Practice:

- Use **public connectivity** for early exploration and testing

- Use **private connectivity** for production systems

Deletion Protection

During graph creation, **deletion protection** is **enabled by default**. You can turn it off under "Advanced settings."

Why It Matters

- Prevents accidental deletion of your graph

- Can be disabled if you're building disposable or test graphs

---

Tagging Your Graph

Tags help you organize, manage, and cost-allocate graphs.

Tag Examples

```
Tags:
  - Key: environment
    Value: production
  - Key: project
    Value: fraud-detection
```

Post-Creation Considerations

Once your graph is created:

1. **Wait for status to become "Available"**

2. **Access your graph** using the endpoint URL

   o   Use SDK, CLI, notebook, or HTTP clients

3. **Load data** (see Chapter 14)

4. **Run queries or algorithms** (see Chapter 17+)

Troubleshooting Graph Creation

If your graph fails to create or is stuck in `Creating`:

- Ensure IAM permissions are sufficient

- Validate VPC, subnet, and security group IDs

- Check for conflicts with existing graph names

- Make sure you selected a supported region

Recap and Recommendations

- Neptune Analytics graphs are fast to provision— **typically under 5 minutes**

- Choose between **empty graphs** or **preloaded graphs**

- Configure **public or private connectivity** depending on your security needs

- Enable **vector indexing** if you plan to use ML embeddings

- Use the AWS Console for simplicity, the CLI for automation, and CloudFormation for infrastructure-as-code workflows

---

Example Use Case: Creating a Graph for Product Recommendations

You're building a product recommendation engine that uses vector embeddings and user-item interactions. Here's how you would approach graph creation:

1. **Use CLI or Console** to create an empty graph with:

   - `vector-search` dimension of 384

   - public connectivity for development

2. **Load user and product nodes** with relationships

3. **Insert embeddings**

4. **Run** `.vectors.topKByNode()` **to generate recommendations**

Your graph becomes the analytical engine behind smart personalization.

Neptune Analytics makes graph creation flexible, fast, and scalable. Whether you're starting with zero data or importing terabytes from S3, you're just minutes away from actionable insights.

Chapter 14: Loading Data

One of the most critical steps in using Amazon Neptune Analytics effectively is loading data into your graph. Whether you're building your graph from scratch, migrating from an existing Neptune database, or importing data from a data lake, understanding how data loading works—and how to do it efficiently—is essential.

In this chapter, we will cover all the supported data loading mechanisms in Neptune Analytics, explore file formats, detail the step-by-step process of using each method, and highlight best practices to avoid common pitfalls.

Overview of Data Loading Methods

Neptune Analytics provides three primary methods to load data into a graph:

1. **Bulk Import**
   The fastest method for large datasets. Designed for one-time or periodic high-volume ingestion into empty graphs.

2. **Batch Load**
   Ideal for incremental data updates. Allows you to append or update existing graph data.

3. **openCypher Queries**
   Best for small data volumes, conditional inserts, or real-time data transformation scenarios.

Each method serves a different use case depending on your scale, frequency of updates, and data source location.

Supported Data Formats

Neptune Analytics supports both **Labeled Property Graph (LPG)** and **RDF** models. The supported file formats include:

- **CSV**
  Standard and simple format for LPG data.

- **Parquet**
  Highly efficient binary columnar format, recommended for large datasets.

- **RDF (N-Triples)**
  For RDF-style graphs.

You can load data from:

- **Amazon S3** buckets

- **Neptune database snapshots or clusters**

  Tip: Always validate your data format before importing to avoid runtime errors.

---

1. Bulk Import

Bulk import is the recommended approach for loading large datasets into a **new empty graph**.

Use Cases

- Initial graph population

- Migrating from Neptune Database

151

- Loading static data from Amazon S3

Key Requirements

- The target graph must be **empty**

- Source data must be stored in **Amazon S3**

- An IAM role with **read access** to the S3 bucket must be provided

Initiating Bulk Import (CLI Example)

```
aws neptune-graph create-graph-using-
import-task \
  --graph-name "analytics-graph" \
  --region "us-east-1" \
  --format "CSV" \
  --role-arn
"arn:aws:iam::123456789012:role/GraphExecut
ionRole" \
  --source "s3://my-data-bucket/graph-
data/" \
  --public-connectivity \
  --min-provisioned-memory 256 \
  --max-provisioned-memory 256
```

Parameters Breakdown

- `--format`: CSV, PARQUET, or RDF

- `--role-arn`: IAM role used by Neptune to access S3

- `--source`: Folder path in S3 (must end with a `/`)

- `--min-provisioned-memory` and `--max-provisioned-memory`: Controls memory allocation

Monitoring Progress

After triggering the import, check the task status using:

```
aws neptune-graph list-import-tasks --graph-identifier g-xxxxxxxxxx
```

> ⚠ **Important**: Only one bulk import can run at a time per graph.

---

2. Batch Load

Batch loading is designed for **incremental updates** on an existing graph. It is flexible but not as fast as bulk import.

Use Cases

- Adding new nodes or edges regularly

- Updating single-valued properties

- Loading periodic data snapshots

API Endpoint

`StartImportTask` is used to begin the batch import process on an existing graph.

CLI Example

```
aws neptune-graph start-import-task \
  --graph-identifier g-0123456789abcdef \
  --format CSV \
  --source "s3://my-bucket/batch-data/" \
  --role-arn
"arn:aws:iam::123456789012:role/GraphExecut
ionRole"
```

Response Example

```
{
  "taskId": "it-1234abcd5678efgh",
  "status": "InProgress"
}
```

Checking Status

```
aws neptune-graph get-import-task \
  --graph-identifier g-0123456789abcdef \
  --task-id it-1234abcd5678efgh
```

Canceling a Task

```
aws neptune-graph cancel-import-task \
  --graph-identifier g-0123456789abcdef \
  --task-id it-1234abcd5678efgh
```

🔍 **Tip**: Use batch load when your graph is already populated and you need to regularly ingest new data.

3. Loading Data via openCypher

You can also load data directly using Cypher queries. This is useful for:

- Small datasets

- Dynamic, on-the-fly inserts

- Real-time event ingestion

Example

```
UNWIND [
  {id: "p1", name: "Alice"},
  {id: "p2", name: "Bob"}
] AS row
CREATE (p:Person {id: row.id, name:
row.name})
```

Submit using the AWS CLI:

```
aws neptune-graph execute-query \
  --graph-identifier g-0123456789 \
  --region us-east-1 \
  --query-string 'UNWIND
[{id:"p1",name:"Alice"}] AS row CREATE
(n:Person {id:row.id,name:row.name})' \
  --language open_cypher \
  out.txt
```

CSV Format Specification

When using CSV, separate files are used for vertices and edges.

Vertex File

~id	label	name	age
p1	Person	Alice	34
p2	Person	Bob	28

Edge File

~id	~from	~to	~label
e1	p1	p2	FRIENDS_WITH

Tips

- Use consistent headers across files

- Avoid loading the same file twice (will create duplicates)

- Use ~id for node/edge IDs, and ~label for types

Parquet Format Specification

Parquet is a preferred format for large-scale ingestion due to compression and faster reads.

Column Type Support

- string, int, float, boolean

- Lists of the above types

Sample Parquet Output Structure

- Vertices and edges stored in separate Parquet datasets

- Each column maps to a property

  For more details, see AWS documentation on supported Parquet column types

---

RDF Format Specification

If you're using RDF (Resource Description Framework), files must be in **N-Triples** format.

Example

```
<http://example.org/Alice>
<http://example.org/knows>
<http://example.org/Bob> .
```

  ! RDF loading is only available through **bulk import** currently.

Permissions for Data Import

Your IAM role must include permissions to access:

- Amazon S3 (for reading data)

- Neptune Graph APIs (`neptune-graph:*`)

Sample IAM Policy

```
{
  "Version": "2012-10-17",
  "Statement": [
    {
      "Effect": "Allow",
      "Action": ["s3:GetObject",
"s3:ListBucket"],
      "Resource": ["arn:aws:s3:::my-
bucket", "arn:aws:s3:::my-bucket/*"]
    },
    {
      "Effect": "Allow",
      "Action": "neptune-graph:*",
      "Resource": "*"
    }
  ]
}
```

Monitoring Import Performance

Track metrics in **Amazon CloudWatch**, such as:

- Import duration

- Bytes read from S3

- Memory utilization

- Errors during parsing or mapping

    Set alarms for import failure to catch errors
early.

Common Pitfalls and How to Avoid Them

Problem	Cause	Solution
Duplicate edges	File reloaded	Deduplicate or use unique IDs
Graph not empty	Using bulk import on a non-empty graph	Use batch load instead
Import stuck	Missing permissions	Verify IAM role permissions
Invalid format	Wrong headers or types	Validate CSV/Parquet before loading

Best Practices for Loading Data

- **Use bulk import** for first-time loads, especially over 10GB

- **Split vertex and edge files** for clarity

- **Batch small updates** instead of frequent single inserts

- **Compress large files** (Parquet preferred over CSV)

- **Include proper metadata** (e.g., labels, IDs)

- **Test imports in dev environments** before production

Summary

Loading data into Neptune Analytics is a versatile and powerful process. From high-speed bulk imports to incremental updates and ad-hoc inserts, Neptune provides all the tools needed to manage and evolve your graph data.

The right loading strategy depends on your use case, data size, and update frequency. With a solid understanding of these loading techniques and best practices, you'll be able to keep your graphs accurate, scalable, and optimized for high-performance analytics.

Chapter 15: Data Formats (CSV, Parquet, RDF)

When working with Neptune Analytics, selecting the right data format is critical for effective data ingestion, compatibility, and performance. Neptune Analytics supports three primary data formats for loading graph data: **CSV**, **Parquet**, and **RDF**. Each format has distinct characteristics, use cases, and integration paths that suit different workflows.

In this chapter, we'll explore each format in depth, covering:

- Structure and syntax

- Use cases and scenarios

- Formatting requirements for Neptune Analytics

- Pros and cons of each format

- Tips for choosing the right format for your project

Why Data Format Matters

Neptune Analytics uses **in-memory, columnar storage** to deliver high-performance analytics. The structure and cleanliness of your data have a direct impact on:

- **Ingestion speed**

- **Query performance**

- **Storage efficiency**

- **Ease of mapping to graph structures (nodes, edges, properties)**

By understanding each supported data format, you can make informed decisions that accelerate your graph analytics workflows.

Supported Data Formats Overview

Format	Type	Ideal For	Compr.	Schema
CSV	Row-based, plain text	Simplicity, manual editing	No	Optional
Parquet	Columnar, binary	Large-scale, performance-critical data	Yes	Yes
RDF	Triple-based, semantic	Ontologies, linked data, RDF-based apps	Optional	No

CSV Format

Overview

CSV (Comma-Separated Values) is the simplest format supported by Neptune Analytics. It's ideal for small to medium-sized datasets or where human-readability and manual data creation are needed.

File Structure

CSV files for Neptune Analytics are typically separated into:

- **Vertex files**: Each row represents a node (or vertex)

- **Edge files**: Each row represents a relationship between nodes

You can use **custom delimiters**, such as commas or semicolons, but ensure consistency and proper escaping.

Example: Vertex CSV

```
~id,name,age:Integer
user1,Alice,30
user2,Bob,45
```

Example: Edge CSV

```
~id,~from,~to,~label,since:Date
e1,user1,user2,FRIENDS,2015-06-23
```

> **Tip:** Prefixes like ~id, ~from, ~to, and ~label are required by Neptune Analytics to interpret the file structure correctly.

Features

- Simple to write, edit, and debug

- No compression; larger files can be slower to ingest

- Schema can be partially inferred (e.g., age:Integer)

- Supports property columns with typed suffixes (`:Integer`, `:Date`, `:Boolean`)

Best Practices

- Use descriptive headers and consistent typing

- Avoid duplicate edges (especially when reloading files)

- Escape delimiters properly (e.g., use `\ ;` for semicolons in values)

When to Use

- Testing or prototyping

- Manual data entry

- Lightweight ETL jobs

Parquet Format

Overview

Parquet is a **columnar, compressed, binary format** designed for big data workloads. It offers faster processing for large datasets and is ideal for use with Neptune Analytics when performance and scalability are key.

File Structure

Parquet files can contain both vertices and edges, usually with clearly defined columns:

- $\sim$id: Unique ID for the node or edge

- $\sim$from / $\sim$to: For edge files, indicating the direction

- $\sim$label: Type of node or relationship

- Additional property columns: Typed automatically based on schema or data

Example: Parquet Schema (Vertices)

~id	name	age
user1	Alice	30
user2	Bob	45

Supported Data Types

- Integer, Float, Boolean, String

- Date, Timestamp

- Lists and Maps (limited support)

   Note: You should define column types consistently; mixed-type columns may cause ingestion failures.

Features

- High-performance for large data loads

- Smaller file size due to compression

- Columnar storage optimizes analytical queries

- Requires schema alignment and careful formatting

Best Practices

- Use Parquet when loading tens of millions of rows or more

- Pre-validate data with tools like AWS Glue or Apache Spark

- Ensure all required fields (~id, ~from, etc.) are present and typed

When to Use

- Large enterprise datasets

- Machine-generated graph data

- Pipelines using Spark, Hive, or AWS Glue

RDF Format

Overview

RDF (Resource Description Framework) is a **W3C standard for semantic data** that represents information as triples (subject, predicate, object). Neptune Analytics supports RDF for loading **knowledge graphs**, ontologies, and linked data.

RDF Triple Structure

Each RDF triple describes one fact:

```
<http://example.org/user1>
<http://example.org/knows>
<http://example.org/user2>
```

This is analogous to:

- Subject: user1

- Predicate: knows

- Object: user2

Supported RDF Formats

- **Turtle (.ttl)** — Compact, human-readable

- **N-Triples (.nt)** — Line-by-line triple encoding

- **RDF/XML** — XML-based serialization (less common)

- **TriG** — Named graph extension of Turtle

Example: Turtle Format

```
@prefix ex: <http://example.org/> .

ex:user1 a ex:Person ;
         ex:name "Alice" ;
         ex:knows ex:user2 .
```

Features

- Ideal for semantic web, reasoning engines, linked data

- Naturally fits ontologies and vocabularies (e.g., FOAF, Schema.org)

- Requires RDF loaders (Neptune does not interpret RDF as LPG)

Best Practices

- Ensure IRIs are unique and valid

- Use namespaces and prefixes consistently

- Validate syntax with tools like RDF4J or Apache Jena

When to Use

- Semantic applications

- Linked data ingestion

- Ontology-driven modeling

Neptune Analytics Data Format Guidelines

Regardless of the format, data must adhere to Neptune's ingestion rules:

- **Identifiers must be unique** within the vertex and edge space

- **Property types must be clearly defined** or inferred correctly

- **UTF-8 encoding is required**

- **Compressed files** (e.g., .gz) are supported for CSV and RDF

Supported File Extensions

Format	Extensions
CSV	.csv, .csv.gz
Parquet	.parquet, .parquet.snappy
RDF	.ttl, .nt, .rdf, .xml, .trig

Edge and Vertex File Separation

When using CSV or Parquet:

- Vertex files must only contain node data

- Edge files must define relationships (~from, ~to, ~label)

- You can load multiple files at once, organized into folders

File Naming Recommendations

To ease debugging and tracking:

- Use clear prefixes: `vertices_person.csv`, `edges_friends.csv`

- Group files by entity type

- Avoid spaces and special characters

Choosing the Right Format

Here's a quick decision table to help you select the best format for your use case:

Use Case	Recommended Format
Manual data creation	CSV
Rapid prototyping	CSV
Large-scale ingestion	Parquet
Spark or Glue data pipelines	Parquet
Semantic knowledge graphs	RDF
External linked data ingestion	RDF
Frequent schema changes	CSV or RDF

Tips for Preparing Data

- **Validate before upload**: Use small files to test schema compatibility.

- **Batch uploads**: Organize large loads into smaller batches per entity type.

- **Use S3 folders**: Group files into folders for logical organization (e.g., `s3://bucket/graph-data/nodes/`, `edges/`)

170

- **Leverage AWS Glue**: For converting source data (e.g., JSON to Parquet) before ingestion.

Troubleshooting Common Format Issues

Problem	Likely Cause	Fix
Missing nodes after load	Incorrect headers or ~id missing	Verify header format and column names
Edge load fails	~from or ~to columns missing	Ensure edges include required references
Mixed-type errors in Parquet	Inconsistent column typing	Standardize types across all rows
Triples not recognized in RDF load	Invalid syntax or namespace issues	Validate RDF with parser tools
CSV delimiter issues	Unescaped commas or semicolons	Use \ ; for semicolon escape

Summary

Neptune Analytics offers flexible and powerful options for loading graph data through CSV, Parquet, and RDF formats. Each format serves a specific set of needs, from ease of editing to big data performance or semantic web compatibility.

By understanding how each format works and following the recommended guidelines, you'll ensure smoother data ingestion, faster query performance, and fewer surprises along the way.

Key Takeaways

- **CSV**: Great for simplicity, quick testing, and small to mid-sized data.

- **Parquet**: Ideal for high-volume, high-performance workloads with tight schema control.

- **RDF**: The go-to format for semantic and ontology-based graph data.

- **Headers matter**: Always use correct identifiers like `~id`, `~from`, and `~label`.

- **Prepare and validate** your data before ingestion to save time during analysis.

Let me know if you'd like visual schema diagrams or conversion code snippets for any of these formats!

Chapter 16: Batch Load

Introduction

Efficiently loading data is one of the most critical steps in working with graph databases. In Neptune Analytics, while **bulk import** is ideal for loading large datasets into empty graphs, there are many cases where you need to incrementally add or update data in an existing graph. For these situations, Neptune Analytics provides a powerful and flexible mechanism called **batch load**.

Batch load allows you to load smaller volumes of data— such as new vertices and edges or property updates—into an already running Neptune Analytics graph from files stored in **Amazon S3**. It is particularly useful for **incremental updates, testing**, and **partial dataset refreshes**.

In this chapter, you will learn what batch load is, when to use it, how to structure your data, how to submit a batch load request using the AWS CLI or SDKs, and how to interpret responses and handle errors.

What is Batch Load?

Batch load is a **data ingestion mechanism** in Neptune Analytics that supports **incremental data loading** from Amazon S3 into an **existing** Neptune Analytics graph. Unlike bulk import, which can only be used on empty graphs, batch load is used **after a graph is already created and populated**.

Key Characteristics

- Supports **CSV**, **Parquet**, and **RDF** data formats

- Ideal for **small to medium data volumes**

- Can update **single-cardinality properties**

- Does **not require the graph to be stopped or reloaded**

- Fast and optimized for common use cases like edge additions or property updates

---

When to Use Batch Load

Use batch load in scenarios such as:

- Adding new relationships (edges) or entities (nodes)

- Updating single properties of existing nodes/edges

- Adding new property columns

- Regular data refresh jobs with small changes

- Loading preprocessed outputs from upstream ETL pipelines

Avoid using batch load for:

- Loading full datasets into a **new** or **empty** graph (use bulk import instead)

- Replacing the entire graph content

- Making frequent or real-time updates (use OpenCypher queries for transactional needs)

Supported Data Formats

Neptune Analytics supports the same formats in batch load as in bulk import:

1. **CSV**:

    - Most flexible and human-readable

    - Define nodes, edges, and properties in individual CSV files

2. **Parquet**:

    - Columnar format optimized for big data workflows

    - Better compression and performance for large inputs

3. **RDF** (Resource Description Framework):

    - For semantic graphs

    - Use N-Triples, Turtle, or RDF/XML formats

Your choice depends on the source system and pipeline architecture. CSV is often preferred for its simplicity and ease of transformation.

Batch Load Architecture

The high-level flow of a batch load operation is as follows:

1. **Prepare Data Files** in supported format (CSV, Parquet, RDF).

2. **Upload Files to Amazon S3** bucket.

3. **Call** `StartLoadData` **API** or corresponding AWS CLI/SDK command.

4. Neptune Analytics fetches and parses the data.

5. Nodes, edges, and properties are added or updated in the graph.

Permissions Required

Ensure the IAM role you assign to Neptune Analytics includes the following:

- `s3:GetObject` and `s3:ListBucket` permissions on the S3 data bucket

- Neptune Analytics permissions like:

    - `neptune-graph:StartLoadData`

    - `neptune-graph:GetLoadDataStatus`

You'll also need to pass the role's ARN during the batch load request.

Preparing Your Data for Batch Load

Let's take a quick look at how to structure a CSV batch load.

Example: Node File (`persons.csv`)

```
~id,~label,name,age
p1,Person,Alice,34
p2,Person,Bob,42
```

Example: Edge File (`knows.csv`)

```
~id,~from,~to,~label,since
e1,p1,p2,KNOWS,2012
```

- Use the `~id`, `~from`, `~to`, and `~label` headers for node and edge definitions.

- Add additional columns as properties.

- Upload files to an accessible S3 path, e.g., `s3://your-bucket/graph-data/`.

Submitting a Batch Load Request

You can initiate a batch load via:

- AWS CLI

- AWS SDKs (Python, Java, etc.)

- Neptune Analytics console (GUI)

Let's explore the CLI approach first.

Batch Load via AWS CLI

```
aws neptune-graph start-load-data \
  --graph-identifier g-0123456789 \
  --format CSV \
  --role-arn
arn:aws:iam::123456789012:role/NeptuneGraph
LoaderRole \
  --source s3://your-bucket/graph-data/ \
  --region us-east-1
```

CLI Parameters Explained

- `--graph-identifier`: Your Neptune Analytics graph ID

- `--format`: CSV, PARQUET, or RDF

- `--role-arn`: IAM role with S3 access

- `--source`: S3 prefix or file path (must end with a slash)

- `--region`: AWS Region where the graph is hosted

Tracking Load Progress

After submitting the load request, Neptune Analytics processes the data in the background.

Use this CLI command to monitor the status:

```
aws neptune-graph get-load-data-status \
  --graph-identifier g-0123456789 \
  --load-id abcd1234-5678-efgh-ijkl-
12345678mnop \
  --region us-east-1
```

Possible Status Values

- IN_PROGRESS: Data is still being loaded

- COMPLETED: Load was successful

- FAILED: Load encountered an error

- CANCELLED: Load was manually stopped

Handling Errors

If a batch load fails, review the **response logs** returned by the get-load-data-status command. Common issues include:

- **Invalid column names** or missing headers (~id, ~label)

- **Malformed data** (e.g., missing edge targets)

- **S3 access errors** (IAM role lacks `s3:GetObject` permission)

- **Graph constraints** (e.g., attempting to set multi-cardinality properties)

Use these logs to debug and fix your data before retrying the batch load.

Batch Load via Python SDK (Boto3)

```python
import boto3

client = boto3.client('neptune-graph',
region_name='us-east-1')

response = client.start_load_data(
    graphIdentifier='g-0123456789',
    format='CSV',

roleArn='arn:aws:iam::123456789012:role/Nep
tuneGraphLoaderRole',
    source='s3://your-bucket/graph-data/'
)

print("Load ID:", response['loadId'])
```

Use the returned `loadId` to track the load progress via `get_load_data_status`.

Best Practices for Batch Load

- **Validate Data Before Uploading**
  Ensure correct headers and data types to prevent load-time errors.

- **Use Separate Files for Nodes and Edges**
  Helps organize complex graphs and simplifies troubleshooting.

- **Minimize Property Overwrites**
  Only include columns you intend to update. Existing properties will be replaced.

- **Limit File Size**
  Keep files below 500 MB for faster load performance and easier error handling.

- **Use Descriptive Load IDs (via Tags)**
  Helps track different batch jobs across teams or environments.

Example: Batch Load Workflow

Prepare CSV files: `persons.csv`, `knows.csv`

Upload to: `s3://social-graph-dataset/2025/`

Assign IAM role: `NeptuneGraphLoaderRole`

Submit load request:

```
 aws neptune-graph start-load-data \

  --graph-identifier g-987654321 \
  --format CSV \
  --role-arn
arn:aws:iam::123456789012:role/NeptuneGraph
LoaderRole \
  --source s3://social-graph-dataset/2025/
```

Check status:

```
aws neptune-graph get-load-data-status --
graph-identifier g-987654321 --load-id
<LOAD_ID>
```

Canceling a Batch Load

If needed, you can cancel an in-progress batch load:

```
aws neptune-graph cancel-load-data \
  --graph-identifier g-0123456789 \
  --load-id <LOAD_ID>
```

This is useful when:

- Incorrect data was used

- Load is stuck or taking too long

- You need to rerun the job with fixes

Summary

Batch loading in Neptune Analytics is a powerful way to **incrementally update** your graph without disrupting ongoing queries or rebuilding the entire structure. It's perfect for agile data workflows and periodic refreshes.

In this chapter, you've learned:

- What batch load is and when to use it

- How to prepare and structure your data files

- How to execute and monitor batch loads using CLI and SDKs

- Best practices and error handling strategies

Chapter 17: Bulk Import

In this chapter, we dive into the **bulk import** capability of **Amazon Neptune Analytics**—a high-performance feature that allows you to rapidly ingest large volumes of graph data from Amazon S3 into Neptune Analytics graphs. Bulk import is designed for **initial data population** or large-scale updates and is often the fastest, most efficient way to move graph datasets from your data lake into memory for analysis.

We'll cover:

- What bulk import is and when to use it

- Supported file formats and schemas

- How to initiate a bulk import

- Permissions and IAM requirements

- Monitoring, troubleshooting, and best practices

- Examples of bulk import in action

What is Bulk Import?

Bulk import is a mechanism to load **large-scale datasets** into a **new or empty Neptune Analytics graph** from Amazon S3. Unlike batch loading or insert queries, which are better suited for incremental or smaller data additions, bulk import is optimized for **speed and throughput**.

Key Characteristics:

- Loads directly from **Amazon S3** into memory

- Must be performed on an **empty graph**

- Supports **CSV**, **Parquet**, and **RDF** formats

- Enables **parallel processing** for fast ingest

- Integrates with IAM for secure access

- Can be triggered via **AWS CLI**, **API**, or **CloudFormation**

🚀 Bulk import is the recommended method when loading **tens of gigabytes or more** of graph data.

When Should You Use Bulk Import?

Use bulk import in the following scenarios:

- **Initial population of a new Neptune Analytics graph**

- **Migrating data from Neptune Database to Neptune Analytics**

- **Loading datasets from a data lake or S3 archive**

- **Rehydrating a graph for experimentation or analysis**

- **Preloading data for graph algorithms or ML pipelines**

Avoid bulk import if:

- Your graph already has existing data

- You need to load small, incremental updates (use batch load instead)

- You need to conditionally insert or upsert records (use openCypher queries)

Supported Formats

Bulk import supports the same file formats as Neptune Analytics:

Format	Description	Use Cases
CSV	Tabular format, easy to generate	Simple property graphs, edge lists
Parquet	Columnar format, efficient storage	High-volume, structured datasets
RDF	Triple format, semantic data	Knowledge graphs, linked data

Format Selection Tips:

- Use **CSV** for ease of use and human readability.

- Use **Parquet** for performance with large or nested datasets.

- Use **RDF** if you're working with semantic triples or data from SPARQL endpoints.

Graph Requirements for Bulk Import

Before starting a bulk import:

- Your target graph **must be empty** (no existing nodes or edges).

- You must specify the **source location** in S3.

- An appropriate **IAM role** with permissions to read from S3 and write to Neptune Analytics must be attached.

  ⬤ You cannot bulk import into a graph that already contains data. If your graph isn't empty, consider creating a new one or using batch load.

IAM Permissions for Bulk Import

You need an **IAM role** that Neptune Analytics can assume to access your S3 data. This role must include the following permissions:

S3 Permissions:

```
{
  "Effect": "Allow",
  "Action": [
    "s3:GetObject",
    "s3:ListBucket"
  ],
  "Resource": [
    "arn:aws:s3:::my-bucket-name",
    "arn:aws:s3:::my-bucket-name/*"
```

```
  ]
}
```

Neptune Analytics Permissions:

```json
{
  "Effect": "Allow",
  "Action": [
    "neptune-graph:StartImportTask",
    "neptune-graph:GetGraph",
    "neptune-graph:GetImportTask",
    "neptune-graph:ListImportTasks"
  ],
  "Resource": "*"
}
```

Initiating a Bulk Import

You can start a bulk import in several ways:

Option 1: During Graph Creation (One-Time Setup)

You can create a graph and immediately initiate a bulk import using the AWS CLI:

```
aws neptune-graph create-graph-using-
import-task \
  --graph-name "my-new-graph" \
  --region "us-east-1" \
  --format "CSV" \
```

```
  --role-arn
"arn:aws:iam::123456789012:role/MyGraphRole
" \
  --source "s3://my-bucket/graph-data/" \
  --public-connectivity \
  --min-provisioned-memory 256 \
  --max-provisioned-memory 256
```

Option 2: Import Into Existing Empty Graph

```
aws neptune-graph start-import-task \
  --graph-identifier "g-0123456789" \
  --format "CSV" \
  --role-arn
"arn:aws:iam::123456789012:role/MyGraphRole
" \
  --source "s3://my-bucket/graph-data/"
```

Use Parquet or RDF as the --format if applicable.

Monitoring Import Progress

Once an import is initiated, you can check its progress:

```
aws neptune-graph get-import-task \
  --graph-identifier "g-0123456789" \
  --task-identifier "import-task-abc123"
```

Or list all import tasks:

```
aws neptune-graph list-import-tasks \
  --graph-identifier "g-0123456789"
```

Canceling an Import

If needed, you can cancel a running import:

```
aws neptune-graph cancel-import-task \
  --graph-identifier "g-0123456789" \
  --task-identifier "import-task-abc123"
```

Note that canceling may still leave partial data in the graph, and cleanup may be required.

Inspecting Import Results

Once an import completes, check the response payload from `get-import-task`:

```
{
  "status": "SUCCEEDED",
  "startTime": "2025-03-15T12:34:56Z",
  "endTime": "2025-03-15T12:35:42Z",
  "metrics": {
    "nodesImported": 235670,
    "edgesImported": 678934,
    "warnings": 12
  }
}
```

Warnings may indicate:

- Duplicate IDs

- Invalid data types

- Missing properties

Troubleshooting Bulk Imports

Problem	Likely Cause	Resolution
Task stuck in `IN_PROGRESS`	Large file, network lag, or IAM permissions issue	Check IAM role, network logs, or reduce file size
`AccessDeniedExceptio n`	IAM role lacks permission	Update S3 or Neptune IAM policy
`GraphNotEmptyExcepti on`	Trying to bulk import into a graph with existing data	Use batch load or create a new empty graph
Missing or corrupted rows	File format mismatch or unsupporte d characters	Validate CSV/Parqu et schema
Unexpected import failure	Schema issues,	Check logs via `get-`

	resource limits, malformed files	import-task and validate dataset
.		

Best Practices for Bulk Import

- **Use consistent formatting**: Avoid mixing data types or formats across files.

- **Split large datasets**: Break large files into chunks to improve parallelism.

- **Validate data schema**: Ensure headers and data types match Neptune expectations.

- **Compress your data**: Use GZIP to reduce transfer time from S3.

- **Use structured folder naming**: Makes debugging and task auditing easier.

- **Pre-test with sample data**: Helps identify issues before a full-scale import.

- **Ensure graph is empty**: Only bulk load into graphs with no existing content.

Real-World Example

Let's walk through a realistic case:

You're importing a social graph from a CSV dataset stored in S3. The structure includes Person nodes and KNOWS edges.

CSV Files:

- nodes.csv

```
~id,~label,name,age
1,Person,Alice,34
2,Person,Bob,29
```

- edges.csv

```
~from,~to,~label,since
1,2,KNOWS,2020
```

S3 Path: s3://my-social-data/csv/

CLI Command:

```
aws neptune-graph create-graph-using-
import-task \
  --graph-name "social-graph" \
  --region "us-east-1" \
  --format "CSV" \
  --role-arn
"arn:aws:iam::123456789012:role/SocialGraph
Role" \
  --source "s3://my-social-data/csv/" \
  --public-connectivity \
  --min-provisioned-memory 128 \
  --max-provisioned-memory 128
```

After a successful load, you can start querying:

```
MATCH (p:Person)-[:KNOWS]->(f:Person)
RETURN p.name, f.name
```

Summary

Bulk import is a **critical foundation** for leveraging Neptune Analytics at scale. It enables high-throughput, schema-flexible ingestion from Amazon S3 and allows you to bring massive graph datasets into memory in minutes.

Remember:

- Use it for initial data loads only

- Graphs must be empty before importing

- Choose the format (CSV, Parquet, RDF) that best fits your data

- Use IAM roles with precise permissions

- Monitor and troubleshoot tasks via CLI/API

- Apply best practices to improve speed and reliability

With a well-structured bulk import pipeline, you're set to unleash the full power of Neptune Analytics for advanced graph analytics and insight generation.

Troubleshooting and Queries

Chapter 18: Troubleshooting

Working with Neptune Analytics provides a powerful platform for running large-scale graph analytics at speed. However, like any cloud-based, multi-layered system, issues can occasionally arise—from access and configuration problems to query performance and data ingestion errors. In this chapter, we'll walk through a comprehensive set of **troubleshooting tips**, **error resolution guides**, and **debugging tools** to help you quickly identify and fix common problems encountered when using Neptune Analytics.

Overview: Where Troubles Typically Occur

Troubleshooting Neptune Analytics can be grouped into several main categories:

1. **Graph creation and configuration issues**

2. **Access and authentication problems**

3. **Data loading errors**

4. **Query execution issues**

5. **Vector search complications**

6. **Performance bottlenecks**

7. **Permissions and IAM role errors**

Each section below addresses these categories with actionable steps and example errors.

Graph Creation Issues

Creating a graph is usually straightforward, but errors can occur if required configurations are missing or misconfigured.

Common Symptoms

- Graph stuck in `Creating` state

- API errors like `InvalidParameterException`

- Missing or incorrect VPC/subnet IDs

Resolutions

- **Check required permissions**: Make sure your IAM role has the following actions:

  - `ec2:DescribeVpcs`, `ec2:DescribeSubnets`, `ec2:CreateVpcEndpoint`, etc.

- **Validate your input**:

  - Ensure `graph-name` is unique and conforms to AWS naming rules.

  - Verify that VPC ID and subnet IDs are correct.

- **Provisioning timeout**: If graph provisioning takes longer than 20 minutes, check:

    ○ VPC has DNS resolution and DNS hostnames enabled.

    ○ Subnets belong to availability zones in the same region.

Tips

Use the `get-graph` CLI command to monitor status:

```
aws neptune-graph get-graph --graph-
identifier <graph-id>
```

-

Access and Authentication Problems

Neptune Analytics relies heavily on **AWS IAM and SIGV4** authentication. If you can't connect to the graph, authentication is often the root cause.

Common Errors

- `AccessDeniedException`

- `403 Forbidden` when executing queries

- Connection timeouts or name resolution failures

Checklist

IAM Policy: Ensure your user/role has access to Neptune Analytics actions like:

```
"Action": [
  "neptune-graph:ExecuteQuery",
  "neptune-graph:GetGraph",
  "neptune-graph:ListGraphs"
]
```

-
- **SIGV4 signing**: Required for all HTTP requests. If using `curl`, switch to `awscurl`.

- **Endpoint**: Confirm the correct DNS and region for your graph.

Tools

Use AWSCurl to test requests:

```
awscurl -X POST <graph-endpoint>/queries \
--region us-east-1 \
--service neptune-graph \
-d "query=MATCH (n) RETURN n LIMIT 1"
```

Data Loading Errors

Neptune Analytics supports multiple data formats (CSV, Parquet, RDF), and loading errors can be caused by formatting issues or access problems with Amazon S3.

Common Messages

- `DataParsingException`

- `AccessDeniedException`

- `InvalidFormatException`

- `TooManyEdgesException`

Troubleshooting Steps

1. **Check your S3 path**:

    - Must be in the format `s3://bucket-name/folder/`

    - Folder path must end with a slash

2. **Validate IAM Role**:

    - Role used for import must have:

        - `s3:GetObject`, `s3:ListBucket`

        - Trust relationship with Neptune Analytics

3. **Check data format**:

    - Use Neptune's sample format templates

    - Ensure CSV/Parquet schema matches expectations (e.g., for edge files: `~id`, `~from`, `~to`)

4. **Examine batch load logs**:

Use `get-import-task` CLI command to check progress and error logs:

```
aws neptune-graph get-import-task --task-id
<task-id>
```

   o

Query Execution Issues

Even after successful graph creation and data loading, queries can sometimes fail due to syntax, timeout, or internal errors.

Common Problems

- `InternalFailureException`

- Empty result sets from valid queries

- Unexpected output format

Solutions

- **Query plan cache**:
   - Can cause issues with parameterized mutation querles

Use hint to disable:

```
CYPHER QUERY:PLANCACHE "disabled"
MATCH (n) RETURN n
```

- ○
- **Check input parameters**:

    - ○ Avoid passing null values or unsupported types

    - ○ For example: `sum("abc")` is invalid

- **Named paths**:

Avoid using named paths unless necessary:

```
MATCH path=(a)-[:FRIEND]->(b) RETURN path
-- Avoid unless required
```

- ○

Timeout and Retry Settings

By default, SDKs and CLI time out after 60 seconds and retry failed queries.

Set these explicitly to avoid long queries being retried:

CLI:

```
export AWS_MAX_ATTEMPTS=1
aws neptune-graph execute-query \
--cli-read-timeout 0 \
--query-string "MATCH (n) RETURN n"
```

Python SDK:

```
from botocore.config import Config
config =
Config(retries={"total_max_attempts": 1},
read_timeout=None)
```

Vector Search Issues

If you use vector similarity or embeddings, errors can arise during vector upserts or queries.

Common Symptoms

- `VectorIndexNotFoundException`

- `DimensionMismatchException`

- Poor or no results from `.topKByNode()` or `.distance()` queries

Diagnosis & Fixes

- **Vector dimension mismatch**:

  - Ensure the embedding vector dimension matches the graph's configured `dimension`

  - Set at graph creation (e.g., 384)

- **Missing index**:

- If you forgot to enable vector search, you'll need to recreate the graph with vector search configuration.

Query format:

```
CALL algo.vectors.topKByNode({node: "p123",
k: 5})
RETURN similarNode, score
```

-

Performance Bottlenecks

Neptune Analytics is built for speed, but poorly written queries or large datasets can still lead to performance degradation.

Signs of Poor Performance

- Queries take longer than expected

- Resource throttling (check metrics)

- High memory usage

Best Practices

- **Avoid COLLECT(DISTINCT())** — replace with `.distinct()` or filtering

- **Use parameterized queries**

- **Avoid named paths** unless required

- **Apply filters early** in the query

- **Use `UNWIND` for batch inserts**, not individual statements

Query Optimization Tips

- Flatten maps: avoid nested map structures in `UNWIND`

- Remove unused variables from `WITH` clauses

- Prefer custom node IDs

- Avoid expensive pattern matches on `~id`

IAM and Role-Related Errors

IAM misconfigurations are a common cause of access or operation failures.

Error Examples

- `UnauthorizedOperation`

- `PrincipalNotFound`

- Graph or import task fails silently

Checklist

- Ensure the IAM role:

  - Has correct trust relationship with `neptune-graph.amazonaws.com`

  - Includes necessary policies (Neptune, S3, logs)

- For import tasks:

  - Verify `s3:GetObject`, `s3:ListBucket` permissions

  - Confirm `kms:Decrypt` if using encrypted buckets

Tools for Debugging

Neptune Analytics integrates with AWS-native observability tools:

Tool	Use
AWS CloudTrail	Logs API requests (e.g., CreateGraph, ExecuteQuery)
Amazon CloudWatch	Monitors memory usage, query count, latency
Reachability Analyzer	Checks VPC connectivity to private endpoints
GetGraph API	View status, memory settings, endpoint info

Example: CloudWatch Metrics

You can view:

- QueryCount

- QueryLatency

- MemoryUtilization

Use this to detect bottlenecks or runaway queries.

Common Troubleshooting Scenarios

Problem	Likely Cause	Solution
Graph won't create	Missing permissions or invalid VPC/subnet	Check IAM and VPC settings
Query fails with `InternalFailureException`	Plan cache issue or invalid input	Disable plan cache, fix query syntax
No results from vector query	Embedding not indexed or dimension mismatch	Verify vector config and input
Data import fails	Bad S3 path or IAM role issue	Validate URI and permissions
`403 Forbidden` when querying	Missing IAM permissions or bad credentials	Update IAM policy, check credentials

Summary

Troubleshooting Neptune Analytics requires a structured approach:

- **Start with logs**: CloudTrail and import task outputs are essential

- **Validate your environment**: VPC, endpoints, IAM, and S3 roles must all align

- **Break down the problem**: Is it graph-level, network-level, data-level, or query-level?

- **Use the right tool for the job**: CLI, SDKs, AWSCurl, and graph-notebooks all have strengths

- **Follow best practices** to avoid common pitfalls (especially with query design and vector configuration)

With a solid understanding of these troubleshooting techniques, you'll be well-equipped to resolve issues quickly and keep your analytics workloads running smoothly.

Chapter 19: `neptune.read()`

The `neptune.read()` function is a key utility in Amazon Neptune Analytics that allows users to retrieve data from a Neptune Analytics graph into an interactive environment such as a Jupyter notebook or a data analysis tool. It is particularly valuable for data scientists and engineers who want to analyze graph data using Python libraries like Pandas or visualize graph structures with tools like NetworkX or Matplotlib.

This chapter explores the `neptune.read()` functionality in detail, including its syntax, usage patterns, supported formats, use cases, and best practices.

What is `neptune.read()`?

`neptune.read()` is a Python function provided through the graph-notebook project. It allows you to run an openCypher query on a Neptune Analytics graph and return the results as a Python-readable structure, such as a Pandas DataFrame or raw JSON.

It is typically used in Neptune graph notebooks, which run on Amazon SageMaker or JupyterLab environments configured to connect to Neptune Analytics.

Key Benefits

- **Integrates graph results with Python-based tools**

- **Allows structured analysis of graph query output**

- **Supports openCypher queries**

- **Simple and intuitive for data scientists familiar with Pandas or NumPy**

Basic Syntax

```
neptune.read(query: str,
language="openCypher")
```

Parameters:

- `query`: A string containing a valid openCypher query.

- `language`: The query language. Currently, only `"openCypher"` is supported.

Returns:

- A structured data object (typically a Pandas DataFrame)

- Nested structures (nodes, edges, paths) are returned as JSON within the DataFrame columns

---

Setup and Requirements

To use `neptune.read()`:

1. **Install the Neptune graph-notebook extension**:

   - Either through SageMaker setup

   - Or by installing locally via pip from the graph-notebook GitHub repository

2. **Set up your notebook environment** using:

```
%graph_notebook_config
```

Or set environment variables for host, port, and authentication.

3. **Authenticate** using IAM credentials, either from:

   - Notebook instance IAM role (in SageMaker)

   - AWS CLI credentials (locally)

Example Usage

Simple openCypher Query

```
from graph_notebook.neptune.client import neptune
result = neptune.read("MATCH (p:Person) RETURN p.name AS name, p.age AS age")
```

Display Results as a DataFrame

```
import pandas as pd
```

```
df = pd.DataFrame(result)
df.head()
```

Visualizing Data (Optional)

```
import matplotlib.pyplot as plt

df.plot(kind='bar', x='name', y='age')
plt.title("Age of People in the Graph")
plt.show()
```

Query Result Structures

`neptune.read()` wraps the HTTP response from
Neptune Analytics and parses it into structured rows.

Return Types:

Graph Element	Python Representation
Nodes	Dictionary (JSON)
Relationships	Dictionary (JSON)
Paths	Nested dictionaries
Scalar values	String, Int, Float

Example Output Row:

```
{
  "p.name": "Alice",
  "p.age": 32,
  "p": {
    "~id": "123",
    "~label": "Person",
    "name": "Alice",
    "age": 32
```

```
    }
}
```

> ⚡ Use `.apply(json.loads)` if you want to
> manipulate nested JSON node structures in
> Pandas.

Advanced Query Example

```
query = """
MATCH (c:Customer)-[:PURCHASED]-
>(p:Product)
RETURN c.name AS customer, p.name AS
product
"""

results = neptune.read(query)
```

Convert to DataFrame:

```
df = pd.DataFrame(results)
print(df)
```

Use Cases for `neptune.read()`

- **Graph-based exploratory data analysis (EDA)**

- **Combining graph queries with traditional ML workflows**

- **Visualizing graph structures using Python libraries**

- **Transforming graph output into tabular data for BI tools**

- **Running ad-hoc queries during model development**

Best Practices

Keep Queries Focused and Limited

Avoid retrieving thousands of records in a single call. Use LIMIT to restrict your output.

```
neptune.read("MATCH (n) RETURN n LIMIT 50")
```

Flatten Nested Structures (If Needed)

Convert nested dictionaries into flat columns using Pandas utilities for easier analysis.

```
df['name'] = df['p'].apply(lambda x:
x['name'])
```

Use Graph Visualization for Complex Relationships

For graph-centric data (e.g., paths, multi-hop relationships), use visualization tools:

```
import networkx as nx

G = nx.Graph()
for index, row in df.iterrows():
    G.add_edge(row['source'],
row['target'])
nx.draw(G, with_labels=True)
```

Handle Pagination in Large Results

For massive datasets, break down queries using
parameters like SKIP and LIMIT.

```
query = "MATCH (n) RETURN n SKIP 100 LIMIT
100"
```

Troubleshooting neptune.read()

Issue	Cause	Solution
Empty result	Query returned no rows	Validate your query syntax and filters
Timeout error	Query too large	Reduce dataset size or increase notebook timeout
Permission denied	Missing IAM permissions	Ensure the notebook has access to the graph
ValueError on DataFrame	Bad JSON structure	Flatten nested objects before converting

Security Considerations

- **Use IAM roles** for graph access from notebooks

- Avoid embedding access keys in scripts

- Always sign requests using AWS SigV4 (handled by the notebook)

Summary

The `neptune.read()` function is a user-friendly, powerful interface for bridging Neptune Analytics with Python-based analytics environments. It enables interactive exploration, data wrangling, and rapid prototyping with graph data.

By combining the expressive power of openCypher with the flexibility of Pandas and visualization tools, `neptune.read()` becomes an essential part of a graph data scientist's toolkit.

Chapter 20: Query Examples (CSV & Parquet)

Querying data is at the heart of graph analytics, and with Neptune Analytics, users can quickly extract insights from datasets loaded in either **CSV** or **Parquet** formats. This chapter provides practical, ready-to-use **query examples** for both formats using **openCypher**, the supported query language in Neptune Analytics.

We'll cover:

- The structure of CSV and Parquet-based graphs

- How data maps into graph models (nodes, edges, properties)

- Query examples using openCypher syntax

- Use cases like filtering, aggregating, traversing, and analyzing

- Output structure samples

This chapter is designed to help you move from **data loading to data querying** with clarity and confidence, using real-world scenarios.

Understanding CSV and Parquet in Neptune Analytics

Although the file formats are different (plain text vs. columnar binary), once the data is loaded into Neptune Analytics, **both CSV and Parquet** result in the same in-memory graph structure. Your queries, therefore, use the same openCypher syntax regardless of the source format.

Data Model Assumptions

For the examples in this chapter, assume the following simplified graph:

- **Nodes (Vertices):**

  - Person nodes with properties: name, age, location

  - Company nodes with properties: name, industry

- **Edges (Relationships):**

  - WORKS_FOR relationships from Person to Company

  - KNOWS relationships between Person nodes

These entities are loaded using either CSV or Parquet. We'll show the loading structure briefly and focus primarily on **querying**.

Sample Data – CSV Example

CSV Vertex: Person

```
~id,~label,name,age:Integer,location
person1,Person,Alice,29,Seattle
person2,Person,Bob,34,San Francisco
person3,Person,Charlie,31,Austin
```

CSV Vertex: Company

```
~id,~label,name,industry
company1,Company,TechCorp,Software
company2,Company,HealthX,Healthcare
```

CSV Edge: WORKS_FOR

```
~id,~from,~to,~label,role
e1,person1,company1,WORKS_FOR,Engineer
e2,person2,company2,WORKS_FOR,Analyst
e3,person3,company1,WORKS_FOR,Manager
```

CSV Edge: KNOWS

```
~id,~from,~to,~label,since:Date
e4,person1,person2,KNOWS,2019-06-12
e5,person2,person3,KNOWS,2020-01-08
```

Sample Data – Parquet Example

The same structure can be represented in Parquet files. Here's a simplified schema view:

Parquet Vertices: Person

~id	~label	name	age	location
person1	Person	Alice	29	Seattle
person2	Person	Bob	34	San Francisco
person3	Person	Charlie	31	Austin

Parquet Edges: WORKS_FOR

~id	~from	~to	~label	role
e1	person1	company1	WORKS_FOR	Engineer
e2	person2	company2	WORKS_FOR	Analyst

Query Language: openCypher

All examples below use **openCypher**, a pattern-matching query language similar to SQL but designed for graphs. Cypher syntax is used to match patterns like:

```
MATCH (n:Label)-[:RELATION]->(m:Label)
```

You can run these queries using:

- AWS CLI: `aws neptune-graph execute-query`

- Neptune Workbench notebooks: `%%oc` cell magic

- SDKs or the Neptune Analytics HTTPS endpoint

Query Examples – Basics

1. Return All Persons

```
MATCH (p:Person)
RETURN p.name, p.age, p.location
```

Expected Output:

p.name	p.age	p.location
Alice	29	Seattle
Bob	34	San Francisco
Charlie	31	Austin

2. Find All People Working at "TechCorp"

```
MATCH (p:Person)-[:WORKS_FOR]->(c:Company)
WHERE c.name = "TechCorp"
RETURN p.name, c.name
```

3. List People and Their Coworkers

```
MATCH (p1:Person)-[:WORKS_FOR]-
>(c:Company)<-[:WORKS_FOR]-(p2:Person)
WHERE p1.name < p2.name
RETURN p1.name AS person, p2.name AS
coworker, c.name AS company
```

> **Tip:** The p1.name < p2.name condition prevents duplicate pairs.

Query Examples – Filters and Aggregations

4. Count Employees by Company

```
MATCH (p:Person)-[:WORKS_FOR]->(c:Company)
RETURN c.name AS company, count(p) AS
num_employees
ORDER BY num_employees DESC
```

5. People Over Age 30

```
MATCH (p:Person)
WHERE p.age > 30
RETURN p.name, p.age
```

6. Locations with the Most Employees

```
MATCH (p:Person)
RETURN p.location, count(*) AS total
ORDER BY total DESC
```

Query Examples – Relationships and Traversals

7. Find Who Knows Whom

```
MATCH (a:Person)-[k:KNOWS]->(b:Person)
RETURN a.name AS source, b.name AS target,
k.since
```

8. Two-Hop Connections (Friends of Friends)

```
MATCH (a:Person)-[:KNOWS]->(:Person)-
[:KNOWS]->(c:Person)
WHERE a <> c
RETURN DISTINCT a.name AS person, c.name AS
friend_of_friend
```

9. Chain of Employment

Find a person and who they know that works at the same company.

```
MATCH (p1:Person)-[:WORKS_FOR]-
>(c:Company)<-[:WORKS_FOR]-(p2:Person),
      (p1)-[:KNOWS]->(p2)
RETURN p1.name, p2.name, c.name
```

Advanced Examples – Using Properties

10. Match by Job Role

```
MATCH (p:Person)-[w:WORKS_FOR]->(c:Company)
WHERE w.role = "Engineer"
RETURN p.name, c.name
```

11. Find Most Connected Person

```
MATCH (p:Person)-[:KNOWS]->()
RETURN p.name, count(*) AS num_connections
ORDER BY num_connections DESC
```

```
LIMIT 1
```

12. Who Works in Healthcare?

```
MATCH (p:Person)-[:WORKS_FOR]->(c:Company)
WHERE c.industry = "Healthcare"
RETURN p.name
```

Output Format Differences

While queries work the same regardless of format, the output can vary depending on:

- Execution environment (CLI, SDK, notebook)

- Output format (JSON, CSV, table)

Sample Output in CLI (CSV)

```
p.name,p.age
Alice,29
Bob,34
```

Sample Output in Notebook

Rendered as a table or graph visualization, with ability to toggle node/edge types.

Tips for Querying CSV & Parquet Data

- **Be type-aware**: Ensure types match your Cypher filters (e.g., don't compare strings to integers).

- **Use indexes**: While Neptune Analytics does in-memory indexing, filters on properties like `age`, `name`, or `location` perform better with smaller result sets.

- **Watch naming**: Avoid using reserved keywords or special characters in column names.

- **Test on small samples**: Before running on a full dataset, test on a subset to refine your query logic.

Troubleshooting Query Errors

Error Message	Likely Cause	Suggested Fix
Unknown label or property	Typos or missing fields in data	Validate data format and spelling
Type mismatch in filter expression	Comparing different types	Use explicit casting or check field types
No matches found	Filters too strict or missing data	Broaden query or inspect loaded data
Invalid syntax near	Typo in Cypher query	Use a linter or simpler pattern to debug

Summary

Once your data is loaded into Neptune Analytics—whether from CSV or Parquet—you unlock powerful querying capabilities with openCypher. This chapter has provided a toolkit of example queries that cover:

- Entity filtering and selection

- Relationship traversal

- Aggregation and counts

- Multi-hop pattern matching

These patterns will help you answer complex business questions, explore your graph data more intuitively, and validate your data model through practical usage.

Key Takeaways

- Queries are the same for CSV and Parquet once data is loaded.

- Focus on labels (`:Person`, `:Company`) and properties (`name`, `age`) when building filters.

- Use aggregation and relationship queries to uncover structure and meaning.

- Combine Cypher logic and domain knowledge to build powerful graph insights.

Exporting Data

Chapter 21: SDK/CLI Commands

Introduction

Amazon Neptune Analytics offers a robust set of **command-line interface (CLI)** and **software development kit (SDK)** operations for interacting with graph data and managing the analytics environment programmatically. Whether you're deploying in a CI/CD pipeline, building data science workflows, or automating graph updates, mastering these commands is crucial for efficiency, reproducibility, and scalability.

In this chapter, we'll explore the essential CLI and SDK commands available in Neptune Analytics, including:

- Graph management (create, delete, update)

- Data loading and export

- Query execution and control

- Monitoring and diagnostics

- IAM and security considerations

You'll learn how to use these commands with practical examples and best practices for working in both development and production environments.

Why Use the CLI and SDK?

Neptune Analytics can be accessed via:

- **AWS CLI**: Useful for scripting, automation, and one-off tasks.

- **AWS SDKs**: Integrate graph operations into applications using Python, Java, JavaScript, Go, and more.

Both methods use the same underlying Neptune Analytics API and require **SigV4 signing**, which is handled automatically by the AWS CLI and SDKs.

Prerequisites

Before using any command, ensure the following:

- AWS CLI v2 or a supported SDK is installed and configured

- IAM credentials are set up with necessary permissions (e.g., `neptune-graph:*`)

- Your Neptune Analytics graph is in the **Available** state

- You know the **graph identifier**, e.g., `g-0123456789`

CLI Commands Overview

Let's start with the CLI, which is available via:

```
aws neptune-graph <operation>
```

1. Create a Graph

```
aws neptune-graph create-graph \
  --graph-name "demo-graph" \
  --region us-east-1 \
  --provisioned-memory 256 \
  --replica-count 1 \
  --public-connectivity
```

Optional: Enable vector search

```
--vector-search '{"dimension": 384}'
```

2. Get Graph Details

```
aws neptune-graph get-graph \
  --graph-identifier g-0123456789
```

3. List All Graphs

```
aws neptune-graph list-graphs
```

4. Delete a Graph

```
aws neptune-graph delete-graph \
  --graph-identifier g-0123456789
```

Querying with the CLI

5. Execute a Query

```
aws neptune-graph execute-query \
  --graph-identifier g-0123456789 \
  --region us-east-1 \
  --query-string "MATCH (n) RETURN n LIMIT
10" \
  --language open_cypher \
  out.json
```

6. Get Query Status

```
aws neptune-graph get-query \
  --graph-identifier g-0123456789 \
  --query-id abcdef12-3456-7890-ghij-
klmnopqrstuv
```

7. List All Queries

```
aws neptune-graph list-queries \
  --graph-identifier g-0123456789
```

8. Cancel a Running Query

```
aws neptune-graph cancel-query \
  --graph-identifier g-0123456789 \
  --query-id abcdef12-3456-7890-ghij-
klmnopqrstuv
```

Data Loading Commands

9. Start a Batch Load

```
aws neptune-graph start-load-data \
  --graph-identifier g-0123456789 \
  --format CSV \
  --source s3://your-bucket/graph-data/ \
  --role-arn
arn:aws:iam::123456789012:role/NeptuneGraph
LoaderRole
```

10. Get Load Status

```
aws neptune-graph get-load-data-status \
  --graph-identifier g-0123456789 \
  --load-id abc1234-load-id
```

11. Cancel a Load Job

```
aws neptune-graph cancel-load-data \
  --graph-identifier g-0123456789 \
  --load-id abc1234-load-id
```

Data Export Commands

12. Start Export Task

```
aws neptune-graph start-export-task \
  --graph-identifier g-0123456789 \
  --format CSV \
  --output-location s3://your-bucket/graph-
exports/ \
```

```
  --role-arn
arn:aws:iam::123456789012:role/NeptuneExpor
tRole
```

13. Get Export Task Status

```
aws neptune-graph get-export-task \
  --graph-identifier g-0123456789 \
  --task-id export-task-abc123
```

14. List Export Tasks

```
aws neptune-graph list-export-task \
  --graph-identifier g-0123456789
```

15. Cancel Export Task

```
aws neptune-graph cancel-export-task \
  --graph-identifier g-0123456789 \
  --task-id export-task-abc123
```

SDK Integration Examples

Python (Boto3)

```
import boto3

client = boto3.client('neptune-graph')

response = client.execute_query(
    graphIdentifier='g-0123456789',
```

```
    queryString='MATCH (n) RETURN n LIMIT
5',
    language='open_cypher'
)

print(response['payload'].read().decode('ut
f-8'))
```

JavaScript (Node.js)

```
const { NeptuneGraphClient,
ExecuteQueryCommand } = require("@aws-
sdk/client-neptune-graph");

const client = new NeptuneGraphClient({
region: "us-east-1" });

const command = new ExecuteQueryCommand({
  graphIdentifier: "g-0123456789",
  queryString: "MATCH (n) RETURN n LIMIT
5",
  language: "open_cypher"
});

const response = await
client.send(command);
const result = await
response.payload.transformToString("utf-
8");
console.log(result);
```

Java (v2 SDK)

```
NeptuneGraphClient client =
NeptuneGraphClient.builder()
    .region(Region.US_EAST_1)
    .build();

ExecuteQueryRequest request =
ExecuteQueryRequest.builder()
    .graphIdentifier("g-0123456789")
    .queryString("MATCH (n) RETURN n LIMIT
5")
    .language("open_cypher")
    .build();

ResponseInputStream<ExecuteQueryResponse>
response = client.executeQuery(request);
BufferedReader reader = new
BufferedReader(new
InputStreamReader(response));
reader.lines().forEach(System.out::println)
;
```

Query Plan Cache and Tuning

You can disable or enable the query plan cache by using
the QUERY:PLANCACHE hint:

```
MATCH (n) RETURN n LIMIT 1 /*
QUERY:PLANCACHE "disabled" */
```

For long-running queries via CLI or SDK, set higher timeout and retry settings:

```
export AWS_MAX_ATTEMPTS=1
aws neptune-graph execute-query \
  --cli-read-timeout 0 \
  --graph-identifier g-0123456789 \
  --query-string "MATCH (n) RETURN n LIMIT
100000"
```

Monitoring and Logs

You can monitor graph activity via:

- **CloudWatch metrics** for CPU, memory, and query count

- **CloudTrail logs** for API events

- **VPC flow logs** for networking behavior

IAM Permissions and Policy Examples

To allow a user or service to execute all graph-related operations:

```
{
  "Version": "2012-10-17",
  "Statement": [
    {
      "Effect": "Allow",
```

```
    "Action": "neptune-graph:*",
    "Resource": "*"
  }
]
}
```

For more restrictive policies, limit actions to specific graphs
and operations.

Best Practices

- **Use parameterized queries** to improve cache
  efficiency and reduce injection risk.

- **Limit query concurrency** for large datasets to
  avoid memory saturation.

- **Use** `MAX_ATTEMPTS=1` to avoid retries for long-
  running analytic queries.

- **Log and audit** all CLI/SDK calls using CloudTrail.

- **Automate** batch loads, exports, and snapshots
  using scheduled scripts or Lambda functions.

Summary

Neptune Analytics provides a comprehensive CLI and SDK
interface for managing and interacting with graph data.
Whether you're a developer building graph-powered apps
or a data engineer orchestrating ETL pipelines,
understanding these commands enables full lifecycle
control of your graph environment.

In this chapter, we covered:

- Graph lifecycle management commands

- How to execute and manage queries

- Data load and export operations

- SDK usage across languages

- Tips for automation, performance, and security

Chapter 22: Export Task APIs (start, get, list, cancel)

Amazon Neptune Analytics enables not only the powerful ingestion and analysis of large graph datasets, but also the **export of graph data** when needed. This chapter provides a deep dive into the **Export Task APIs**, which allow you to programmatically **start, monitor, list, and cancel** data export operations from your Neptune Analytics graph.

Whether you're creating backups, transferring data to another system, or generating exportable insights for reporting or ML workflows, the Export Task APIs provide a flexible way to extract graph data in **CSV** or **Parquet** formats directly to **Amazon S3**.

Overview of Export Task Workflow

The export process in Neptune Analytics follows a **task-based model**. Each export is initiated as a background task that can be monitored and controlled via APIs or the AWS CLI.

Export Task Lifecycle:

1. **Start** an export task using `start-export-task`

2. **Monitor** its progress using `get-export-task`

3. **List** all tasks with `list-export-task`

4. **Cancel** a task (if needed) using `cancel-export-task`

Supported Output Formats

You can export graph data in two formats:

Format	Description	Use Cases
CSV	Human-readable tabular data	Quick inspection, manual processing
Parquet	Columnar, compressed format	Data lakes, big data processing

Each export will output a set of files to an **Amazon S3 bucket** that you specify.

Required Permissions

Before you begin using export APIs, ensure you have the necessary IAM permissions for:

Neptune Analytics API Access:

```
{
  "Effect": "Allow",
  "Action": [
    "neptune-graph:startExportTask",
    "neptune-graph:getExportTask",
    "neptune-graph:listExportTasks",
    "neptune-graph:cancelExportTask"
  ],
  "Resource": "*"
}
```

S3 Access:

```
{
  "Effect": "Allow",
  "Action": [
    "s3:PutObject",
    "s3:AbortMultipartUpload"
  ],
  "Resource": [
    "arn:aws:s3:::your-export-bucket",
    "arn:aws:s3:::your-export-bucket/*"
  ]
}
```

☑ You must also provide an IAM role with these permissions when initiating an export task.

Starting an Export Task

Use the `start-export-task` API to export graph data to an Amazon S3 location.

Syntax (CLI):

```
aws neptune-graph start-export-task \
  --graph-identifier g-0123456789 \
  --format CSV \
  --output-location "s3://my-export-bucket/exports/" \
  --role-arn arn:aws:iam::123456789012:role/MyExportRole
```

239

Parameters:

- `--graph-identifier`: Your Neptune Analytics graph ID

- `--format`: Output format (`CSV` or `PARQUET`)

- `--output-location`: Amazon S3 path where files will be saved

- `--role-arn`: IAM role Neptune will assume to write to S3

Sample Output:

```
{
  "taskIdentifier": "export-task-abc123",
  "status": "IN_PROGRESS"
}
```

Retrieving an Export Task (get-export-task)

Use `get-export-task` to check the status or result of a specific export task.

Syntax (CLI):

```
aws neptune-graph get-export-task \
  --graph-identifier g-0123456789 \
  --task-identifier export-task-abc123
```

Sample Response:

```
{
  "taskIdentifier": "export-task-abc123",
  "status": "SUCCEEDED",
  "outputLocation": "s3://my-export-
bucket/exports/",
  "startTime": "2025-03-27T12:00:00Z",
  "endTime": "2025-03-27T12:01:20Z",
  "format": "CSV",
  "metrics": {
    "nodesExported": 15234,
    "edgesExported": 39857
  }
}
```

Possible Status Values:

- IN_PROGRESS

- SUCCEEDED

- FAILED

- CANCELLED

🔍 Use the output location to retrieve exported files once the task is complete.

Listing All Export Tasks (list-export-task)

To view the export history or check multiple tasks, use the `list-export-task` command.

241

Syntax (CLI):

```
aws neptune-graph list-export-task \
  --graph-identifier g-0123456789
```

Sample Response:

```
{
  "exportTasks": [
    {
      "taskIdentifier": "export-task-
abc123",
      "status": "SUCCEEDED",
      "format": "CSV",
      "startTime": "2025-03-27T12:00:00Z"
    },
    {
      "taskIdentifier": "export-task-
def456",
      "status": "IN_PROGRESS",
      "format": "PARQUET",
      "startTime": "2025-03-27T13:00:00Z"
    }
  ]
}
```

Canceling an Export Task (cancel-export-task)

Use this command to stop an export that is currently in progress.

Syntax (CLI):

```
aws neptune-graph cancel-export-task \
  --graph-identifier g-0123456789 \
  --task-identifier export-task-def456
```

Sample Output:

```
{
  "taskIdentifier": "export-task-def456",
  "status": "CANCELLED"
}
```

> ⚠ Canceling a task does not delete partially written files in S3. You must clean them up manually.

Structure of Exported Files

Each export generates multiple files in the specified S3 path:

- **Nodes and edges** are split into separate files.

- For **CSV** format:

    o `nodes-*.csv`

    o `edges-*.csv`

- For **Parquet**:

    o `nodes-*.parquet`

243

○　`edges-*.parquet`

You can specify a **filter** (optional) to restrict which parts of the graph are exported (see the "Filter syntax" chapter for more).

Best Practices for Export Tasks

Practice	Benefit
Use IAM roles with least privilege	Prevent accidental overexposure or access to other S3 buckets
Export to time-stamped folders	Avoid overwriting old exports and aid in historical tracking
Monitor metrics after each export	Understand graph growth and export efficiency
Automate exports with Lambda	Useful for scheduled snapshots or integration with data lakes
Use Parquet for downstream analytics	Better for big data tools like Athena, Redshift, or EMR

Example: Scheduled Export Pipeline

A team needs to archive daily snapshots of their customer interaction graph.

1. Set up an S3 prefix like `s3://company-exports/customer-graph/daily/YYYY-MM-DD/`

2. Use an AWS Lambda function triggered by EventBridge (cron) to:

　　　○　Start export

244

- ○ Monitor export status

- ○ Send success/failure notifications

3. Use Athena or Redshift Spectrum to query exported Parquet files

This architecture enables a serverless, fully automated data export and archive pipeline.

Summary

Export Task APIs give you full control over extracting graph data from Neptune Analytics into formats ready for further processing, storage, or analysis.

Core APIs:

API	Function
`start-export-task`	Begins a new export to S3
`get-export-task`	Checks the status and output of a task
`list-export-task`	Lists all export tasks for a graph
`cancel-export-task`	Cancels a running export

With these APIs, you can confidently export graph data at scale, integrate with your analytics platforms, or build repeatable export workflows for reporting, compliance, and AI workloads.

Chapter 23: File Structure and Filters

In Neptune Analytics, how you structure your data files and apply filters determines not only how efficiently data is loaded but also how effectively you can analyze and query it. Whether you're importing billions of graph relationships or exporting query results, getting the file formats and filtering options right is key to success.

This chapter provides an in-depth look at:

- The **structure of imported and exported files**

- Supported **file formats** (CSV and Parquet)

- **Column naming conventions**

- How to apply **filters** to your data operations

- Syntax examples for filter expressions

Let's explore how to set up your files and fine-tune your workflows using filters in Neptune Analytics.

Overview of File Formats in Neptune Analytics

Neptune Analytics supports **two primary file formats** for data import and export:

- **CSV (Comma-Separated Values)**

- **Parquet (Apache columnar storage format)**

Both formats can represent **nodes** and **edges**, and are used in **batch load**, **bulk import**, and **export** tasks.

File Structure: Importing Graph Data

To import data into Neptune Analytics, you structure your files into **node** and **edge** records with required and optional fields.

Node File Requirements

Each row represents a node (vertex).

Required fields:

- `~id`: Unique identifier for the node

- `~label`: Label for the node type

Optional fields:

- Additional properties (e.g., name, age, created_at)

Example CSV (nodes.csv):

```
~id,~label,name,created_at
u1,User,Alice,2024-01-01
u2,User,Bob,2024-01-03
```

Edge File Requirements

Each row represents a relationship between two nodes.

Required fields:

- `~id`: Unique edge ID

- `~from`: Source node ID

- `~to`: Target node ID

- `~label`: Relationship type (e.g., KNOWS, BOUGHT)

Optional fields:

- Properties (e.g., weight, timestamp)

Example CSV (edges.csv):

```
~id,~from,~to,~label,weight
e1,u1,u2,KNOWS,0.8
```

Tips:

- All file paths must end in / for folder-level imports from Amazon S3.

- Duplicate edges will be inserted if the same edge file is loaded more than once.

- Use unique `~id` values to avoid duplication conflicts.

File Structure: Exporting Graph Data

When you export data using `start-export-task`, Neptune Analytics outputs files in **CSV** or **Parquet** format depending on your configuration.

Exported File Naming

Each export creates a structured directory in the specified Amazon S3 location, typically organized as:

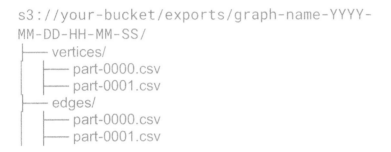

```
s3://your-bucket/exports/graph-name-YYYY-
MM-DD-HH-MM-SS/
├── vertices/
│   ├── part-0000.csv
│   ├── part-0001.csv
├── edges/
│   ├── part-0000.csv
│   ├── part-0001.csv
```

Each `part-xxxx` file contains a chunk of the data based on parallelism during export.

Vertex Output Structure (CSV or Parquet)

Column Name	Description
~id	Unique identifier for the node
~label	Node label
<property>	One or more user-defined properties

Edge Output Structure

Column Name	Description
~id	Unique edge ID
~from	Source node ID
~to	Target node ID
~label	Relationship type
<property>	User-defined edge properties

Data Types and Column Support

Neptune Analytics supports the following types in CSV and Parquet files:

Supported CSV Column Types

- string

- int

- float

- boolean

- date, timestamp

- list (e.g., ["item1", "item2"])

- map (JSON-style maps as strings)

Supported Parquet Column Types

- INT32, INT64

- FLOAT, DOUBLE

- BOOLEAN

- BINARY (for strings)

- LIST, MAP, and nested structures

Sample Parquet Schema for Vertices

```
{
  "fields": [
    {"name": "~id", "type": "BINARY"},
    {"name": "~label", "type": "BINARY"},
    {"name": "created_at", "type": "INT64",
"logicalType": "timestamp-millis"},
    {"name": "tags", "type": {"type":
"LIST", "elementType": "BINARY"}}
  ]
}
```

Using Filters in Export Operations

To control which parts of your graph are exported, Neptune Analytics supports **filters** in the start-export-task API.

Filters can be used to:

- Select specific nodes or edges by label

- Filter by property values

- Limit export to certain connected components

- Perform conditional exports based on timestamp or other fields

Filter Syntax Overview

Filters are provided in JSON syntax and support the following operators:

Operator	Description
=	Equal to
!=	Not equal to
> < >= <=	Numerical comparisons
AND OR	Logical conjunction
IN	Set inclusion
NOT IN	Set exclusion

Basic Filter Example

Export only nodes labeled User:

```
{
  "vertexFilter": {
    "label": "User"
  }
}
```

Filter by Property

Export nodes labeled User with age > 30:

```
{
  "vertexFilter": {
    "label": "User",
    "properties": {
      "age": {
        "gt": 30
      }
```

```
      }
    }
}
```

Complex Filter with Logical Operators

Export edges where `weight > 0.5 AND type = "FRIEND"`:

```
{
  "edgeFilter": {
    "label": "FRIEND",
    "properties": {
      "weight": {
        "gt": 0.5
      }
    }
  }
}
```

Using IN and NOT IN

```
{
  "vertexFilter": {
    "label": "User",
    "properties": {
      "status": {
        "in": ["active", "pending"]
      }
    }
  }
}
```

Applying Filters to Export Tasks (CLI)

Here's how to apply filters using the AWS CLI:

```
aws neptune-graph start-export-task \
--graph-identifier g-0123456789 \
--region us-east-1 \
--output-location s3://my-export-bucket/ \
--format CSV \
--filter-spec file://filter.json
```

Where `filter.json` contains your JSON-formatted filter rules.

Sample Filter Use Cases

Use Case	Filter Description
Export only user data	Use `vertexFilter` with label `User`
Export recent transactions	Use `edgeFilter` with timestamp comparison
Export relationships with weight > 0.8	Filter edges on `weight` property
Export by ID	Filter using `~id` or property values
Export specific node groups	Use `IN` on labels or property values

Best Practices for File and Filter Usage

- **Use consistent property names** across your graph

- **Flatten nested maps** where possible for performance

- Keep edge and node files **separate and clearly labeled**

- Use **filters to avoid exporting unnecessary data**

- Optimize export and import performance by:

    - Using Parquet for large datasets

    - Chunking large files into parts

    - Filtering before exporting instead of post-processing

Troubleshooting File and Filter Issues

Issue	Cause	Resolution
Data import fails	Invalid CSV structure	Check for missing headers like ~id, ~label
Properties not recognized	Incorrect data type or formatting	Ensure supported types are used
Empty export result	Filter too restrictive	Test filter expression with relaxed criteria
Errors during filter parsing	Malformed JSON	Validate JSON structure and syntax

Unexpected property values	Mismatched property names	Align property keys in your filters and files

Summary

In Neptune Analytics, file structure and filters are foundational tools for managing large-scale graph data effectively. Structuring your files correctly ensures smooth ingestion and export processes, while filters help you isolate the exact data you need—saving time, storage, and compute costs.

Key takeaways:

- Use `~id`, `~label`, `~from`, `~to` fields in files to define nodes and edges clearly

- Choose **CSV** for simplicity, **Parquet** for scale and performance

- Use filters to fine-tune data operations and export only relevant subsets

- Always validate your filter logic before running large-scale exports

Graph Snapshots

Chapter 24: Creating, Listing, Restoring, and Deleting Snapshots

Graph snapshots are a critical part of managing data lifecycle and resilience in Amazon Neptune Analytics. Snapshots allow you to preserve the state of your graph at a given point in time, making it possible to restore to a known-good configuration, back up data before large transformations, or migrate graph data between environments.

In this chapter, we'll walk through:

- What graph snapshots are

- How to **create**, **list**, **restore**, and **delete** snapshots

- Use cases and best practices for using snapshots

- How snapshot functionality ties into Neptune Analytics workflows

---

What Is a Graph Snapshot?

A **graph snapshot** in Neptune Analytics is a **read-only, point-in-time backup** of your graph data. It captures the full state of a Neptune Analytics graph—including all vertices, edges, properties, and configuration—at the moment it is taken.

Snapshots are stored within the Neptune Analytics service and can later be restored to create a **new graph** with the exact same data.

Snapshots help with:

- Disaster recovery

- Development and testing

- Periodic backups

- Data migration across environments or regions

> Snapshots are only available for graphs in a *healthy* AVAILABLE state. You cannot snapshot a graph while it's being updated or imported.

---

1. Creating a Snapshot

You can create a snapshot using the AWS Management Console, AWS CLI, or SDK.

Console Method

1. Navigate to the Neptune Analytics console.

2. Under the **Analytics** section, click **Graphs**.

3. Select the graph for which you want to create a snapshot.

4. Click **Actions** → **Create snapshot**.

5. Provide a **snapshot name** and confirm the operation.

CLI Method

```
aws neptune-graph create-snapshot \
  --graph-identifier g-0123456789abcdef \
  --snapshot-name my-graph-snapshot \
  --region us-east-1
```

Notes

- Snapshot names must be unique within an AWS account and region.

- Snapshot creation is asynchronous. Use `get-snapshot` to check its status.

- Snapshot creation can take several minutes depending on graph size.

Common Use Case

Before performing large data transformations (like running `.pageRank.mutate` or deleting edges), create a snapshot to ensure rollback capability.

---

2. Listing Snapshots

You can list all snapshots associated with your AWS account and region.

CLI Example

```
aws neptune-graph list-snapshots \
  --region us-east-1
```

Output Example

```
{
  "snapshots": [
    {
      "snapshotName": "my-graph-snapshot",
      "graphIdentifier": "g-
0123456789abcdef",
      "status": "AVAILABLE",
      "creationTime": "2025-03-
26T10:45:12Z"
    }
  ]
}
```

Filter by Graph

To only view snapshots of a particular graph:

```
aws neptune-graph list-snapshots \
  --graph-identifier g-0123456789abcdef
```

3. Restoring from a Snapshot

Restoring from a snapshot creates a **new Neptune Analytics graph** initialized with the snapshot data. The original snapshot and graph remain unaffected.

Console Method

1. Go to the **Snapshots** section in the Neptune Analytics console.

2. Select the snapshot.

3. Click **Restore snapshot**.

4. Provide a **new graph name**.

5. Configure memory, replicas, and network settings as you would for a new graph.

6. Click **Create graph**.

CLI Method

```
aws neptune-graph restore-snapshot \
  --snapshot-name my-graph-snapshot \
  --graph-name restored-graph \
  --region us-east-1 \
  --provisioned-memory 256 \
  --public-connectivity \
  --replica-count 1
```

Parameters

- --graph-name: New graph name (must be unique)

- --provisioned-memory: Memory in m-NCUs

- --replica-count: Number of replicas

- --public-connectivity: Set to enable internet access

Restoration Time

Typically takes 5–15 minutes, depending on graph size and settings.

Use Case

Create isolated development or testing environments by restoring a production snapshot into a sandboxed graph.

---

4. Deleting Snapshots

Over time, snapshots can accumulate and may consume metadata storage limits or clutter your workspace. It's good practice to delete unused snapshots.

Console Method

1. Navigate to the **Snapshots** section in the Neptune Analytics console.

2. Select the snapshot(s) you want to delete.

3. Click **Delete** and confirm.

CLI Method

```
aws neptune-graph delete-snapshot \
  --snapshot-name my-graph-snapshot \
  --region us-east-1
```

Notes

- Deletion is permanent and cannot be undone.

- Always ensure the snapshot is no longer needed before deleting.

Snapshot Lifecycle Workflow

Here's a typical lifecycle using snapshots effectively:

1. **Create Snapshot**
   Backup before major changes or scheduled batch loads.

2. **Perform Graph Operations**
   Run algorithms or modify data (e.g., add labels, mutate properties).

3. **Validate Changes**
   Test query output or application integration.

4. **Restore Snapshot (Optional)**
   Roll back if the changes produced unexpected results.

5. **Delete Old Snapshots**
   Clean up unnecessary backups.

Monitoring Snapshot Status

Use this CLI to check the status of any snapshot:

```
aws neptune-graph get-snapshot \
  --snapshot-name my-graph-snapshot \
  --region us-east-1
```

Possible statuses include:

- CREATING

- AVAILABLE

- DELETING

- FAILED

IAM Permissions for Snapshot Operations

Ensure your IAM role or user has the following permissions:

```
{
  "Effect": "Allow",
  "Action": [
    "neptune-graph:CreateSnapshot",
    "neptune-graph:ListSnapshots",
    "neptune-graph:GetSnapshot",
    "neptune-graph:RestoreSnapshot",
    "neptune-graph:DeleteSnapshot"
  ],
  "Resource": "*"
}
```

You may also need permissions for managing graphs (CreateGraph, DeleteGraph) during restoration.

Best Practices

- **Name snapshots clearly**, using timestamps or descriptive labels (e.g., `prod-pre-cleanup-2025-03-26`).

- **Tag snapshots** with project or environment metadata for cost tracking and automation.

- **Automate snapshot creation** as part of your CI/CD pipeline for staging and testing environments.

- **Avoid snapshotting graphs with running import tasks**—wait for imports to complete.

Common Issues and Troubleshooting

Issue	Cause	Solution
Snapshot stuck in `CREATING`	Graph is busy or large	Wait; if it persists, contact AWS support
Cannot restore snapshot	Duplicate graph name	Use a unique name for restored graph
Deleted wrong snapshot	Irreversible	Maintain backup policy and retention rules
Snapshot restore missing stats	Bug from earlier versions	May require re-generating statistics after restore

Summary

Graph snapshots in Neptune Analytics offer a powerful way to manage graph state over time. With snapshot capabilities, you can confidently perform transformations, automate environment setup, and back up valuable graph data.

Understanding how to create, manage, and restore from snapshots is essential to any robust Neptune Analytics deployment. By integrating snapshots into your workflow, you build resilience, agility, and confidence in your graph-based systems.

Graph Management

Chapter 25: Modifying, Maintaining, Deleting Graphs

Managing a Neptune Analytics graph over its lifecycle involves more than just creation and querying. As your analytical needs evolve, you'll often need to **modify configurations**, perform **ongoing maintenance**, or eventually **delete** graphs you no longer use. This chapter covers the complete lifecycle management of Neptune Analytics graphs, including best practices for safely managing resources.

We'll explore:

- How to modify a Neptune Analytics graph (scaling, tags, public access, etc.)

- Maintenance tasks (monitoring, backups, updates)

- How to safely delete graphs

- IAM and security considerations for these operations

- Best practices to avoid data loss or unexpected charges

Overview of Graph Lifecycle Management

Neptune Analytics is a **managed, memory-optimized** graph analytics service. Once provisioned, your graphs reside in a scalable infrastructure managed by AWS. However, there are still important **user-managed aspects**, including:

- Adjusting memory and connectivity settings

- Updating graph metadata (tags, descriptions)

- Performing backups (via snapshots)

- Deleting graphs when no longer needed

- Ensuring secure and efficient access

Modifying a Neptune Analytics Graph

You can modify an existing Neptune Analytics graph through:

- **AWS Console**

- **AWS CLI**

- **Neptune Analytics APIs**

What Can Be Modified?

Property	Modifiable After Creation?	Notes
Memory (Provisioned m-NCUs)	☑ Yes	Can scale up or down within limits
Public connectivity	☑ Yes	Switch between public/private access
Tags	☑ Yes	Add, edit, or delete tags
IAM role mappings	☑ Yes	Modify role permissions
Graph name	✘ No	Fixed at creation
VPC and subnet settings	✘ No	Immutable once set
Vector index configuration	✘ No	Must be defined at creation

Important: If you need to change unmodifiable settings (e.g., vector index), you'll need to **create a new graph** and reload your data.

Modifying Memory or Public Access (Console)

1. Open the Neptune Console.

2. Go to **Analytics > Graphs**.

3. Select your graph.

4. Click **Modify graph**.

5. Change:

    ○ **Provisioned memory (m-NCUs)**

    ○ **Enable/disable public connectivity**

6. Save changes.

Changes typically apply within minutes. Scaling may take longer for very large graphs.

Modifying via CLI

Use the update-graph command:

```
aws neptune-graph update-graph \
  --graph-identifier g-0123456789 \
  --provisioned-memory 512 \
```

```
--public-connectivity-enabled
```

You can change memory, toggle public access, or update tags using this method.

Maintaining Neptune Analytics Graphs

Even though Neptune Analytics is managed, you're responsible for some **operational hygiene** to ensure consistent performance and availability.

1. Monitor Usage and Health

Use the following tools:

- **Amazon CloudWatch**: Monitors memory usage, query volume, and errors.

- **AWS CloudTrail**: Tracks API calls and user actions for audit purposes.

- **GraphSummary API**: Provides metadata like node/edge counts and storage footprint.

```
aws neptune-graph get-graph-summary \
  --graph-identifier g-0123456789
```

2. Snapshot Your Graphs Regularly

Neptune Analytics supports **graph snapshots**, which serve as backups.

- Snapshots are stored in Amazon S3.

- You can restore a graph from a snapshot at any time.

- Useful for version control, disaster recovery, or A/B testing.

Creating a snapshot (CLI):

```
aws neptune-graph create-snapshot \
  --graph-identifier g-0123456789 \
  --snapshot-name graph-backup-2025-03
```

> Snapshots can't be used to roll back an existing graph. You'll need to create a new graph from a snapshot.

---

3. Rotate Access Credentials

- Use **IAM roles** to manage access.

- Rotate roles and credentials periodically.

- Apply **least privilege** principles for all users and applications.

4. Optimize Query Performance

- Use **query caching** where appropriate.

- Minimize large, unfiltered queries.

- Place **restrictive filters early** in Cypher queries.

- Avoid repeated graph mutations (especially inside loops).

Deleting a Neptune Analytics Graph

When a graph is no longer needed, delete it to **avoid ongoing charges**. Deletion is permanent unless you have created a snapshot.

Deletion Steps via Console

1. Go to **Amazon Neptune Console**.

2. Select your graph under **Analytics > Graphs**.

3. Click **Actions > Delete**.

4. Confirm deletion.

Deletion via CLI

```
aws neptune-graph delete-graph \
  --graph-identifier g-0123456789
```

You can optionally tag snapshots before deletion to preserve your data.

Important Notes Before Deletion

- **Check for dependent services** (e.g., notebooks, IAM roles).

- **Export data** or **snapshot** your graph before deleting.

- Deleted graphs **cannot be recovered**.

Tagging and Organizing Graphs

Tags help track and manage multiple graphs, especially in large environments.

Example Tags

```
[
  {"Key": "Project", "Value":
"MarketingAnalytics"},
  {"Key": "Owner", "Value":
"data.team@example.com"},
  {"Key": "Environment", "Value":
"staging"}
]
```

Use tags to:

- Organize by team or use case

- Control costs (via billing reports)

- Automate lifecycle policies

Updating Tags (CLI)

```
aws neptune-graph tag-resource \
  --resource-arn arn:aws:neptune-graph:us-
east-1:123456789012:graph/g-0123456789 \
  --tags Key=Environment,Value=dev
Key=Owner,Value=analytics-team
```

IAM & Security Considerations

Neptune Analytics graphs use **IAM-based access control**.

Key Recommendations

- Define **fine-grained IAM policies** for graph operations.

- Use **role-based access** for automation (e.g., ETL jobs, apps).

- Enable **AWS PrivateLink** for secure, internal-only access.

Example IAM Policy Snippet

```
{
  "Effect": "Allow",
  "Action": [
    "neptune-graph:UpdateGraph",
    "neptune-graph:DeleteGraph",
    "neptune-graph:CreateSnapshot"
  ],
  "Resource": "arn:aws:neptune-graph:us-east-1:123456789012:graph/g-0123456789"
}
```

Best Practices

1. **Always snapshot before deleting or modifying a graph**.

2. **Monitor usage regularly** via CloudWatch and summary APIs.

3. **Tag your graphs** for tracking, billing, and automation.

4. **Avoid unnecessary scaling changes** to prevent downtime.

5. **Rotate IAM roles** and audit permissions routinely.

6. **Use deletion protection** for critical or production graphs.

7. **Document ownership** of each graph using tags or descriptions.

Common Pitfalls to Avoid

Mistake	Impact	Solution
Deleting graphs without snapshot	Permanent data loss	Always snapshot first
Forgetting to tag graphs	Difficult cost attribution and tracking	Apply tags during or post-creation
Over-provisioning memory	Unnecessary cost	Monitor and adjust based on usage
Not scaling memory for larger datasets	Performance degradation	Increase m-NCUs when needed
Using wide-open IAM roles	Security risk	Apply least-privilege policies

Summary

Managing Neptune Analytics graphs is straightforward but essential. With a few strategic actions—like tagging, snapshotting, monitoring, and controlled modification—you can ensure your graph workloads are secure, efficient, and cost-effective.

Whether you're scaling up for a big analysis job or winding down an old project, the ability to safely modify, maintain, and delete Neptune Analytics graphs helps you manage resources with confidence.

Key Takeaways

- You can **scale memory and toggle connectivity** after creation.

- **Snapshots** are vital for backups and safe iteration.

- **Deletion is permanent**, so snapshot before removing a graph.

- Use **tags and IAM policies** to organize and secure your graphs.

- Follow **best practices** to maintain performance and reduce risk.

Chapter 26: Tagging and ARNs

Introduction

As you manage more graphs, users, and automation in Amazon Neptune Analytics, **resource organization and access control** become essential. This is where **tagging** and **Amazon Resource Names (ARNs)** come into play.

Tagging helps you label and organize Neptune Analytics resources, making it easier to track costs, enforce compliance, and manage large environments. ARNs provide a standardized way to uniquely reference Neptune Analytics resources in IAM policies, automation scripts, and logs.

This chapter dives deep into how **tagging and ARNs work in Neptune Analytics**, with examples of how to use them effectively for security, automation, and resource management.

What Are Tags?

Tags in AWS are key-value pairs attached to AWS resources. They provide metadata to help you **identify, organize, and control access** to resources.

Tag Structure

Each tag has:

- **Key**: The name (e.g., `"Environment"`, `"Owner"`, `"CostCenter"`)

- **Value**: The value (e.g., `"Production"`, `"Alice"`, `"1234"`)

Example

```
[
  { "Key": "Project", "Value":
"FraudDetection" },
  { "Key": "Environment", "Value":
"Development" }
]
```

Benefits of Tagging Neptune Analytics Resources

- **Cost Allocation**: Assign cost center tags to track and manage billing by project or team.

- **Access Control**: Use **tag-based IAM policies** to restrict who can access which graphs.

- **Automation**: Filter or select graphs dynamically by tag in scripts or Lambda functions.

- **Search and Management**: Find and manage graphs more easily via the console or CLI.

What Can You Tag in Neptune Analytics?

As of 2025, the following Neptune Analytics resource can be tagged:

- **Graphs**

Each graph supports up to **50 tags**.

Adding Tags When Creating a Graph

You can add tags when you create a graph via the AWS CLI or SDK.

CLI Example

```
aws neptune-graph create-graph \
  --graph-name analytics-prod \
  --region us-east-1 \
  --provisioned-memory 256 \
  --tags Key=Environment,Value=Production
Key=Owner,Value=TeamA
```

Python SDK Example

```
client.create_graph(
    graphName='analytics-prod',
    provisionedMemory=256,
    tags=[
        {'Key': 'Environment', 'Value':
'Production'},
        {'Key': 'Owner', 'Value': 'TeamA'}
    ]
)
```

Adding or Updating Tags on an Existing Graph

CLI: Tag Resource

```
aws neptune-graph tag-resource \
  --resource-arn arn:aws:neptune-graph:us-
east-1:123456789012:graph/g-0123456789 \
```

```
  --tags Key=Department,Value=Marketing
Key=Project,Value=AdTargeting
```

CLI: Untag Resource

```
aws neptune-graph untag-resource \
  --resource-arn arn:aws:neptune-graph:us-
east-1:123456789012:graph/g-0123456789 \
  --tag-keys Department Project
```

CLI: List Tags

```
aws neptune-graph list-tags-for-resource \
  --resource-arn arn:aws:neptune-graph:us-
east-1:123456789012:graph/g-0123456789
```

Example Use Case: Automating with Tags

You can use tags to automate behavior across multiple graphs. For example:

- Start exports only for graphs tagged with `"Export" = "Enabled"`

- Send alerts if graphs with `"Environment" = "Production"` exceed query thresholds

- Rotate IAM roles based on `"Owner"` tag value

Using tools like Lambda, EventBridge, or Step Functions, you can query tags and apply logic accordingly.

What Is an ARN?

ARN stands for **Amazon Resource Name**. It is a **globally unique identifier** for any AWS resource, including Neptune Analytics graphs.

ARN Format for Neptune Analytics Graphs

```
arn:aws:neptune-graph:<region>:<account-id>:graph/<graph-id>
```

Example

```
arn:aws:neptune-graph:us-east-1:123456789012:graph/g-0123456789
```

Using ARNs in IAM Policies

You can write IAM policies that reference specific Neptune Analytics graphs using ARNs.

Example: Allow Access to One Graph

```
{
  "Effect": "Allow",
  "Action": "neptune-graph:*",
  "Resource": "arn:aws:neptune-graph:us-east-1:123456789012:graph/g-0123456789"
}
```

Example: Deny Access to Graphs in Production

```
{
  "Effect": "Deny",
  "Action": "neptune-graph:*",
  "Resource": "*",
  "Condition": {
    "StringEquals": {
      "aws:ResourceTag/Environment":
"Production"
    }
  }
}
```

Tag-Based Access Control (TBAC)

AWS allows you to control access **based on tags** through **IAM Conditions**. This is called **tag-based access control (TBAC)**.

Example: Allow Access Only to Graphs with Matching Owner Tag

```
{
  "Version": "2012-10-17",
  "Statement": [
    {
      "Sid": "AccessGraphsByOwnerTag",
      "Effect": "Allow",
      "Action": "neptune-graph:*",
      "Resource": "*",
      "Condition": {
        "StringEquals": {
```

```
        "aws:ResourceTag/Owner":
"${aws:username}"
          }
        }
      }
    ]
}
```

This policy ensures that a user can only access graphs where the `Owner` tag matches their IAM username.

Best Practices for Tagging

- **Standardize Tag Keys**: Use a controlled vocabulary for keys like `"Environment"`, `"Team"`, `"Project"`, `"CostCenter"`.

- **Use Tags in Naming Conventions**: Reinforce tag-based logic with consistent resource names.

- **Automate Tagging**: Use Lambda triggers, templates, or provisioning tools to enforce tags on graph creation.

- **Audit Tag Usage**: Periodically review tags to clean up unused or inconsistent entries.

- **Use Tags for Reporting**: Combine Neptune Analytics tags with Cost Explorer or Athena to generate cost and usage reports.

Example Workflow: Tag-Driven Graph Management

A data engineering team manages 20+ Neptune Analytics graphs across dev, test, and prod. They implement:

- A Lambda that checks every graph's `Environment` tag

- If `Environment = Production`, it enables additional logging

- If `Environment = Development`, it automatically deletes idle graphs after 30 days

This ensures efficient use of resources and aligns with governance policies—all powered by tags and ARNs.

Summary

Tags and ARNs are foundational tools for managing, securing, and scaling your Neptune Analytics environment. Tags add metadata that improves organization, cost tracking, and automation. ARNs give you precise control over permissions and resource targeting in IAM policies and automation scripts.

In this chapter, you learned:

- How to tag graphs using CLI and SDKs

- How ARNs identify Neptune Analytics resources

- How to use tag-based IAM conditions for access control

- Best practices for tagging strategy

Chapter 27: CloudTrail and CloudWatch Integration

Monitoring, auditing, and troubleshooting are essential components of any production-grade system, especially when dealing with complex and highly connected data like graphs. Amazon Neptune Analytics integrates natively with **AWS CloudTrail** and **Amazon CloudWatch**, providing a full suite of tools for **observability, security auditing, performance monitoring, and alerting**.

In this chapter, we'll walk through:

- What CloudTrail and CloudWatch are

- How Neptune Analytics integrates with each

- Use cases for monitoring and auditing

- Step-by-step configuration guides

- Best practices for logs and metrics

- Example alerts and queries

Introduction to AWS Observability Tools

What is AWS CloudTrail?

AWS CloudTrail records **API activity across your AWS account**, giving you a detailed log of every request made to Neptune Analytics—whether from the AWS CLI, SDKs, console, or other AWS services.

Key capabilities:

- Log who did what and when

- Track IAM user or role actions

- Detect unusual or unauthorized access

- Support compliance, auditing, and forensic analysis

What is Amazon CloudWatch?

Amazon CloudWatch is AWS's observability platform that collects **logs**, **metrics**, and **events** from your Neptune Analytics environment. It helps with:

- Operational dashboards and insights

- Alerting and thresholds

- Root cause analysis and troubleshooting

- Long-term performance analysis

CloudTrail Integration with Neptune Analytics

Every API call made to Neptune Analytics is recorded in CloudTrail, including actions like:

- `CreateGraph`

- `StartImportTask`

- `ExecuteQuery`

- StartExportTask

- GetGraphSummary

- And many others

Where CloudTrail Fits In:

Purpose	Example Use Case
Audit API usage	Who created or deleted a graph?
Track access patterns	Which users are querying the graph most frequently?
Detect misconfigurations	Why was a graph deleted or an export canceled?
Security and compliance	Prove to auditors that sensitive data is protected

CloudTrail Log Sample:

```
{
  "eventTime": "2025-03-27T12:45:00Z",
  "eventName": "ExecuteQuery",
  "userIdentity": {
    "type": "IAMUser",
    "userName": "data-analyst"
  },
  "requestParameters": {
    "graphIdentifier": "g-0123456789",
    "language": "openCypher",
    "queryString": "MATCH (n) RETURN n
LIMIT 5"
  },
  "sourceIPAddress": "203.0.113.45"
}
```

Setting Up CloudTrail for Neptune Analytics

Neptune Analytics automatically integrates with CloudTrail—**no manual instrumentation is required**. However, you must:

1. Ensure **CloudTrail is enabled** in your AWS account.

2. Create a **trail** that delivers logs to **S3** or **CloudWatch Logs** for analysis.

3. (Optional) Use **Amazon Athena** to query logs or set up **EventBridge rules** for alerting.

Quick Setup via Console:

- Go to **CloudTrail > Trails > Create Trail**

- Choose "Apply trail to all regions"

- Choose delivery to an S3 bucket or CloudWatch Logs

- Click **Create**

You'll now see Neptune Analytics events like `StartExportTask`, `GetGraph`, `ListGraphs`, etc., recorded automatically.

CloudWatch Integration with Neptune Analytics

Neptune Analytics provides two main integration points with CloudWatch:

1. **CloudWatch Logs** – For operational log output from the system

2. **CloudWatch Metrics** – For graph-level metrics on memory usage, task status, and performance

---

CloudWatch Metrics from Neptune Analytics

Neptune Analytics automatically emits **key performance metrics** to CloudWatch for every graph.

Common Metrics:

Metric Name	Description
MemoryUtilization	% of provisioned memory currently in use
QueryCount	Number of queries executed
ImportTaskCount	Running or completed bulk import tasks
ExportTaskCount	Running or completed export tasks
QueryDuration	Average duration of queries over time
GraphSizeInMB	Size of the graph in memory
NodeCount / EdgeCount	Number of nodes and edges loaded into memory

Accessing Metrics:

- Go to **CloudWatch > Metrics**

- Choose **"NeptuneAnalytics" namespace**

- Select your **graph ID** as the dimension

- Create dashboards or alarms as needed

You can set **threshold alarms** on `MemoryUtilization` to avoid memory overflows or unnecessary scaling.

CloudWatch Logs (Custom Logging)

Currently, Neptune Analytics **does not emit detailed query logs** to CloudWatch by default, but you can:

- **Log from client-side notebooks or applications** (e.g., via Lambda, Jupyter)

- **Capture errors or anomalies** using CloudWatch Logs in your app layers

- **Combine logs from EventBridge triggers or step functions** for full workflow visibility

---

Creating CloudWatch Alarms

Here's how to create an alarm for memory usage exceeding 80%:

Step-by-Step (Console):

1. Navigate to **CloudWatch > Alarms > Create Alarm**

2. Choose metric: `MemoryUtilization` for your graph

3. Set threshold: **Greater than 80 for 2 consecutive periods**

4. Set notification: Use an **SNS topic** or **email**

5. Name the alarm: `HighMemoryUsage-GraphX`

6. Review and create

Alarm Use Cases:

- Alert on **excessive memory usage**

- Notify on **sudden spike in query failures**

- Detect a **long-running import/export task**

EventBridge + Neptune Analytics (Advanced Monitoring)

Want to trigger automated actions when a graph event occurs?

Use **Amazon EventBridge** to listen for Neptune Analytics events such as:

- `CreateGraph`

- `StartExportTask`

- `ExecuteQuery`

Sample Rule to Log Export Task Events:

```json
{
  "source": ["aws.neptune-graph"],
  "detail-type": ["AWS API Call via
CloudTrail"],
  "detail": {
    "eventName": ["StartExportTask"]
  }
}
```

You can route matching events to:

- **Lambda functions** for post-processing

- **SNS topics** for notifications

- **Step Functions** for automation workflows

Example: Monitoring a Graph Import Pipeline

You have a pipeline that bulk imports user data into Neptune Analytics every day.

1. Use CloudTrail to **audit who started the import**

2. Use CloudWatch Metrics to **monitor import task status**

3. Set an alarm if memory crosses 90%

4. Use EventBridge to **trigger post-import cleanup or validation**

This architecture ensures **complete visibility, traceability, and response automation**.

Best Practices for Observability

Practice	Why It Matters
Enable CloudTrail in all regions	Captures full API activity
Centralize logs to S3 or CloudWatch Logs	Easier querying and long-term retention
Set up metric-based alarms	Real-time visibility into anomalies
Automate alerts using SNS or EventBridge	Faster reaction to issues or workload changes
Use dashboards for key metrics	Track memory, query counts, and task performance at a glance

Summary

Amazon Neptune Analytics integrates seamlessly with AWS observability services to provide **security, transparency, and operational intelligence**.

Tool	What It Provides
CloudTrail	Records every API call for auditing
CloudWatch Metrics	Monitors performance, usage, and scaling
CloudWatch Logs	Enables custom logs from apps or pipelines
EventBridge	Automates workflows based on events

With proper observability in place, you can detect issues early, prove compliance, and continuously optimize your Neptune Analytics deployments.

Security

Chapter 28: Data Protection, IAM, and Compliance

As organizations increasingly rely on graph-based analytics to power insights in critical domains such as finance, healthcare, and cybersecurity, **data protection** and **compliance** become essential components of any Neptune Analytics deployment. Amazon Neptune Analytics is built on the AWS shared responsibility model and integrates tightly with AWS's security and compliance ecosystem.

In this chapter, we will explore:

- How Neptune Analytics handles **data protection**

- The role of **IAM (Identity and Access Management)** in securing graph operations

- Compliance features and integrations

- Best practices for secure access, encryption, auditing, and regulatory alignment

---

Understanding the Shared Responsibility Model

Amazon Neptune Analytics, like all AWS services, operates under the **AWS Shared Responsibility Model**:

- **AWS is responsible for**: security *of* the cloud (e.g., hardware, infrastructure, managed services).

- **You are responsible for**: security *in* the cloud (e.g., IAM policies, data access, encryption settings, compliance configuration).

This means customers must actively configure and monitor their Neptune Analytics environment to meet organizational and regulatory requirements.

Data Protection in Neptune Analytics

Data protection in Neptune Analytics covers multiple layers, including:

- **Encryption at rest**

- **Encryption in transit**

- **Network isolation and endpoint control**

- **Access control through IAM**

- **Auditing and logging**

Let's explore each.

Encryption at Rest

All data in Neptune Analytics is encrypted at rest using **AWS Key Management Service (KMS)**. This includes:

- Data loaded into the in-memory graph

- Graph metadata

- Snapshots (when applicable)

Key Features

- **KMS Integration**: Neptune Analytics uses customer-managed keys (CMKs) or AWS-managed keys (default).

- **Granular control**: Customers can audit key usage and rotate keys as required.

- **Compliant encryption**: Uses industry-standard AES-256.

How to Specify a CMK

When creating a graph using the CLI:

```
aws neptune-graph create-graph \
  --graph-name "secure-graph" \
  --provisioned-memory 128 \
  --kms-key-identifier arn:aws:kms:us-east-
1:123456789012:key/abcd1234
```

Encryption in Transit

All communications with Neptune Analytics are encrypted using **TLS (Transport Layer Security)**.

- Graph endpoints are served over **HTTPS (port 443)**.

- All API requests and query executions are protected with **SIGV4 signing**.

- AWS SDKs and CLI automatically use HTTPS and sign requests.

IAM: Identity and Access Management

IAM is at the core of access control in Neptune Analytics. It ensures only authorized users, roles, and services can interact with graphs.

IAM Roles and Policies

You can define permissions using **IAM policies** and attach them to users, roles, or services.

Example Policy for Graph Access

```
{
  "Version": "2012-10-17",
  "Statement": [
    {
      "Effect": "Allow",
      "Action": [
        "neptune-graph:CreateGraph",
        "neptune-graph:ExecuteQuery",
        "neptune-graph:ListGraphs",
        "neptune-graph:GetGraph"
      ],
      "Resource": "*"
    }
  ]
}
```

> 📌 **Best Practice**: Always follow the principle of **least privilege**—grant only the permissions needed for the task.

IAM Authentication for Query Execution

Neptune Analytics supports **IAM-based request signing (SigV4)**. All requests to the service must be signed with valid AWS credentials.

Supported Authentication Methods

- IAM users

- IAM roles (e.g., EC2 instance roles, SageMaker execution roles)

- Federated identities via AWS STS (e.g., SSO or Cognito)

Tools That Use IAM Authentication

- **AWS CLI**

- **Boto3 / SDKs**

- **Jupyter graph-notebook**

- **AWSCurl**

IAM Trust Relationships for Import/Export

When performing **import/export tasks** from S3, Neptune Analytics assumes a role you specify. That role must trust Neptune and include proper S3 permissions.

Trust Policy Example

```
{
  "Version": "2012-10-17",
  "Statement": [
    {
      "Effect": "Allow",
      "Principal": {
        "Service": "neptune-
graph.amazonaws.com"
      },
      "Action": "sts:AssumeRole"
    }
  ]
}
```

Role Policy for S3 Access

```
{
  "Effect": "Allow",
  "Action": [
    "s3:GetObject",
    "s3:ListBucket"
  ],
  "Resource": [
    "arn:aws:s3:::my-graph-data",
    "arn:aws:s3:::my-graph-data/*"
  ]
}
```

Network Isolation and Endpoint Security

Neptune Analytics supports **both public and private connectivity** options for graphs:

Option	Description	Best For
Public endpoint	Accessible over the internet (IAM protected)	Development and testing
Private endpoint	Resides in your VPC	Production, secure environments

Best Practices

- Use **private connectivity** for production workloads

- Use **AWS PrivateLink** and **VPC endpoints** for secure, private access

- Use **security groups** to restrict inbound/outbound traffic

- **Disable public access** unless explicitly needed

Compliance and Certifications

Amazon Neptune and its associated services comply with a wide range of **industry standards and regulations**, including:

- **SOC 1, 2, 3**

- **ISO 27001, 27017, 27018**

- **HIPAA eligible**

- **FedRAMP Moderate**

- **GDPR aligned**

- **PCI DSS**

Neptune Analytics inherits compliance guarantees from the AWS infrastructure on which it's built.

> **Note**: Compliance alignment still requires customers to configure their environment properly (e.g., logging, access control, encryption keys).

Logging and Auditing with CloudTrail

AWS CloudTrail automatically records API activity for Neptune Analytics, including:

- Graph creation and deletion

- Query execution events

- Import/export task management

- IAM policy evaluations

Enable CloudTrail to:

- Track usage for security audits

- Detect anomalous activity

- Investigate data access issues

Example CloudTrail Event

```
{
  "eventSource": "neptune-
graph.amazonaws.com",
  "eventName": "ExecuteQuery",
  "userIdentity": {
    "type": "IAMUser",
    "userName": "data-analyst"
  },
  "requestParameters": {
    "queryString": "MATCH (n) RETURN n
LIMIT 10"
  }
}
```

Multi-Tenant Isolation and Data Residency

Each Neptune Analytics graph is isolated per account and region.

- **Multi-tenant protection**: Graphs are not shared across accounts.

- **Regional residency**: Data does not leave the region unless explicitly exported.

  🌐 **Data Residency Tip**: If your organization has regional compliance requirements (e.g., GDPR), be sure to deploy graphs in the correct AWS region.

Security Best Practices for Neptune Analytics

Here's a consolidated checklist of recommendations for protecting your graph workloads:

Access Control

- ☑ Use IAM roles for applications, not long-lived IAM users

- ☑ Apply the principle of least privilege to IAM policies

- ☑ Rotate credentials and access keys regularly

Network Security

- ☑ Use VPC endpoints and security groups

- ☑ Restrict outbound internet access from compute nodes

- ☑ Disable public graph endpoints in production

Data Protection

- ☑ Use customer-managed KMS keys (CMKs)

- ☑ Encrypt data in transit and at rest (enabled by default)

- ☑ Periodically rotate KMS keys

Audit and Monitoring

- ☑ Enable CloudTrail logging for Neptune API calls

- ☑ Monitor usage patterns for anomalies

- ☑ Integrate with AWS Config and GuardDuty for compliance automation

---

Example: Secure Graph Access Pattern

Let's say you're deploying Neptune Analytics in a healthcare context under HIPAA:

1. **Create a private graph** in a VPC

2. **Use a CMK** for encryption at rest

3. **Restrict access via IAM role** with limited permissions

4. **Create a SageMaker notebook** in the same VPC with that IAM role

5. **Enable CloudTrail logging** for all Neptune actions

6. **Apply security group rules** to restrict network access

7. **Limit data exports** to a controlled S3 bucket with bucket policies

---

Summary

Data protection and compliance are not optional—they're critical to responsible graph analytics. Neptune Analytics supports enterprise-grade security out of the box, but it's up to you to configure and enforce the right protections.

Key takeaways:

- Encryption in transit and at rest is built in

- IAM is the foundation for secure access and query execution

- CloudTrail and VPC controls help monitor and isolate workloads

- Compliance features align with major frameworks like HIPAA, GDPR, and SOC

By applying these principles, you can safely operate Neptune Analytics in high-security, regulated environments.

Chapter 29: Service-Linked Roles

Amazon Neptune Analytics integrates deeply with AWS Identity and Access Management (IAM) to ensure secure and auditable operations. One of the key IAM features Neptune leverages is **service-linked roles**—a special type of IAM role that is directly managed by an AWS service.

In this chapter, we'll explore what service-linked roles are, why they are important for Neptune Analytics, how they are created and used, and best practices for managing them securely in your AWS environment.

What is a Service-Linked Role?

A **service-linked role** is a unique type of IAM role that is **predefined by an AWS service** to perform actions on your behalf. Unlike custom IAM roles you create manually, service-linked roles are tightly coupled with specific services and include all necessary permissions that the service requires to function.

For **Amazon Neptune Analytics**, the service-linked role allows Neptune to access other AWS resources in your account (such as Amazon S3) and to manage internal components required for provisioning and operating graph environments.

Why Service-Linked Roles Matter in Neptune Analytics

Neptune Analytics is a managed service, and much of its backend orchestration—like provisioning compute, accessing data in S3, logging events, and applying configuration—requires AWS-level permissions. Instead of requiring users to manually set all permissions, AWS provides a **Neptune-managed IAM role** with predefined permissions: the **service-linked role**.

Key Responsibilities of the Neptune Service-Linked Role:

- Accessing and retrieving data from Amazon S3 buckets (for loading data)

- Creating or modifying network interfaces for private graph endpoints

- Managing logs and monitoring integrations (CloudWatch, CloudTrail)

- Handling internal data movement for operations like restore or snapshot

---

Service-Linked Role for Neptune Analytics

The specific role used by Neptune Analytics is:

```
AWSServiceRoleForNeptuneGraph
```

Role ARN Example:

```
arn:aws:iam::<account-id>:role/aws-service-role/neptune-graph.amazonaws.com/AWSServiceRoleForNeptuneGraph
```

Service Principal:

```
neptune-graph.amazonaws.com
```

This service principal identifies the Neptune Analytics service as the entity that can assume the role.

Creating the Service-Linked Role

You don't usually need to manually create the service-linked role. It is automatically created by AWS the first time you:

- Create a Neptune Analytics graph using the AWS Console

- Run an operation (like a graph import) that requires the role

- Use an API operation such as `create-graph` with IAM permissions

However, if you want to **manually create** the service-linked role, you can do so using the AWS CLI:

```
aws iam create-service-linked-role \
  --aws-service-name neptune-graph.amazonaws.com
```

Response Example:

```
{
  "Role": {
    "Path": "/aws-service-role/neptune-graph.amazonaws.com/",
```

```
    "RoleName":
"AWSServiceRoleForNeptuneGraph",
    ...
  }
}
```

Viewing and Auditing the Role

To inspect the role, use the AWS CLI or the IAM Console.

View Role Permissions:

```
aws iam get-role --role-name
AWSServiceRoleForNeptuneGraph
```

View Inline Policies:

```
aws iam list-role-policies --role-name
AWSServiceRoleForNeptuneGraph
```

IAM Console Navigation:

1. Open the IAM Console

2. Choose **Roles**

3. Filter by **Service-Linked Roles**

4. Select AWSServiceRoleForNeptuneGraph

Managing the Role

Deleting the Role

You can only delete a service-linked role if no Neptune Analytics graphs are using it. To delete the role:

```
aws iam delete-service-linked-role \
  --role-name AWSServiceRoleForNeptuneGraph
```

This is useful when cleaning up unused Neptune resources in dev/test environments.

> ⚠ **Caution**: Deleting the service-linked role while graphs are still active will result in failures for operations like data import or snapshot creation.

Recreating the Role

If the role was deleted, it will be recreated automatically the next time you create or manage a graph—assuming your IAM user has `iam:CreateServiceLinkedRole` permission.

IAM Policies Attached to the Role

The service-linked role automatically includes managed permissions tailored to Neptune Analytics operations.

These typically allow access to:

- **S3 buckets** for reading data during bulk import or batch load

- **EC2/VPC** resources for network operations (e.g., creating endpoints)

- **CloudWatch Logs and Metrics**

- **KMS** for encryption (if customer-managed keys are used)

IAM Permissions Needed to Work with the Service-Linked Role

To allow your users or applications to use Neptune Analytics (and let the service manage the role), ensure they have IAM permissions like:

```
{
  "Effect": "Allow",
  "Action": [
    "iam:PassRole",
    "iam:CreateServiceLinkedRole",
    "iam:GetRole"
  ],
  "Resource": "*"
}
```

> You can scope this policy down further by specifying the Neptune service role ARN as the resource.

Common Issues and Troubleshooting

Issue	Cause	Solution
"AccessDeniedException: Not authorized to perform iam:PassRole"	Missing permissions to use the service-linked role	Grant `iam:PassRole` for `AWSServiceRoleForNeptuneGraph`
Graph stuck in "Creating" state	Role does not exist or is missing required permissions	Recreate the role or check trust relationship
Import task fails to read S3	IAM role not allowed to access S3	Attach a policy that grants `s3:GetObject` to the service role
Deleted role and graphs won't start	Service-linked role missing	Re-run a graph creation to auto-recreate the role

Best Practices

- **Do not modify** the policies attached to service-linked roles directly.

- **Do not reuse** this role for other services or custom operations.

- **Audit role usage** with AWS CloudTrail to monitor access.

- **Use tags** on Neptune graphs to identify which roles and policies they depend on.

- **Grant least privilege** to IAM users working with Neptune to ensure controlled role usage.

Summary

Service-linked roles are a foundational component of Neptune Analytics' secure, automated operation model. By delegating key actions like S3 access and endpoint creation to a managed role, Neptune can deliver a seamless user experience while keeping security boundaries tight.

As a Neptune administrator or developer, understanding how this role functions and how to manage it responsibly helps you troubleshoot issues, enforce security policies, and maintain confidence in your infrastructure.

Querying

Chapter 30: Query APIs (ExecuteQuery, ListQueries, etc.)

Amazon Neptune Analytics provides a robust set of **Query APIs** that allow developers to execute openCypher queries, monitor running or completed queries, and manage query lifecycles programmatically. These APIs are essential for building automated graph analytics pipelines, integrating Neptune Analytics with custom applications, and managing long-running or batch graph queries.

In this chapter, we'll explore:

- Core Query APIs supported by Neptune Analytics

- How to execute queries using the `ExecuteQuery` API

- Managing queries with `ListQueries`, `GetQuery`, and `CancelQuery`

- API parameters and expected responses

- Practical usage examples via CLI and SDKs

- Best practices and error handling

Why Use Query APIs?

While notebooks and the AWS Console are great for interactive exploration, the **Query APIs** provide:

- **Automation** for pipelines and applications

- **Fine-grained control** over query execution

- **Visibility** into running or historical queries

- **Cancellation mechanisms** for runaway or unoptimized queries

They support **openCypher queries only** (as of this writing), and are available via:

- AWS CLI

- AWS SDKs (Python, Java, etc.)

- HTTPS/REST interface

Overview of Supported Query APIs

API Name	Description
ExecuteQuery	Submit an openCypher query to a Neptune Analytics graph
GetQuery	Retrieve metadata and status of a specific query
ListQueries	List running or recently executed queries
CancelQuery	Cancel a running query

These APIs are part of the **Amazon Neptune Analytics Data Plane** and are scoped to specific graph instances.

Prerequisites

Before calling these APIs, ensure:

- You have a **provisioned Neptune Analytics graph**

- The graph is in an AVAILABLE state

- You have an IAM role or credentials with neptune-graph:ExecuteQuery and related permissions

- The graph supports **openCypher** (required for query execution)

ExecuteQuery API

Purpose

Submits an openCypher query to the Neptune Analytics engine for execution.

CLI Syntax

```
aws neptune-graph execute-query \
  --graph-identifier g-0123456789abcdef0 \
  --query-string "MATCH (p:Person) RETURN
p.name LIMIT 5"
```

Parameters

Parameter	Description
graph-identifier	Unique ID of the Neptune Analytics graph
query-string	The openCypher query to execute
parameters (optional)	JSON map of query parameters ($param)

Example with Parameters

```
aws neptune-graph execute-query \
  --graph-identifier g-0123456789abcdef0 \
  --query-string "MATCH (p:Person) WHERE
p.age > $minAge RETURN p.name" \
  --parameters '{ "minAge": 30 }'
```

Output

Returns metadata about the query execution:

```
{
  "queryId": "q-abcdef123456",
  "status": "QUEUED"
}
```

You can use this `queryId` to track the query or cancel it later.

GetQuery API

Purpose

Retrieves the status and metadata of a specific query using its `queryId`.

CLI Syntax

```
aws neptune-graph get-query \
  --graph-identifier g-0123456789abcdef0 \
  --query-id q-abcdef123456
```

Output

```
{
  "queryId": "q-abcdef123456",
  "status": "COMPLETED",
  "elapsed": "3.2s",
  "queryString": "MATCH (p:Person) RETURN
p.name"
}
```

You can monitor the lifecycle of the query from QUEUED →
RUNNING → COMPLETED or FAILED.

ListQueries API

Purpose

Lists recent or active queries for a given graph. This is
helpful for monitoring current load or checking for long-
running operations.

CLI Syntax

```
aws neptune-graph list-queries \
  --graph-identifier g-0123456789abcdef0
```

Optional Parameters

- status: Filter by status (RUNNING, FAILED,
  COMPLETED, CANCELLED)

- max-results: Limit the number of queries
  returned

- `next-token`: For pagination

Output

```
{
  "queries": [
    {
      "queryId": "q-xyz123",
      "status": "RUNNING",
      "queryString": "MATCH (p:Person)-
[:KNOWS]->(f) RETURN p.name, f.name"
    },
    {
      "queryId": "q-abc456",
      "status": "COMPLETED",
      "queryString": "MATCH (p:Person)
RETURN count(p)"
    }
  ]
}
```

CancelQuery API

Purpose

Cancels a running query using its `queryId`.

CLI Syntax

```
aws neptune-graph cancel-query \
  --graph-identifier g-0123456789abcdef0 \
  --query-id q-xyz123
```

Output

```
{
  "queryId": "q-xyz123",
  "status": "CANCELLATION_REQUESTED"
}
```

> **Note:** Cancellation is best-effort. If a query is
> already near completion, cancellation may
> have no effect.

Example Workflow: Long-Running Query Monitoring

Here's how you might build a basic query management
workflow:

1. **Submit query** with ExecuteQuery → capture
   queryId

2. **Poll status** with GetQuery

3. **Timeout after 10s?** → call CancelQuery

4. **Log results or errors**

You can automate this logic in Python using boto3:

```python
import boto3, time

client = boto3.client('neptune-graph')

response = client.execute_query(
```

```python
    graphIdentifier='g-0123456789abcdef0',
    queryString='MATCH (n) RETURN count(n)'
)

query_id = response['queryId']

for _ in range(20):
    status = client.get_query(
        graphIdentifier='g-
0123456789abcdef0',
        queryId=query_id
    )['status']

    if status in ['COMPLETED', 'FAILED']:
        print(f"Query finished with status:
{status}")
        break
    elif status == 'RUNNING':
        print("Still running...")
    time.sleep(1)
```

API Permissions

To call these APIs, your IAM role or user must have
appropriate permissions.

Example IAM Policy

```json
{
  "Version": "2012-10-17",
  "Statement": [
    {
      "Effect": "Allow",
      "Action": [
```

```
      "neptune-graph:ExecuteQuery",
      "neptune-graph:GetQuery",
      "neptune-graph:ListQueries",
      "neptune-graph:CancelQuery"
    ],
    "Resource": "arn:aws:neptune-
graph:*:*:graph/*"
  }
]
}
```

Apply this to notebook roles, Lambda functions, or EC2 instances used for graph querying.

Best Practices for Using Query APIs

- **Avoid blocking clients** with long queries—use `GetQuery` to poll status

- **Use parameters** for secure, reusable query templates

- **Log `queryId` values** for auditing and debugging

- **Use `CancelQuery`** if queries exceed expected duration

- **Throttle query submissions** to prevent overwhelming the graph

Common Errors & Troubleshooting

Error	Cause	Solution
InvalidParameterException	Malformed query or missing parameters	Check syntax and ensure valid input
GraphNotFoundException	Wrong graph identifier	Verify graph ID
QueryTimeoutException	Long-running query timed out	Optimize query or split into parts
AccessDeniedException	IAM permissions missing	Attach appropriate policy

Summary

The Query APIs in Neptune Analytics are a powerful, flexible interface for submitting and managing openCypher queries programmatically. They support automation, batch jobs, observability, and error recovery, making them essential for production-grade graph applications.

Key Takeaways

- Use `ExecuteQuery` to run Cypher queries on-demand.

- Use `GetQuery` and `ListQueries` to monitor query execution.

- Use `CancelQuery` to manage long-running or problematic queries.

- Always capture and handle `queryId` for tracking and debugging.

- Automate query workflows with SDKs and scripts for repeatable analysis.

Chapter 31: Query Plan Cache

Introduction

Amazon Neptune Analytics is designed to deliver high-performance graph queries at scale. One of the powerful features it provides to optimize query performance is the **Query Plan Cache**. Much like a traditional database execution plan cache, the query plan cache in Neptune Analytics stores **parsed and optimized query plans** for reuse. This dramatically reduces query execution overhead for repeated or similar queries.

In this chapter, you will learn what the query plan cache is, how it works in Neptune Analytics, how to control its behavior, and best practices to leverage it for optimal performance. We'll also cover diagnostic tips and how to disable it when necessary.

What Is the Query Plan Cache?

The **query plan cache** stores **compiled query execution plans** for OpenCypher queries. When Neptune Analytics receives a query, it:

1. Parses the OpenCypher syntax.

2. Builds an internal representation of the query graph.

3. Optimizes the traversal and access patterns.

4. Generates an execution plan.

With the query plan cache enabled, Neptune Analytics **skips steps 1–3 for cached queries**, reducing both latency and resource consumption.

325

Benefits of Query Plan Caching

- **Lower latency** for repeated queries

- **Reduced CPU usage** on parsing and planning

- **Faster response times** in applications or notebooks

- **More consistent performance** for complex queries

How Neptune Analytics Uses the Cache

Neptune Analytics uses a **normalized representation** of OpenCypher queries to match them in the cache. This means:

- The cache key is based on the **structure** of the query, not its literal form.

- Variable names and minor formatting differences do **not affect** cache hits.

- Parameters can still be used in conjunction with caching.

Example

Both of these queries will likely hit the same cache plan:

```
MATCH (p:Person)-[:FRIEND]->(f:Person)
RETURN f.name
```

```
MATCH (a:Person)-[:FRIEND]->(b:Person)
RETURN b.name
```

Even though the variable names differ, the structural query is identical.

How to View Query Cache Behavior

You can **control and inspect** query cache usage using **query hints** and **logging**.

Using Query Hints

Neptune Analytics supports special comments to alter query behavior. These hints do **not affect the query semantics**, but control execution options.

Disable the Query Plan Cache

```
MATCH (n) RETURN n LIMIT 1 /*
QUERY:PLANCACHE "disabled" */
```

Enable the Cache Explicitly

```
MATCH (n) RETURN n LIMIT 1 /*
QUERY:PLANCACHE "enabled" */
```

Hint Syntax

- Must be placed **at the end** of the query.

The format must be exactly:

```
/* QUERY:PLANCACHE "<mode>" */
```

-
- Accepted modes: `"enabled"`, `"disabled"`

Controlling Query Cache Behavior

There are three ways to influence how Neptune Analytics handles the query plan cache:

1. Default Behavior

By default, Neptune Analytics attempts to use the plan cache **whenever possible**. If a matching plan is found, it is reused.

2. Explicit Hints

Use query hints to override the default:

- **Enabled**: Forces caching for this query (if possible)

- **Disabled**: Skips cache and builds a new plan from scratch

3. SDK or CLI Overrides (Advanced)

If you're using the AWS CLI or SDK, query caching can still be controlled using query strings with hints, just like in notebooks or code.

When to Disable the Cache

While the cache is helpful in most cases, there are scenarios where you might want to **disable it**:

- You're **tuning performance** and want to test different execution paths.

- You suspect **stale plans** are causing performance issues.

- Your query structure changes slightly but still shares the same normalized form (leading to incorrect reuse).

- You're running **long-running analytical queries** that benefit from custom optimization.

Diagnosing Cache Issues

To identify whether query cache is impacting performance:

1. Run the query with the cache enabled.

2. Time the response and record performance metrics.

3. Run the same query with `/* QUERY:PLANCACHE "disabled" */`.

4. Compare execution times and resource usage.

If the no-cache version is consistently faster or more correct, consider updating the structure of your queries or using cache hints.

Best Practices for Using the Query Plan Cache

- ☑ **Write clean, normalized queries**
  Reuse structure to benefit from caching.

- ☑ **Use query parameters**
  Avoid changing literal values directly in the query string.

- ☑ **Avoid dynamic query generation**
  Instead of string concatenation, parameterize queries in SDKs.

- ☑ **Use cache hints in tuning**
  Disable the cache when benchmarking or profiling queries.

- ☑ **Log and monitor**
  Log query durations with and without caching to understand patterns.

- ✗ **Don't over-rely on cache**
  Cached plans are helpful but not a silver bullet for poor query design.

Example: Caching vs. No Caching

```
-- With cache
MATCH (p:Person)-[:FOLLOWS]->(c:Company)
RETURN p.name, c.name

-- Without cache
```

330

```
MATCH (p:Person)-[:FOLLOWS]->(c:Company)
RETURN p.name, c.name /* QUERY:PLANCACHE
"disabled" */
```

In environments where this query runs thousands of times per hour, enabling the cache can yield massive performance savings.

Query Plan Cache in the Console and CLI

When running queries via the AWS CLI, cache hints are passed in the query string:

```
aws neptune-graph execute-query \
  --graph-identifier g-0123456789 \
  --query-string "MATCH (n) RETURN n LIMIT
1 /* QUERY:PLANCACHE \"disabled\" */" \
  --language open_cypher \
  out.json
```

Similarly, SDKs can send the same hint in the query string.

Common Pitfalls

- **Using different whitespace or formatting** may still match the same cache entry. If you're debugging, rely on **explicit hints** instead.

- **Not escaping query hint quotes** correctly in CLI may result in syntax errors.

- **Assuming plan cache = faster query** — caching removes compilation overhead, but the actual execution still depends on graph size and structure.

Summary

The query plan cache in Neptune Analytics is a powerful feature that can significantly improve the performance and consistency of repeated queries. By reusing optimized plans, it reduces the work done during query execution. However, it's important to understand how it works and when to override it to gain full control over performance.

In this chapter, we explored:

- What the query plan cache is and how it works

- How to enable or disable it using query hints

- Scenarios where disabling the cache is helpful

- Best practices and common pitfalls

- How to test and tune query performance using cache behavior

Chapter 32: Query Explain

Understanding how your graph queries are executed is critical for building efficient, performant, and cost-effective graph applications. **Amazon Neptune Analytics** offers a powerful feature known as **Query Explain**, which allows you to inspect and analyze how openCypher queries are interpreted, planned, and executed by the engine.

In this chapter, we'll dive into the **query explain mechanism**, explore how it works, what insights it provides, and how to use it effectively to:

- Diagnose slow queries

- Optimize query patterns

- Understand internal execution strategies

- Reduce memory usage and improve response times

Let's begin by understanding what "query explain" means in Neptune Analytics and how it differs from just executing a query.

What is Query Explain?

The **Query Explain** feature in Neptune Analytics provides a **detailed breakdown of the execution plan** for a given openCypher query without actually running the query. Instead of returning the result set, it returns **how** the engine would process the query internally—step by step.

This is invaluable for:

- **Query optimization**

- **Understanding complex joins or traversals**

- **Diagnosing inefficiencies in patterns**

- **Training and educational purposes**

It works similarly to the EXPLAIN or EXPLAIN ANALYZE statements in traditional SQL databases.

How to Run a Query Explain in Neptune Analytics

There are two main ways to request a query plan:

Option 1: Using the AWS CLI

```
aws neptune-graph explain-query \
  --graph-identifier g-0123456789 \
  --language openCypher \
  --query-string "MATCH (p:Person)-
[:FRIEND_OF]->(f:Person) RETURN p.name,
f.name"
```

Output Example:

```
{
  "plan": {
    "steps": [
      {
        "operator": "NodeByLabelScan",
        "args": {
```

```
        "label": "Person"
      }
    },
    {
      "operator": "Expand",
      "args": {
        "relationship": "FRIEND_OF",
        "direction": "OUTGOING"
      }
    },
    {
      "operator": "Projection",
      "args": {
        "columns": ["p.name", "f.name"]
      }
    }
  ]
 }
}
```

Option 2: From a Jupyter Notebook

Using the %explain magic command:

```
%%explain

MATCH (p:Person)-[:FRIEND_OF]->(f:Person)
RETURN p.name, f.name
```

This returns a formatted table of execution steps directly in the notebook interface.

Anatomy of a Query Plan

The query plan is made up of a series of **logical operators**, each representing a step in the process of evaluating your openCypher query.

Common Operators:

Operator	Description
NodeByLabelScan	Scans all nodes with a given label
NodeIndexSeek	Uses an index to retrieve specific nodes
Expand	Traverses edges from a node to related nodes
Filter	Applies a WHERE condition
Projection	Projects or selects the final result columns
Sort	Applies an ORDER BY operation
Limit	Applies a row limit to the result
Aggregation	Performs COUNT, AVG, SUM, or other aggregations

Example Breakdown:

Query:

```
MATCH (m:Movie) WHERE m.year > 2000 RETURN
m.title ORDER BY m.title
```

Plan:

1. NodeByLabelScan – Scan nodes with label Movie

2. Filter – Keep only nodes where year > 2000

3. Projection – Select m.title

336

4. `Sort` – Order by `title`

Interpreting and Optimizing Queries

Let's go through several real-world examples to understand how query plans can help you optimize performance.

Example 1: Missing Index

Query:

```
MATCH (u:User) WHERE u.username = "alice"
RETURN u
```

Plan:

- `NodeByLabelScan` on `User`

- `Filter` on `username`

Problem: Full label scan — no index used
Fix: Define an index on `User.username`

Once indexed, the plan will show:

- `NodeIndexSeek` instead of `NodeByLabelScan`

☑ Always index fields used in equality filters for performance.

Example 2: Inefficient Traversal

Query:

```
MATCH (a)-[:FOLLOWS]->(b)-[:FOLLOWS]->(c)
RETURN a, c
```

Plan:

- `NodeByLabelScan` on all starting nodes

- Multiple `Expand` operations

Issue: Traversal pattern is too broad
Optimization: Use labels or filters to constrain nodes:

```
MATCH (a:User)-[:FOLLOWS]->(b:User)-
[:FOLLOWS]->(c:User) RETURN a, c
```

> 🧠 Add label constraints wherever possible to avoid scanning unnecessary nodes.

Example 3: Aggregation Optimization

Query:

```
MATCH (m:Movie) RETURN COUNT(m)
```

Plan:

- NodeByLabelScan

- Aggregation

This is a simple and efficient pattern. If Movie has an index, the scan may be optimized internally.

☑ Aggregations are cheap if the dataset is filtered first.

Tips for Reading and Using Query Plans

- **Start at the top**: Plans are usually top-down—start with what's scanned or matched.

- **Look for full scans**: NodeByLabelScan may be slow on large datasets.

- **Check for Expand operations**: Expanding relationships is expensive without filters.

- **Use projections wisely**: Only return what you need (RETURN n.name vs RETURN n).

- **Understand sorting**: ORDER BY forces a sort operation; consider if it's necessary.

When to Use Query Explain

Use Case	Benefit
Slow-running query	See where performance bottlenecks are
Complex pattern matching	Understand traversal paths
Building queries for production	Optimize early before scaling
Teaching/training openCypher	Explain how the engine thinks
Query regression after data changes	Check how execution plan adapts

Limitations of Query Explain

While Query Explain is powerful, there are a few things to keep in mind:

- It provides a **logical plan**, not a physical cost-based optimizer

- It does **not show execution times** or data volumes (use metrics/logs for that)

- It assumes **current graph structure**, so results may differ as data changes

- Plans are not cached — they reflect current indexing and stats

Best Practices for Query Optimization

Best Practice	Reason
Index frequently filtered properties	Reduces scans and speeds up lookups
Use labels on all MATCH patterns	Narrows search space for traversal
Limit result sets where possible	Avoid loading large results unnecessarily
Profile queries with and without indexes	Quantify benefits of indexing

340

Run EXPLAIN before EXECUTE	Understand performance impact ahead of time

Summary

The **Query Explain** feature in Neptune Analytics is a powerful tool for developers and data engineers who want to write efficient, performant graph queries. It reveals the **execution plan**, giving insight into how the engine thinks, scans, and traverses the graph.

Use it to:

- Avoid slow queries

- Reduce memory usage

- Understand performance implications

- Improve data modeling

By regularly using query explain during development and review, you can build graph applications that are not only powerful, but also fast and scalable.

Chapter 33: Statistics and Exceptions

Neptune Analytics is designed for speed, scale, and reliability, but like any complex analytical system, it generates **runtime statistics** and may raise **exceptions** under certain conditions. Understanding how to interpret these statistics and handle exceptions gracefully is critical to building robust, scalable graph-based applications.

In this chapter, we'll explore:

- How to retrieve and interpret **query statistics**

- Common **exceptions and error messages**

- Techniques for handling failures

- Best practices for **query planning**, **validation**, and **error recovery**

Let's dive into how Neptune Analytics communicates what's happening under the hood—and how you can respond when things go wrong.

Understanding Runtime Statistics

Every time you execute a query in Neptune Analytics, the system provides runtime metadata alongside your results. These statistics are valuable for:

- Performance tuning

- Query debugging

- Monitoring data volume and shape

- Analyzing resource usage

Accessing Query Statistics

You can retrieve query statistics using:

- **AWS SDKs (Boto3, Java, etc.)**

- **Graph notebook output**

- **CLI responses**

- **CloudTrail logs (for metadata)**

Each successful query execution returns a `statistics` block (when enabled or available), which may include:

Statistic	Description
queryExecutionTime	Time taken to process the query (in ms)
rowsReturned	Number of rows in the result set
nodesVisited	Number of nodes scanned or visited
edgesVisited	Number of edges traversed
memoryUsed	Peak memory used by the query
queryPlanUsed	Boolean; was a cached plan used?

Example Output (Python SDK)

```
{
  "result": [
    {"name": "Alice", "id": "u1"},
    {"name": "Bob", "id": "u2"}
  ],
  "statistics": {
```

```
    "queryExecutionTime": 42,
    "rowsReturned": 2,
    "nodesVisited": 10,
    "edgesVisited": 20
  }
}
```

> 🧠 **Tip**: High nodesVisited or
> edgesVisited values with low
> rowsReturned can indicate inefficient
> patterns or missing filters.

Measuring Query Performance

To optimize queries using runtime statistics:

- **Compare nodesVisited and edgesVisited to result count**. If high, add filters earlier.

- **Use queryExecutionTime to detect slow paths. Avoid nested pattern matching.

- **Monitor memoryUsed for large graph operations like PageRank or label propagation.

Using Explain Plans (Upcoming)

AWS plans to add **query plan introspection** in Neptune Analytics. Until then, query statistics are your main visibility into execution performance.

Common Exceptions in Neptune Analytics

When something goes wrong, Neptune Analytics returns an **exception** in the form of an HTTP error code, usually wrapped with a detailed message. Understanding these errors will help you debug quickly.

Categories of Exceptions

Type	Description
Syntax	Malformed queries
Validation	Schema or data type mismatch
Resource	Memory, timeout, or concurrency limits
Access	IAM or endpoint-related
Execution	Internal engine errors or malformed results

Syntax Errors

Most common when writing Cypher queries.

Example:

```
SyntaxError: Invalid input '[': expected
whitespace, comment, or a string literal
```

Fix:

- Double-check function arguments and list syntax

- Ensure UNWIND blocks or property lists are properly formatted

Bad Query

```
MATCH (n) WHERE n.tags IN ["finance",
"tech"] RETURN n
```

Fixed Version

```
MATCH (n) WHERE ANY(tag IN n.tags WHERE tag
IN ["finance", "tech"]) RETURN n
```

Validation Exceptions

Occur when the query logic or data types are invalid.

Common Examples:

Error	Cause
ValidationException	Invalid node/edge structure or references
UnsupportedOperationException	Using an operation not yet supported
IllegalArgumentException	Wrong argument type (e.g., string instead of number)

Fixes:

- Validate property types before filtering

- Avoid undefined variables in WITH clauses

- Check that required labels and properties exist

Resource Exceptions

These errors happen due to memory or system-level constraints.

Examples:

- OutOfMemoryException

- TimeoutException

- RequestEntityTooLarge

- QueryLimitExceeded

Solutions:

- Break large queries into smaller pieces

- Add LIMIT clauses for intermediate steps

- Reduce recursion depth or traversal complexity

- Use batchSize if ingesting large data sets via UNWIND

Tip: Disable Retries to Prevent Repeats

For expensive queries, set:

```
export AWS_MAX_ATTEMPTS=1
```

Or use the Python SDK with:

```
Config(retries={"total_max_attempts": 1},
read_timeout=None)
```

Access and IAM Exceptions

These errors stem from permission or connectivity issues.

Common Errors:

Error Code	Cause	Resolution
`AccessDeniedException`	IAM policy is missing required action	Update IAM role or user
`403 Forbidden`	Invalid SIGV4 signature or expired credentials	Regenerate credentials
`GraphNotFoundException`	Graph ID is incorrect or deleted	Check graph name or identifier

Execution Exceptions

Sometimes the engine hits unexpected conditions, such as:

- `InternalFailureException`: Usually caused by buggy Cypher or malformed data

- `QueryCanceledException`: User or system-initiated cancellation

- `GraphServiceException`: Backend engine failed to handle the request

What to Do:

- Retry with reduced query complexity

- Log and report consistent failures to AWS Support

- Monitor memory and query metrics in CloudWatch

Handling Exceptions Programmatically

If you're building applications on top of Neptune Analytics, you should always catch exceptions and handle them gracefully.

Python SDK Example

```python
import boto3
from botocore.exceptions import ClientError

client = boto3.client('neptune-graph')

try:
    response = client.execute_query(
        graphIdentifier='g-0123456789',
        queryString='MATCH (n) RETURN n LIMIT 10',
        language='OPEN_CYPHER'
    )

print(response['payload'].read().decode('utf-8'))
except ClientError as e:
    print("Error executing query:",
e.response['Error']['Message'])
```

Monitoring and Alerts

Use **Amazon CloudWatch** and **CloudTrail** for ongoing tracking:

- `QueryCount` – number of queries run

- `QueryLatency` – average response time

- `FailedQueryCount` – number of queries that raised exceptions

- **Set alarms** for spikes in error rates or memory usage

Exception Messages to Watch For

Message	Likely Cause	Action
`Cannot deserialize`	Malformed data in import	Validate input files
`Function not found`	Typo or unsupported function	Check spelling or documentation
`IllegalArgumentException`	Wrong type in function	Use `toString()`, `toInteger()` as needed
`NullPointerException`	NULL property access	Use `EXISTS()` or coalesce logic
`InvalidVectorDimensions`	Mismatch with graph config	Ensure correct vector dimension
`TooManyResultsException`	Query returns >10k results	Add `LIMIT`, paginate

Best Practices for Error Prevention

1. **Always use parameter validation**

2. **Break large queries** into reusable subqueries or scripts

3. **Log errors with context**, including input values and query string

4. **Retry smartly** — only on transient or known recoverable errors

5. **Use statistics** to proactively catch performance issues before they turn into failures

---

Summary

Understanding statistics and exceptions helps you master the behavior of Neptune Analytics at runtime. Whether you're tuning queries or managing errors at scale, this knowledge empowers you to:

- Analyze query performance via `statistics` fields

- Respond gracefully to common exceptions

- Harden your applications with structured error handling

- Monitor and optimize graph workloads using CloudWatch

Graph Data Model

Chapter 34: Data Model

Understanding the **data model** used by Amazon Neptune Analytics is essential for building scalable, efficient, and expressive graph applications. Neptune Analytics supports the **Labeled Property Graph (LPG)** model, a flexible and widely adopted structure in modern graph systems. This model allows you to represent complex, real-world entities and relationships naturally, and enables advanced querying through the **openCypher** language.

In this chapter, we'll explore the LPG model as implemented in Neptune Analytics, its core building blocks, how to design effective schemas, and best practices for modeling real-world domains.

What is a Labeled Property Graph (LPG)?

A **Labeled Property Graph** is a graph structure made up of:

- **Nodes (vertices)** that represent entities

- **Edges (relationships)** that represent connections between entities

- **Labels** that categorize nodes and edges

- **Properties** (key-value pairs) attached to nodes and edges for metadata and filtering

LPG is different from RDF (Resource Description Framework), which Neptune Core also supports. Neptune Analytics, however, is built around the LPG model.

Core Components of the Neptune Analytics Data Model

Let's break down the key elements that make up a Neptune Analytics graph.

1. Nodes (Vertices)

Nodes represent individual entities or objects in your domain.

- Each node has a **label** (e.g., `:Person`, `:Movie`)

- Nodes have **properties**, which are key-value pairs

- Each node has a unique `~id` (can be user-defined or auto-generated)

Example:

```
CREATE (:Person {id: "p123", name: "Alice",
age: 34})
```

2. Edges (Relationships)

Edges connect nodes and define how they are related.

- Each edge has a **type** or **label** (e.g., `:FRIENDS_WITH`, `:ACTED_IN`)

- Edges can also have **properties**

- Direction matters in edges: `(a)-[:TYPE]->(b)`

Example:

```
MATCH (a:Person {id: "p123"}), (b:Person
{id: "p456"})
CREATE (a)-[:FRIENDS_WITH {since: 2020}]-
>(b)
```

3. Labels

Labels categorize both nodes and relationships.

- A node can have **one or more labels**

- An edge has **one label only**

Best practice: Use labels consistently for filtering and grouping in queries.

4. Properties

Properties are how you describe your entities and relationships.

- Can be string, number, boolean, list, or null

- Used in filtering, sorting, and aggregations

Example:

```
(:Book {title: "1984", author: "George
Orwell", year: 1949})
```

Understanding ~id, ~label, and System Properties

When loading or exporting data, Neptune Analytics uses special columns:

Column	Description
~id	Unique identifier for a node or edge
~label	Label/type of node or relationship
~from	Source node ID for an edge
~to	Target node ID for an edge

These columns are required when loading data using CSV or Parquet files.

Example: A Movie Recommendation Graph

Here's an example schema representing users, movies, and ratings.

Node Types:

- :User – represents a user

- :Movie – represents a movie

- :Genre – categorizes movies

355

Edge Types:

- `:RATED` – links a `User` to a `Movie` with a rating score

- `:BELONGS_TO` – links a `Movie` to a `Genre`

Sample Data (openCypher):

```
CREATE (:User {id: "u1", name: "Alice"})
CREATE (:Movie {id: "m1", title:
"Inception", year: 2010})
CREATE (:Genre {name: "Sci-Fi"})
MATCH (u:User {id: "u1"}), (m:Movie {id:
"m1"}), (g:Genre {name: "Sci-Fi"})
CREATE (u)-[:RATED {score: 5}]->(m)
CREATE (m)-[:BELONGS_TO]->(g)
```

Modeling Guidelines for Neptune Analytics

Designing your graph well from the start leads to better performance and usability.

Use Meaningful IDs (`id` Property)

While Neptune generates internal ~ids, it's best to define your own identifier fields (`id`, `userId`, etc.) for readability and consistency across environments.

Limit Label Explosion

Avoid assigning too many labels to a node. Use **1–2 focused labels** per node to maintain clean schema and fast filtering.

Normalize Dense Relationships

For very high-degree nodes (e.g., millions of followers), consider:

- Breaking them into **intermediate nodes**

- Using **edge filtering** to limit traversal scope

Avoid Overloading Nodes

Don't pack too many unrelated properties into one node. Instead, use linked nodes for distinct data (e.g., a `Profile` node connected to a `User`).

Schema Flexibility

LPG is schema-optional, but **schema consistency** is highly recommended.

Tips:

- Use naming conventions for property names (`camelCase` or `snake_case`)

- Keep property types consistent (e.g., don't mix int and string for the same field)

- Establish domain-driven node and edge types

Using Vector Properties in the Model

If your use case includes **vector search** (e.g., semantic similarity or recommendations), include vector embeddings as properties on nodes.

Example:

```
CREATE (:Document {
  id: "doc1",
  title: "Neptune Graphs",
  embedding: [0.12, 0.09, -0.23, ...]
})
```

Use these embeddings with `topKByEmbedding()` queries for similarity-based retrieval.

> 🔍 **Important**: Vector properties must match the defined dimension set in the graph (e.g., 384, 768).

Property Data Types

Supported property types in Neptune Analytics include:

Type	Examples
String	"Alice", "NYC"
Integer	34, 2025
Float	3.14, -0.001
Boolean	true, false
List	[1, 2, 3], ["a", "b"]
Null	For missing or empty fields

☑ Use consistent types across similar node or edge types to avoid query errors.

Modeling Time-Based Data

You can store timestamps as:

- ISO 8601 strings: `"2025-03-27T15:30:00Z"`

- Epoch seconds/milliseconds: `1679942400`

Apply best practices depending on your query needs and performance goals.

Loading the Model from CSV

To load a model using CSV files, structure them as follows:

Nodes CSV:

```
~id,~label,name,age
p1,Person,Alice,34
p2,Person,Bob,28
```

Edges CSV:

```
~id,~from,~to,~label,since
e1,p1,p2,FRIENDS_WITH,2019
```

Use **bulk import** or **batch load** APIs to ingest this structure into Neptune Analytics.

Evolving the Data Model

You can safely evolve your graph model over time:

- Add new labels or edge types

- Add new properties to nodes or edges

- Migrate relationships by duplicating, then deleting old edges

But avoid:

- Changing the meaning of existing labels or fields

- Using multiple types in the same property (`status = "active"` vs `status = 1`)

Best Practices Summary

Area	Practice
IDs	Use user-defined `id` property instead of relying on internal `~id`
Labels	Use 1–2 descriptive labels per node; avoid overlabeling
Relationships	Use directionality to model real-world semantics
Properties	Keep types consistent; use lists sparingly
Vectors	Ensure vector dimensions match graph configuration
Performance	Normalize high-degree relationships; use filters on queries

360

Summary

A well-designed data model is the backbone of a high-performing Neptune Analytics graph. By leveraging the flexibility of the Labeled Property Graph model and adhering to modeling best practices, you ensure your graph is intuitive, extensible, and optimized for both analytical and transactional workloads.

Chapter 35: openCypher Specification Compliance

Amazon Neptune Analytics supports querying with the **openCypher** language—a declarative graph query language built around pattern matching. However, like many graph databases, Neptune Analytics implements **a subset of the full openCypher specification** and may include some **extensions** or **limitations** based on its underlying engine and architectural choices.

In this chapter, we'll dive into:

- What openCypher is and how it's used in Neptune Analytics

- Levels of compliance with the openCypher specification

- Supported and unsupported features

- Language-specific behaviors and known limitations

- Querying best practices within Neptune Analytics' supported dialect

---

What is openCypher?

openCypher is an open-source project based on the Cypher query language originally developed by Neo4j. It allows users to express graph patterns and operations in a concise, SQL-like syntax.

Example:

```
MATCH (a:Person)-[:KNOWS]->(b:Person)
RETURN a.name, b.name
```

openCypher is designed to make querying intuitive for both developers and data scientists by using **ASCII-art-style patterns** to represent node and relationship traversals.

Neptune Analytics adopts openCypher to let users:

- Write expressive graph queries for pattern matching

- Traverse relationships between entities

- Filter and return property-based results

- Execute graph algorithms through procedure-like extensions

Neptune Analytics and openCypher

Neptune Analytics supports **openCypher exclusively** for querying graph data, as opposed to Neptune Database, which supports Gremlin, SPARQL, and openCypher.

While Neptune Analytics aims to be broadly compatible with the openCypher specification, it currently supports a **practical and performance-optimized subset** of the full language.

Specification Compliance: Overview

Category	Compliance Level	Notes
Basic pattern matching	☑ Full	Core MATCH/RETURN syntax fully supported
WHERE clauses & filters	☑ Full	Supports logical ops, ranges, functions
Aggregation & grouping	☑ Full	Standard COUNT, SUM, AVG, etc.
WITH and subqueries	⚠ Partial	Supported in simple flows, not nested
UNWIND and collections	⚠ Partial	Basic usage supported; complex UNWIND may fail
Optional matches	☑ Full	OPTIONAL MATCH behaves as expected
CREATE/MERGE/SET/DELETE	✘ Unsupported	Neptune Analytics is **read-only**
Procedures (e.g. algo)	☑ Neptune-specific	Implemented as Neptune-specific extensions
Labels and properties	☑ Full	Multi-label nodes and typed properties supported
Path expressions	☑ Partial	Variable-length paths supported with some limits
Pattern comprehensions	⚠ Partial	Some constructs may be unsupported

Supported openCypher Constructs

Here are common query patterns and expressions that **work as expected** in Neptune Analytics.

Basic Pattern Matching

```
MATCH (n:Person)-[:FRIENDS_WITH]-
>(f:Person)
RETURN n.name, f.name
```

WHERE Clauses

```
MATCH (p:Person)
WHERE p.age > 30 AND p.location = 'Seattle'
RETURN p.name
```

Aggregations

```
MATCH (p:Person)-[:WORKS_FOR]->(c:Company)
RETURN c.name, count(p) AS employee_count
```

Variable-Length Paths

```
MATCH (a:Person)-[:KNOWS*1..3]->(b:Person)
RETURN a.name, b.name
```

OPTIONAL MATCH

```
MATCH (p:Person)
OPTIONAL MATCH (p)-[:KNOWS]->(f:Person)
RETURN p.name, f.name
```

UNWIND (Basic)

```
WITH ['Alice', 'Bob'] AS names
UNWIND names AS name
```

```
RETURN name
```

Functions

- String: `toLower()`, `substring()`, `replace()`

- Numeric: `abs()`, `round()`, `sqrt()`

- Date: `date()`, `datetime()`

- Collection: `size()`, `collect()`, `exists()`

Partially Supported Features

WITH and Subqueries

`WITH` clauses work for breaking pipelines, renaming columns, or ordering:

```
MATCH (p:Person)
WITH p.name AS name
RETURN name
```

However, **nested subqueries or correlated subqueries** are currently not supported.

Complex UNWIND and List Comprehensions

Basic `UNWIND` works, but list comprehension like:

```
RETURN [x IN [1, 2, 3] WHERE x > 1 | x * 2]
AS doubled
```

...may not behave as expected in Neptune Analytics.

Pattern Comprehensions

Syntax like:

```
MATCH (p:Person)
RETURN [(p)-[:KNOWS]->(f) | f.name] AS
friends
```

May not be fully supported and could return errors
depending on the use case.

Unsupported openCypher Features

Neptune Analytics is **read-only**, so any mutation
operations from Cypher are not supported.

Unsupported Commands

Cypher Operation	Reason
CREATE	No mutation support
MERGE	No mutation support
SET	No mutation support
DELETE	No mutation support
REMOVE	No mutation support

Workaround

If you need to update or mutate data, you must:

1. Modify your source data (CSV, Parquet, RDF)

2. Reload the data into a new Neptune Analytics graph

3. Use snapshots to preserve versioned states

Neptune Analytics-Specific Extensions

While Neptune Analytics doesn't support the full openCypher spec, it does provide **graph algorithm procedures** that behave like custom extensions.

Example: Running PageRank

```
CALL
neptunealgo.pageRank.mutate({maxIterations:
10, dampingFactor: 0.85})
YIELD node, score
RETURN node.id, score
```

Other Supported Procedures

Procedure	Description
pageRank.mutate()	Ranks nodes by influence
wcc.mutate()	Finds weakly connected components
labelPropagation.mutate()	Community detection
closeness.mutate()	Measures node centrality
similarity.jaccard()	Measures node similarity

These are **not part of the openCypher spec**, but provide powerful analytical capabilities unique to Neptune Analytics.

Best Practices for Query Portability

- Avoid mutation queries (CREATE, MERGE)—
  Neptune Analytics does not support them.

- Use **simple UNWIND** and **linear WITH flows** for
  compatibility.

- Avoid advanced list/pattern comprehensions unless
  tested.

- Prefer **basic Cypher constructs** like MATCH,
  OPTIONAL MATCH, WHERE, and RETURN.

- Always test queries with a small dataset before
  scaling.

Tips for Debugging Cypher Queries in Neptune Analytics

Issue	Likely Cause	Suggested Fix
Invalid query syntax	Using unsupported construct or typo	Simplify query, check for subqueries
Query timeout	Query too large or complex	Add filters, reduce path length
Procedure not found	Typo in CALL or wrong procedure name	Refer to Neptune docs for correct syntax
Property does not exist	Property was missing or misnamed	Check schema via RETURN keys(n)

369

Summary

Neptune Analytics provides strong support for openCypher, especially for analytical, read-only workloads. While not fully compliant with every part of the openCypher specification, it supports the most critical and commonly used features, along with specialized extensions for graph algorithms.

Understanding the boundaries of this support helps you write performant, compatible queries and design applications that play to Neptune Analytics' strengths.

Key Takeaways

- Neptune Analytics supports a **subset** of the openCypher specification.

- **Read-only operations** like MATCH, WHERE, RETURN, and aggregations are fully supported.

- **Mutations** like CREATE, MERGE, DELETE are **not supported**.

- Graph algorithms are implemented as **custom procedure calls**, not standard openCypher.

- Follow best practices and test queries iteratively for maximum compatibility.

Chapter 36: Isolation Levels

Introduction

When working with data systems, especially databases that support concurrent queries and updates, **isolation levels** play a critical role in ensuring data consistency and correctness. Isolation levels define how transactions interact with each other when executed simultaneously.

In the context of **Amazon Neptune Analytics**, isolation levels help determine what kind of data consistency you can expect when multiple queries are running on the same graph—particularly in scenarios involving updates or long-running analytical queries.

Although Neptune Analytics is **primarily an analytics engine**, not a transactional OLTP (online transaction processing) system like Amazon Neptune Database, it **does support write operations** (mutations) and concurrent query execution. Understanding how isolation is handled allows developers and data scientists to write reliable, predictable queries in shared environments.

In this chapter, we'll explore what isolation levels mean in Neptune Analytics, how the engine ensures consistency during concurrent access, and what guarantees are provided during reads, writes, and mixed workloads.

What Are Isolation Levels?

In traditional database systems, **isolation levels** define how the system behaves when multiple transactions occur concurrently. The main goal is to avoid problems like:

- **Dirty reads**: Reading data that hasn't been committed

- **Non-repeatable reads**: Data changes between two reads in the same transaction

- **Phantom reads**: New rows appear during a transaction's execution

These issues are typically addressed through transaction isolation levels such as:

- **Read Uncommitted**

- **Read Committed**

- **Repeatable Read**

- **Serializable**

However, Neptune Analytics is **not a transactional engine** in the same sense. Instead, it operates with an **in-memory graph structure** and provides a different, simplified model of **concurrent query execution and isolation**, tailored for graph analytics.

How Isolation Works in Neptune Analytics

In Neptune Analytics:

- The graph is **loaded entirely into memory**

- Query execution is **isolated per request**

- Write operations (mutations) are **applied sequentially**

- Reads see the graph **as it was at the start of the query**

Let's break down each of these points in more detail.

Snapshot Isolation for Queries

Neptune Analytics provides **snapshot isolation** for analytical queries. This means:

- When a query begins, it sees a **consistent snapshot** of the graph at that point in time.

- Any changes (mutations) made after the query starts **do not affect the current query**.

- This isolation ensures that queries return stable, repeatable results—even under concurrent write operations.

Example

1. At 12:00 PM, the graph has 100 nodes.

2. A long-running query starts at 12:01 PM.

3. At 12:02 PM, a mutation adds 10 new nodes.

4. The running query at 12:01 PM **does not see the new nodes**, because it operates on a snapshot taken at query start.

This behavior avoids inconsistencies that could arise from reading data mid-update, which is critical in analytical environments.

Mutation Isolation

Mutations in Neptune Analytics (e.g., inserting or updating nodes and edges) are handled differently:

- Mutations are **not part of multi-step transactions** like in OLTP systems.

- Each mutation is applied **atomically** and **independently**.

- Mutations are **sequentially consistent**—each write is immediately visible to queries that start after it completes.

Key Properties

- **No dirty reads**: Because mutations are atomic and not partially visible.

- **No multi-statement transactions**: Each mutation is committed immediately.

- **Sequential visibility**: Later queries see the cumulative result of all completed mutations.

This model simplifies concurrency control and improves scalability, which is ideal for analytics use cases.

Concurrency Control in Neptune Analytics

Although queries are isolated from each other in terms of their snapshot view of the graph, they can still **run concurrently** without affecting one another.

Key Behaviors

- Multiple **read queries** can run concurrently with no interference.

- Reads are isolated from **ongoing mutations** (queries always see a stable snapshot).

- Concurrent **write requests** are serialized— processed in the order received.

There is no locking or blocking between queries, which avoids contention and maximizes throughput.

Isolation Levels Summary Table

Operation Type	Isolation Guarantee	Notes
Read-Only Query	Snapshot Isolation	Consistent view of graph as of query start
Mutation (Write)	Atomic, Sequential	Immediately visible to new queries after completion
Concurrent Queries	Fully Isolated	No locking or interference
Concurrent Writes	Serialized	Applied one at a time in arrival order

Impact of Isolation on Query Design

Knowing that Neptune Analytics uses snapshot isolation can influence how you design queries and workflows.

Best Practices

- ☑ **Run long analytical queries confidently**: They won't be affected by concurrent data changes.

- ☑ **Schedule mutations between query windows** if you require guaranteed freshness.

- ☑ **Avoid assuming in-query updates**: Mutations applied during a query won't be visible in that same query.

- ✗ **Don't expect transactional rollback**: There's no support for rollbacks or multi-statement transactions.

- ☑ **Use time-based metadata**: If freshness or versioning is needed, include timestamp properties on nodes or edges.

Real-World Scenario: Incremental Update and Read

Suppose you run an hourly ETL process that adds new nodes and edges to your graph. During that time, your analytics team is running OpenCypher queries for reporting.

- The queries will run on the **version of the graph as it was before** the ETL batch started.

- After the load completes, **new queries** will include the updates.

- There's **no need to lock the graph** or stop queries during batch loads.

This allows high **concurrency** and **availability** for analytics users, even during graph updates.

FAQs About Isolation in Neptune Analytics

Q: Can I run transactional updates across multiple queries?
 A: No. Each mutation is applied independently and committed immediately. There is no transaction manager like in traditional OLTP systems.

Q: Can a query see changes made by another query that started earlier?
 A: No. Each query sees a snapshot of the graph from when it started, unaffected by other in-flight or subsequent mutations.

Q: Are mutations guaranteed to be consistent?
 A: Yes. Mutations are applied atomically and serialized— so there's no risk of partial or inconsistent updates.

Q: Do queries block each other?
 A: No. Read queries run concurrently without contention. Write operations are serialized but don't block reads.

Limitations

While Neptune Analytics provides strong isolation for analytics, it has limitations compared to a full OLTP system:

- **No multi-statement transactions** (e.g., no BEGIN/COMMIT/ROLLBACK)

- **No isolation levels to configure**—it's always snapshot isolation for reads

- **No fine-grained locking or row-level control**

- **No rollback or undo for mutations**

These trade-offs are intentional and allow the engine to scale and perform well for **read-intensive** and **data science workloads**.

Summary

Neptune Analytics uses a simplified, high-performance concurrency model tailored for analytical workloads:

- Queries execute with **snapshot isolation**, ensuring consistent and repeatable results.

- Mutations are **atomic and sequential**, immediately visible to subsequent queries.

- There is **no support for multi-statement transactions**, but **concurrent reads and writes are safe and efficient**.

Understanding these isolation guarantees helps you design robust query flows, update pipelines, and concurrent access patterns that work seamlessly at scale.

Graph Algorithms

Chapter 37: Path-Finding (BFS, SSSP, Egonet)

Path-finding is one of the most foundational and powerful capabilities in graph analytics. Whether you're trying to find the shortest connection between two people in a social network, trace the flow of money in a fraud ring, or explore local neighborhoods of a node, **Amazon Neptune Analytics** offers built-in support for **path-finding algorithms**.

In this chapter, we'll focus on three of the most essential path-finding techniques supported natively in Neptune Analytics:

- **Breadth-First Search (BFS)**

- **Single-Source Shortest Path (SSSP)**

- **Egonet Extraction**

We'll explain what each algorithm does, when to use it, and how to run it using Neptune Analytics' built-in openCypher-based procedures.

What Is Path-Finding in Graphs?

Path-finding is the process of identifying **sequences of nodes connected by edges** in a graph. These paths may represent:

- The shortest or fastest route between two entities

- All reachable nodes within a distance

- Local influence or neighborhood structure

Neptune Analytics enables high-speed, in-memory traversal and path exploration using built-in graph algorithms, allowing users to analyze even massive graphs interactively.

Breadth-First Search (BFS)

Overview

Breadth-First Search (BFS) is a fundamental graph traversal algorithm that explores all nodes at the current distance before moving to nodes at the next level. It is useful for:

- Discovering all reachable nodes from a starting point

- Exploring hierarchical or layered structures

- Identifying communities or groups

Use Cases

- Find all people within 2 connections of a given user

- Identify reachable systems in a network topology

- Detect indirect influence in social media

How to Run BFS in Neptune Analytics

Neptune Analytics provides a native procedure for BFS:

```
CALL bfs(
  sourceNodeId: STRING,
  edgeLabels: LIST<STRING>,
  maxDepth: INTEGER,
  direction: STRING,
  [filters]
)
YIELD path
```

Parameters

Parameter	Description
sourceNodeId	The ID of the starting node
edgeLabels	A list of edge labels to follow
maxDepth	The maximum number of hops to explore
direction	"OUTGOING", "INCOMING", or "BOTH"
filters	Optional filters for edge or node properties

Example

```
CALL bfs(
  sourceNodeId: "user123",
  edgeLabels: ["FRIEND_OF"],
  maxDepth: 2,
  direction: "OUTGOING"
)
YIELD path
```

This returns all paths up to 2 hops from user123 through the FRIEND_OF relationship.

Output

Each row returns a **path object** that can be processed, visualized, or filtered further.

Overview

Single-Source Shortest Path (SSSP) finds the **minimum-cost path from a single starting node** to all other reachable nodes, where each edge can have a weight (e.g., distance, time, cost).

SSSP is a generalization of Dijkstra's algorithm and is useful when edge weights influence traversal decisions.

Use Cases

- Routing in logistics or transportation networks

- Fraud detection using transactional cost

- Minimizing hops or weighted cost in network traffic

How to Run SSSP in Neptune Analytics

```
CALL sssp(
  sourceNodeId: STRING,
  edgeLabels: LIST<STRING>,
  weightProperty: STRING,
  direction: STRING
)
YIELD nodeId, distance
```

Parameters

Parameter	Description
sourceNodeId	The node where the search starts
edgeLabels	Labels to follow for traversal
weightProperty	Edge property used as cost/weight
direction	"OUTGOING", "INCOMING", or "BOTH"

Example

```
CALL sssp(
  sourceNodeId: "airport_SFO",
  edgeLabels: ["FLIGHT"],
  weightProperty: "duration",
  direction: "OUTGOING"
)
YIELD nodeId, distance
```

This computes the shortest flight path (in minutes) from airport_SFO to all other reachable airports.

Output

Each row includes:

- nodeId: Destination node

- distance: Total weighted cost from the source

SSSP with Filters and Limits

You can combine SSSP with filtering conditions:

```
CALL sssp(
  sourceNodeId: "serverA",
  edgeLabels: ["CONNECTED_TO"],
  weightProperty: "latency",
  direction: "BOTH"
)
YIELD nodeId, distance
WHERE distance < 100
RETURN nodeId, distance
```

> ⚡ Tip: Use edge weight normalization (e.g., converting time to seconds or cost to units) for consistency in large graphs.

Egonet Extraction

Overview

An **Egonet** is the **immediate neighborhood** of a node, including all nodes directly connected to it and the edges among those neighbors. Egonets are useful for understanding a node's local influence and network context.

Use Cases

- Analyzing influencers in a social graph

- Visualizing local business or communication networks

- Detecting fraud rings or cliques

How to Run Egonet in Neptune Analytics

```
CALL egonet(
  nodeId: STRING,
  edgeLabels: LIST<STRING>,
  direction: STRING
)
YIELD nodeId, edges
```

Parameters

Parameter	Description
nodeId	The center node of the egonet
edgeLabels	Labels of relationships to include
direction	"OUTGOING", "INCOMING", or "BOTH"

Example

```
CALL egonet(
  nodeId: "user567",
  edgeLabels: ["FOLLOWS"],
  direction: "BOTH"
)
YIELD nodeId, edges
```

This returns the immediate neighbors of user567, plus any connections among those neighbors.

Output

- A subgraph centered on the target node

- Optionally visualized in Jupyter notebooks or external tools

Comparing the Algorithms

Algorithm	Focus	Depth/Scope	Edge Weights	Common Use Cases
BFS	All paths from source	Fixed depth	✘ No	Friend suggestions, exploration
SSSP	Shortest path to all targets	Dynamic (weighted)	☑ Yes	Routing, latency minimization
Egonet	Local subgraph of a node	1-hop only	✘ No	Influence analysis, local neighborhood view

Visualization in Notebooks

Using the `%graph_notebook_vis_options` and `%visualize` magic commands in Jupyter, you can visualize paths returned from these algorithms:

```
%%oc
CALL bfs("userA", ["FRIEND_OF"], 2,
"OUTGOING") YIELD path


%visualize last_results
```

This renders the paths as an interactive graph for better understanding.

Best Practices

Best Practice	Why It Helps
Limit traversal depth in BFS	Avoids performance issues in dense graphs
Use SSSP with numeric weights only	Ensures correct path cost computation
Pre-filter nodes or edges	Reduces traversal load and memory usage
Visualize results	Easier debugging and analysis of path structures
Combine with centrality metrics	Find important paths from important nodes
Store frequent paths as relationships	Useful for caching or summarizing traversal results

Real-World Use Case: Financial Fraud Network

You're investigating suspicious activity in a financial transaction network. You can:

1. Use **BFS** to find all accounts connected within 3 hops of a known fraudulent account

2. Use **SSSP** to identify the **cheapest money path** between two entities

3. Use **Egonet** to extract and visualize the network around a suspicious account to see if it's part of a fraud ring

This combination provides rich context and allows fraud teams to act faster and with more confidence.

Summary

Amazon Neptune Analytics offers high-performance, built-in support for core path-finding algorithms:

- **BFS**: Broad exploration up to a certain depth

- **SSSP**: Weighted, cost-minimizing paths from a single source

- **Egonet**: One-hop subgraphs revealing local structure

These tools allow analysts and developers to explore, visualize, and act on complex relationships in massive graphs—quickly and at scale.

Chapter 38: Centrality (Degree, PageRank, Closeness Centrality)

In graph theory and network analysis, **centrality** refers to the importance or influence of a node within a graph. Understanding centrality allows you to identify key actors, optimize network performance, detect fraud, and enhance recommendation systems. Neptune Analytics provides built-in algorithms for computing **degree centrality**, **PageRank**, and **closeness centrality**, making it easy to analyze large-scale graphs without external tooling.

This chapter walks you through:

- The core concepts behind centrality metrics

- When and why to use each metric

- How to run these centrality algorithms in Neptune Analytics

- Tips for interpreting results and integrating them into applications

Let's dive into how Neptune Analytics makes graph centrality both scalable and simple to compute.

What Is Centrality?

Centrality measures aim to quantify how **"central"** or **"important"** a node is in a graph. Importance can be based on:

- **Connections** (how many neighbors a node has)

- **Influence** (how likely a node is to affect others)

- **Reachability** (how close a node is to the rest of the graph)

Each centrality metric has a different perspective on importance, and selecting the right one depends on your use case.

---

1. Degree Centrality

Degree centrality is the simplest measure: it counts how many edges are connected to a node.

- **In-degree**: Number of incoming edges

- **Out-degree**: Number of outgoing edges

- **Total degree**: Sum of in- and out-degree

Use Cases

- Identify influencers in a social network

- Detect hubs in a transportation system

- Spot anomalies in graph structure

Neptune Analytics Query

```
CALL algo.degree()
YIELD node, inDegree, outDegree, degree
RETURN node, inDegree, outDegree, degree
ORDER BY degree DESC
```

```
LIMIT 10
```

Sample Output

Node	InDegree	OutDegree	Degree
u123	100	95	195
u456	88	102	190

> **Tip**: Degree centrality is fast to compute and scales well even on massive graphs.

---

2. PageRank

PageRank measures a node's influence based on the number and quality of connections. It was originally developed by Google to rank web pages.

- Nodes earn higher scores if they are linked to by other important nodes.

- Scores propagate through the graph iteratively.

Use Cases

- Rank web pages, products, or users by influence

- Detect authoritative sources in a citation network

- Recommend trending items based on graph influence

Neptune Analytics Query

```
CALL algo.pageRank()
YIELD node, score
```

```
RETURN node, score
ORDER BY score DESC
LIMIT 10
```

Optional Parameters

```
CALL algo.pageRank({
  iterations: 20,
  dampingFactor: 0.85
})
YIELD node, score
RETURN node, score
```

- **iterations**: Number of times the algorithm runs (default: 20)

- **dampingFactor**: Probability of continuing traversal (default: 0.85)

Sample Output

Node	PageRank Score
p987	0.035
p234	0.033
p123	0.030

Interpretation: Higher PageRank nodes are more "influential" or "visited" in the network.

3. Closeness Centrality

Closeness centrality measures how close a node is to all other nodes in the graph, based on shortest paths.

- Nodes with low total distance to others have high closeness.

- Ideal for identifying bridge nodes or information flow facilitators.

Use Cases

- Optimize logistics and routing

- Detect strategic nodes in communication networks

- Pinpoint brokers in social graphs

Neptune Analytics Query

```
CALL algo.closenessCentrality()
YIELD node, closeness
RETURN node, closeness
ORDER BY closeness DESC
LIMIT 10
```

Optional Parameters

```
CALL algo.closenessCentrality({
  sampleSize: 100
})
YIELD node, closeness
```

- **sampleSize**: For large graphs, approximates results by sampling paths

Sample Output

Node	Closeness Score
u456	0.082
u101	0.079

🔍 **Tip**: High closeness scores suggest fast reachability to the rest of the graph.

Comparing the Centrality Algorithms

Metric	Description	Fastest To Compute	Best For
Degree	Counts direct edges	☑	Simple influence detection
PageRank	Propagates influence scores	⚠ (iterative)	Ranking nodes by quality of links
Closeness	Measures shortest-path proximity	✕ (expensive)	Reachability and flow

Performance and Scalability

Neptune Analytics uses an **in-memory execution engine**, making it highly efficient for centrality computations, even on large graphs (millions of nodes and edges).

Performance Tips

- Use `LIMIT` to view top results quickly

- Adjust **iterations** in PageRank for faster completion

- Use **sampling** in closeness centrality for large graphs

- Monitor memory usage for graphs >100M edges

Combining Centrality with Other Metrics

You can enrich your centrality analysis by joining it with node attributes.

Example: Top Influencers by PageRank and Follower Count

```
CALL algo.pageRank()
YIELD node, score
MATCH (node:User)
RETURN node.name, node.followers, score
ORDER BY score DESC
LIMIT 10
```

Use Case Scenarios

Social Networks

- Use **degree** to find highly connected users

- Use **PageRank** to find celebrities or influencers

- Use **closeness** to detect network brokers

Fraud Detection

- High **out-degree** with low **in-degree** may signal fake accounts

- Use **closeness** to find pivot nodes in transaction chains

E-commerce and Recommendations

- Use **PageRank** to prioritize products

- Combine with **vector search** to personalize recommendations

---

Query Variants and Filtering

You can target centrality to subgraphs or labeled relationships.

Example: Degree Centrality on "FOLLOWS" Edges Only

```
CALL algo.degree({
  edgeLabel: "FOLLOWS"
})
YIELD node, degree
RETURN node, degree
ORDER BY degree DESC
```

Example: PageRank on "Article" Nodes Only

```
CALL algo.pageRank({
  nodeLabel: "Article"
})
```

```
YIELD node, score
RETURN node, score
```

Storing and Using Results

After running a centrality algorithm, you can **store results** as properties on nodes:

```
CALL algo.pageRank()
YIELD node, score
SET node.pagerank = score
RETURN count(*)
```

> 🧠 **Tip**: Persisting results allows future queries to sort or filter based on centrality.

Error Handling and Edge Cases

Common Issues

Problem	Cause	Fix
OutOfMemoryException	Graph too large	Reduce size or scale memory
AlgorithmTimeoutException	High iteration count	Lower iterations
NoResultException	Mismatched label or filter	Verify input criteria

Always review logs and **use sample queries first** to validate behavior.

Summary

Centrality is a fundamental concept in graph analytics, and Neptune Analytics makes computing it fast, flexible, and scalable.

Metric	Best For
Degree	Quick identification of highly connected nodes
PageRank	Influence and recommendation systems
Closeness	Reachability and optimization problems

Neptune's built-in `algo` procedures simplify centrality analysis—no need to build your own traversal logic or manage infrastructure.

Chapter 39: Similarity (Jaccard, Overlap, `neighbors.*`)

One of the most powerful capabilities in graph analytics is measuring **similarity** between nodes. In Amazon Neptune Analytics, you can evaluate how closely related two nodes are based on their **neighbor sets** — that is, the nodes to which they are connected. This technique underpins use cases such as recommendation engines, fraud detection, clustering, and link prediction.

This chapter covers how Neptune Analytics supports **set-based similarity algorithms**, including **Jaccard similarity**, **Overlap similarity**, and a family of functions under the `neighbors.*` namespace. You'll learn when and how to use each similarity function, understand their mathematical foundations, and apply them with practical openCypher examples.

What Is Graph Similarity?

Graph similarity is a measure of how alike two nodes are based on their structure, relationships, or properties. In Neptune Analytics, the focus is on **topological similarity** — based on shared neighbors.

The more neighbors two nodes share, the more similar they are likely to be.

> Unlike vector similarity (e.g. cosine distance using embeddings), **Jaccard** and **Overlap** rely entirely on the **connectivity of nodes**.

Key Similarity Functions in Neptune Analytics

Neptune Analytics provides similarity functions via the `neighbors.*` namespace, allowing you to easily calculate similarity between nodes using openCypher queries.

Function	Description
`neighbors.jaccard()`	Measures similarity based on ratio of shared to total neighbors
`neighbors.overlap()`	Measures raw count or ratio of shared neighbors
`neighbors()`	Returns the set of neighbor nodes for a given node

Let's explore each in detail.

Jaccard Similarity (`neighbors.jaccard()`)

The **Jaccard similarity** between two nodes is defined as:

$$J(A,B)=\frac{|N(A) \cap N(B)|}{|N(A) \cup N(B)|}$$

Where:

- $N(A)$ = neighbors of node A

- $N(B)$ = neighbors of node B

The result is a value between **0** (no shared neighbors) and **1** (identical neighbor sets).

Syntax

```
CALL neighbors.jaccard(
    sourceNodeId: STRING,
```

```
   targetNodeId: STRING,
   edgeFilter: MAP
)
YIELD similarity
```

Parameters

- sourceNodeId: ID of the first node

- targetNodeId: ID of the second node

- edgeFilter (optional): Specify relationship type
  and direction

Example: Jaccard Similarity Between Two Users

```
CALL neighbors.jaccard(
   'u1', 'u2', {type: 'FRIENDS_WITH'}
)
YIELD similarity
RETURN similarity
```

Output

similarity
0.6

This means that 60% of the total unique friends of u1 and
u2 are shared.

Overlap Similarity (`neighbors.overlap()`)

Overlap similarity focuses on how many neighbors two nodes share, either in absolute count or as a ratio. It's useful when you care more about **shared connections** than proportional similarity.

Syntax

```
CALL neighbors.overlap(
  sourceNodeId: STRING,
  targetNodeId: STRING,
  edgeFilter: MAP,
  normalize: BOOLEAN
)
YIELD similarity
```

Parameters

- `normalize = true`: returns a ratio

- `normalize = false`: returns count of overlapping neighbors

Example: Overlap Count

```
CALL neighbors.overlap(
  'm1', 'm2',
  {type: 'RATED', direction: 'IN'},
  false
)
YIELD similarity
RETURN similarity
```

Output

similarity
12

In this case, 12 users have rated both movies m1 and m2.

Example: Normalized Overlap

```
CALL neighbors.overlap(
    'm1', 'm2',
    {type: 'RATED', direction: 'IN'},
    true
)
YIELD similarity
RETURN similarity
```

Output

similarity
0.35

Here, 35% of the raters are shared between the two movies.

Retrieving Neighbor Sets with `neighbors()`

You can also retrieve a node's full neighbor set using the `neighbors()` function. This is helpful for understanding the context around a node before calculating similarity.

Syntax

```
CALL neighbors(
    nodeId: STRING,
    edgeFilter: MAP
```

```
)
YIELD neighbor
RETURN neighbor
```

Example

```
CALL neighbors('u1', {type:
'FRIENDS_WITH'})
YIELD neighbor
RETURN neighbor
```

Output

 neighbor

  "u2"

  "u3"

  "u5"

This returns all node IDs connected to u1 via the
FRIENDS_WITH relationship.

Real-World Use Cases

1. Product Recommendations

Use Jaccard or Overlap similarity between products to find
items bought or rated by similar users.

```
CALL neighbors.jaccard('itemA', 'itemB',
{type: 'BOUGHT_BY', direction: 'IN'})
YIELD similarity
RETURN similarity
```

2. Friend Suggestions

Find users with high Jaccard similarity based on mutual friends.

```
CALL neighbors.jaccard('u1', 'u5', {type:
'FRIENDS_WITH'})
YIELD similarity
RETURN similarity
```

3. Detecting Duplicate Accounts

If two accounts share a high overlap in transaction partners or logins, flag them for inspection.

```
CALL neighbors.overlap('acct1', 'acct2',
{type: 'SENT_FUNDS_TO'}, true)
YIELD similarity
RETURN similarity
```

Edge Filter Options

You can filter which edges are used in similarity calculations using:

- type: the relationship label (e.g., FRIENDS_WITH, RATED)

- direction: one of IN, OUT, or BOTH

Example: Only Incoming Ratings

```
CALL neighbors.overlap('m1', 'm2', {
  type: 'RATED',
  direction: 'IN'
}, false)
YIELD similarity
```

This evaluates only users who rated both movies.

Comparing Multiple Node Pairs

To compare many pairs of nodes, use a query with UNWIND:

```
UNWIND [['u1', 'u2'], ['u1', 'u3'], ['u1', 'u4']] AS pair
CALL neighbors.jaccard(pair[0], pair[1], {type: 'FRIENDS_WITH'})
YIELD similarity
RETURN pair[0] AS node1, pair[1] AS node2, similarity
ORDER BY similarity DESC
```

Performance Tips

- Limit the neighbor set size with filters to improve performance

- Avoid calculating similarity on extremely high-degree nodes without purpose

- Cache neighbor sets in application memory for repeated comparisons

Troubleshooting

Problem	Cause	Solution
`similarity = 0`	No shared neighbors	Check edge direction or types
Long query time	High node degree	Use edge filters and pre-aggregation
No results	Node ID mismatch	Ensure you're using the correct `id` field, not internal `~id`

Best Practices

- Use **Jaccard** when proportion matters (e.g., similar user behavior)

- Use **Overlap** when absolute count matters (e.g., common friends)

- Filter by **edge type** and **direction** for precision

- Pre-filter nodes by type to avoid invalid comparisons

- Combine similarity with other signals (e.g., vector, metadata) for hybrid models

407

Summary

Neptune Analytics makes it easy to compute graph-based similarity using powerful, built-in functions like `neighbors.jaccard()` and `neighbors.overlap()`. These tools allow you to go beyond basic queries and uncover nuanced patterns of similarity across your graph — whether you're finding lookalike users, recommending items, or spotting fraud.

By mastering these similarity functions and integrating them into your queries and applications, you'll unlock deeper value from your graph data.

Chapter 35: openCypher Specification Compliance

Amazon Neptune Analytics supports querying graph data using **openCypher**, a declarative query language designed for property graphs. While Neptune Analytics aims to align with the openCypher specification, it does not implement **the full standard**. Instead, it focuses on supporting a **performance-optimized subset** of openCypher, tailored to large-scale, read-only graph analytics.

In this chapter, you'll learn:

- What openCypher is and how it's used in Neptune Analytics

- The scope and limitations of Neptune's openCypher support

- Which openCypher features are supported, partially supported, or unsupported

- Neptune-specific extensions for graph algorithms

- Best practices for writing portable and efficient queries

Understanding these details will help you write better, more compatible queries and avoid unsupported syntax or behavior.

What is openCypher?

openCypher is an open-source graph query language derived from Neo4j's Cypher. It's designed to express graph patterns intuitively using ASCII-art-like syntax and to operate over property graph models (nodes, relationships, labels, properties).

Example:

```
MATCH (p:Person)-[:KNOWS]->(f:Person)
RETURN p.name, f.name
```

This query finds people and their friends in a graph.

openCypher is popular because it combines:

- Familiar SQL-like constructs (MATCH, WHERE, RETURN)

- Pattern-based traversal

- Expressiveness for deep graph analysis

Neptune Analytics uses openCypher as its **primary query interface**, particularly because it's intuitive and powerful for analytical use cases.

Neptune Analytics and openCypher: Overview

While Neptune Analytics uses openCypher for all queries, its implementation is **read-only** and **optimized for speed**. This leads to two key design decisions:

1. **Only a subset of the openCypher specification is supported**

2. **Custom procedures are introduced** for executing graph algorithms

This means that some Cypher features commonly available in transactional databases like Neo4j (e.g., data mutation with CREATE, SET, DELETE) are not available in Neptune Analytics.

Supported openCypher Constructs

Neptune Analytics supports many commonly used openCypher features:

Feature	Supported	Notes
MATCH, WHERE, RETURN	☑	Fully supported
Labels and relationship types	☑	Multi-labels and typed relationships
OPTIONAL MATCH	☑	Useful for left-join-like queries
ORDER BY, LIMIT, SKIP	☑	Works as expected
Aggregations (COUNT, SUM)	☑	Full set of aggregations supported
UNWIND (basic)	☑	Supports simple list expansion
WITH	☑	Supported for query chaining
DISTINCT	☑	Works with both values and paths
Filtering (=, >, IN, etc.)	☑	Standard operators and functions

Example: Aggregation and Filtering

```
MATCH (p:Person)-[:WORKS_FOR]->(c:Company)
WHERE p.age > 30
RETURN c.name, count(p) AS total_employees
```

411

```
ORDER BY total_employees DESC
```

This query counts employees over age 30 per company.

Partially Supported openCypher Features

Some features are **partially implemented**, meaning they work in basic scenarios but have limitations in more advanced forms.

Feature	Status	Notes
UNWIND with list comprehensions	⚠ Partial	Simple arrays work; complex nesting may fail
Pattern comprehensions	⚠ Partial	Limited support; avoid nesting or filters
WITH for subqueries	⚠ Partial	Works for chaining but not for nesting
Path expressions (*1..N)	⚠ Partial	Long paths may cause performance issues
List and map functions	⚠ Partial	Some list functions are not available

Example: UNWIND (Supported)

```
WITH ['Alice', 'Bob'] AS names
UNWIND names AS name
RETURN name
```

Example: Pattern Comprehension (May Fail)

```
MATCH (p:Person)
RETURN [(p)-[:KNOWS]->(f:Person) | f.name]
AS friends
```

This query might not work in Neptune
Analytics depending on the complexity of the
match.

Unsupported Features

As a **read-only** graph service focused on **analytics**,
Neptune Analytics does not support any Cypher
commands that modify the graph.

Feature	Status	Reason
CREATE	✗	Read-only engine
MERGE	✗	Not supported
SET, REMOVE	✗	Cannot mutate node/edge properties
DELETE	✗	No support for data deletion
Transactions	✗	No multi-step or ACID transactions

Unsupported Example:

```
// ✗ Not supported
CREATE (p:Person {name: 'Alice'})
```

If you need to modify graph data, you'll need
to update the source (e.g., CSV or Parquet)
and reimport it into Neptune Analytics.

Neptune-Specific Extensions: Built-in Algorithms

Neptune Analytics introduces custom **procedure calls** for
graph algorithms, implemented as Cypher extensions:

Procedure	Description
pageRank.mutate()	Computes PageRank and stores score
wcc.mutate()	Weakly Connected Components
labelPropagation.mutate()	Community detection
closeness.mutate()	Node centrality based on path length
similarity.jaccard()	Pairwise similarity between nodes

Example: Running PageRank

```
CALL
neptunealgo.pageRank.mutate({maxIterations:
10})
YIELD node, score
RETURN node.id, score
ORDER BY score DESC
```

Notes:

- These procedures **extend openCypher** but are **not part of the official spec**

- Results are written as node properties (e.g., score, communityId)

Function Support

Most commonly used functions are supported:

- **Numeric**: abs(), round(), floor(), ceil()

- **String**: toLower(), substring(), replace()

- **Date/Time**: `date()`, `datetime()`

- **Collection**: `size()`, `exists()`, `collect()`

Best Practices for Compatibility

1. **Avoid write operations** like `CREATE`, `MERGE`, or `SET`.

2. **Test list comprehensions and pattern projections** in small cases first.

3. **Favor simple `UNWIND` patterns**; avoid nested `WITH` + `UNWIND` combos.

4. **Use labels and relationship types** for performance and accuracy.

5. **Modularize logic with `WITH` clauses**, but avoid nested subqueries.

Debugging Unsupported Queries

Error Message	Likely Cause	Suggested Fix
Unknown procedure	Typos or unsupported custom procedure	Check for typos, ensure algorithm exists
Unexpected token	Syntax not supported	Simplify or remove unsupported construct
Procedure does not exist	Not a valid Neptune procedure	Use documented Neptune procedures only
Query plan failed	Feature unsupported or unstable pattern	Break into smaller parts, test incrementally

Summary

Neptune Analytics delivers strong support for openCypher's core querying capabilities—especially for **pattern matching, filtering, aggregation, and traversal**. It does **not implement mutation or transactional features**, and some advanced syntax (like pattern comprehensions or nested subqueries) may be limited.

Instead, it extends openCypher with **Neptune-specific procedures** for running scalable graph algorithms, providing a focused toolset for read-intensive graph analytics.

Key Takeaways

- Neptune Analytics supports a **read-only subset** of openCypher focused on analytics.

- Core querying features (MATCH, WHERE, RETURN, OPTIONAL MATCH, aggregations) are fully supported.

- Mutations (CREATE, DELETE, SET) are **not supported**.

- Use **Neptune algorithm procedures** (e.g., pageRank.mutate) to run analytical algorithms.

- Stick to **simple patterns and avoid nesting** for best performance and compatibility.

Chapter 36: Isolation Levels

Introduction

When working with data systems, especially databases that support concurrent queries and updates, **isolation levels** play a critical role in ensuring data consistency and correctness. Isolation levels define how transactions interact with each other when executed simultaneously.

In the context of **Amazon Neptune Analytics**, isolation levels help determine what kind of data consistency you can expect when multiple queries are running on the same graph—particularly in scenarios involving updates or long-running analytical queries.

Although Neptune Analytics is **primarily an analytics engine**, not a transactional OLTP (online transaction processing) system like Amazon Neptune Database, it **does support write operations** (mutations) and concurrent query execution. Understanding how isolation is handled allows developers and data scientists to write reliable, predictable queries in shared environments.

In this chapter, we'll explore what isolation levels mean in Neptune Analytics, how the engine ensures consistency during concurrent access, and what guarantees are provided during reads, writes, and mixed workloads.

What Are Isolation Levels?

In traditional database systems, **isolation levels** define how the system behaves when multiple transactions occur concurrently. The main goal is to avoid problems like:

- **Dirty reads**: Reading data that hasn't been committed

417

- **Non-repeatable reads**: Data changes between two reads in the same transaction

- **Phantom reads**: New rows appear during a transaction's execution

These issues are typically addressed through transaction isolation levels such as:

- **Read Uncommitted**

- **Read Committed**

- **Repeatable Read**

- **Serializable**

However, Neptune Analytics is **not a transactional engine** in the same sense. Instead, it operates with an **in-memory graph structure** and provides a different, simplified model of **concurrent query execution and isolation**, tailored for graph analytics.

How Isolation Works in Neptune Analytics

In Neptune Analytics:

- The graph is **loaded entirely into memory**

- Query execution is **isolated per request**

- Write operations (mutations) are **applied sequentially**

- Reads see the graph **as it was at the start of the query**

Let's break down each of these points in more detail.

Snapshot Isolation for Queries

Neptune Analytics provides **snapshot isolation** for analytical queries. This means:

- When a query begins, it sees a **consistent snapshot** of the graph at that point in time.

- Any changes (mutations) made after the query starts **do not affect the current query**.

- This isolation ensures that queries return stable, repeatable results—even under concurrent write operations.

Example

1. At 12:00 PM, the graph has 100 nodes.

2. A long-running query starts at 12:01 PM.

3. At 12:02 PM, a mutation adds 10 new nodes.

4. The running query at 12:01 PM **does not see the new nodes**, because it operates on a snapshot taken at query start.

This behavior avoids inconsistencies that could arise from reading data mid-update, which is critical in analytical environments.

Mutation Isolation

Mutations in Neptune Analytics (e.g., inserting or updating nodes and edges) are handled differently:

- Mutations are **not part of multi-step transactions** like in OLTP systems.

- Each mutation is applied **atomically** and **independently**.

- Mutations are **sequentially consistent**—each write is immediately visible to queries that start after it completes.

Key Properties

- **No dirty reads**: Because mutations are atomic and not partially visible.

- **No multi-statement transactions**: Each mutation is committed immediately.

- **Sequential visibility**: Later queries see the cumulative result of all completed mutations.

This model simplifies concurrency control and improves scalability, which is ideal for analytics use cases.

Concurrency Control in Neptune Analytics

Although queries are isolated from each other in terms of their snapshot view of the graph, they can still **run concurrently** without affecting one another.

Key Behaviors

- Multiple **read queries** can run concurrently with no interference.

- Reads are isolated from **ongoing mutations** (queries always see a stable snapshot).

- Concurrent **write requests** are serialized— processed in the order received.

There is no locking or blocking between queries, which avoids contention and maximizes throughput.

Isolation Levels Summary Table

Operation Type	Isolation Guarantee	Notes
Read-Only Query	Snapshot Isolation	Consistent view of graph as of query start
Mutation (Write)	Atomic, Sequential	Immediately visible to new queries after completion
Concurrent Queries	Fully Isolated	No locking or interference
Concurrent Writes	Serialized	Applied one at a time in arrival order

Impact of Isolation on Query Design

Knowing that Neptune Analytics uses snapshot isolation can influence how you design queries and workflows.

Best Practices

- ☑ **Run long analytical queries confidently**: They won't be affected by concurrent data changes.

- ☑ **Schedule mutations between query windows** if you require guaranteed freshness.

- ☑ **Avoid assuming in-query updates**: Mutations applied during a query won't be visible in that same query.

- ✗ **Don't expect transactional rollback**: There's no support for rollbacks or multi-statement transactions.

- ☑ **Use time-based metadata**: If freshness or versioning is needed, include timestamp properties on nodes or edges.

Real-World Scenario: Incremental Update and Read

Suppose you run an hourly ETL process that adds new nodes and edges to your graph. During that time, your analytics team is running OpenCypher queries for reporting.

- The queries will run on the **version of the graph as it was before** the ETL batch started.

- After the load completes, **new queries** will include the updates.

- There's **no need to lock the graph** or stop queries during batch loads.

This allows high **concurrency** and **availability** for analytics users, even during graph updates.

FAQs About Isolation in Neptune Analytics

Q: Can I run transactional updates across multiple queries?
 A: No. Each mutation is applied independently and committed immediately. There is no transaction manager like in traditional OLTP systems.

Q: Can a query see changes made by another query that started earlier?
 A: No. Each query sees a snapshot of the graph from when it started, unaffected by other in-flight or subsequent mutations.

Q: Are mutations guaranteed to be consistent?
 A: Yes. Mutations are applied atomically and serialized— so there's no risk of partial or inconsistent updates.

Q: Do queries block each other?
 A: No. Read queries run concurrently without contention. Write operations are serialized but don't block reads.

Limitations

While Neptune Analytics provides strong isolation for analytics, it has limitations compared to a full OLTP system:

- **No multi-statement transactions** (e.g., no BEGIN/COMMIT/ROLLBACK)

- **No isolation levels to configure**—it's always snapshot isolation for reads

- **No fine-grained locking or row-level control**

- **No rollback or undo for mutations**

These trade-offs are intentional and allow the engine to scale and perform well for **read-intensive** and **data science workloads**.

Summary

Neptune Analytics uses a simplified, high-performance concurrency model tailored for analytical workloads:

- Queries execute with **snapshot isolation**, ensuring consistent and repeatable results.

- Mutations are **atomic and sequential**, immediately visible to subsequent queries.

- There is **no support for multi-statement transactions**, but **concurrent reads and writes are safe and efficient**.

Understanding these isolation guarantees helps you design robust query flows, update pipelines, and concurrent access patterns that work seamlessly at scale.

Chapter 37: Path-Finding (BFS, SSSP, Egonet)

Path-finding is one of the most foundational and powerful capabilities in graph analytics. Whether you're trying to find the shortest connection between two people in a social network, trace the flow of money in a fraud ring, or explore local neighborhoods of a node, **Amazon Neptune Analytics** offers built-in support for **path-finding algorithms**.

In this chapter, we'll focus on three of the most essential path-finding techniques supported natively in Neptune Analytics:

- **Breadth-First Search (BFS)**

- **Single-Source Shortest Path (SSSP)**

- **Egonet Extraction**

We'll explain what each algorithm does, when to use it, and how to run it using Neptune Analytics' built-in openCypher-based procedures.

What Is Path-Finding in Graphs?

Path-finding is the process of identifying **sequences of nodes connected by edges** in a graph. These paths may represent:

- The shortest or fastest route between two entities

- All reachable nodes within a distance

- Local influence or neighborhood structure

Neptune Analytics enables high-speed, in-memory traversal and path exploration using built-in graph algorithms, allowing users to analyze even massive graphs interactively.

Breadth-First Search (BFS)

Overview

Breadth-First Search (BFS) is a fundamental graph traversal algorithm that explores all nodes at the current distance before moving to nodes at the next level. It is useful for:

- Discovering all reachable nodes from a starting point

- Exploring hierarchical or layered structures

- Identifying communities or groups

Use Cases

- Find all people within 2 connections of a given user

- Identify reachable systems in a network topology

- Detect indirect influence in social media

How to Run BFS in Neptune Analytics

Neptune Analytics provides a native procedure for BFS:

```
CALL bfs(
  sourceNodeId: STRING,
  edgeLabels: LIST<STRING>,
  maxDepth: INTEGER,
  direction: STRING,
  [filters]
)
YIELD path
```

Parameters

Parameter	Description
sourceNodeId	The ID of the starting node
edgeLabels	A list of edge labels to follow
maxDepth	The maximum number of hops to explore
direction	"OUTGOING", "INCOMING", or "BOTH"
filters	Optional filters for edge or node properties

Example

```
CALL bfs(
  sourceNodeId: "user123",
  edgeLabels: ["FRIEND_OF"],
  maxDepth: 2,
  direction: "OUTGOING"
)
YIELD path
```

This returns all paths up to 2 hops from user123 through the FRIEND_OF relationship.

Output

Each row returns a **path object** that can be processed, visualized, or filtered further.

Overview

Single-Source Shortest Path (SSSP) finds the **minimum-cost path from a single starting node** to all other reachable nodes, where each edge can have a weight (e.g., distance, time, cost).

SSSP is a generalization of Dijkstra's algorithm and is useful when edge weights influence traversal decisions.

Use Cases

- Routing in logistics or transportation networks

- Fraud detection using transactional cost

- Minimizing hops or weighted cost in network traffic

How to Run SSSP in Neptune Analytics

```
CALL sssp(
  sourceNodeId: STRING,
  edgeLabels: LIST<STRING>,
  weightProperty: STRING,
  direction: STRING
)
YIELD nodeId, distance
```

Parameters

Parameter	Description
sourceNodeId	The node where the search starts
edgeLabels	Labels to follow for traversal
weightProperty	Edge property used as cost/weight
direction	"OUTGOING", "INCOMING", or "BOTH"

Example

```
CALL sssp(
  sourceNodeId: "airport_SFO",
  edgeLabels: ["FLIGHT"],
  weightProperty: "duration",
  direction: "OUTGOING"
)
YIELD nodeId, distance
```

This computes the shortest flight path (in minutes) from airport_SFO to all other reachable airports.

Output

Each row includes:

- nodeId: Destination node

- distance: Total weighted cost from the source

SSSP with Filters and Limits

You can combine SSSP with filtering conditions:

```
CALL sssp(
  sourceNodeId: "serverA",
  edgeLabels: ["CONNECTED_TO"],
  weightProperty: "latency",
  direction: "BOTH"
)
YIELD nodeId, distance
WHERE distance < 100
RETURN nodeId, distance
```

> ⚡ Tip: Use edge weight normalization (e.g., converting time to seconds or cost to units) for consistency in large graphs.

Egonet Extraction

Overview

An **Egonet** is the **immediate neighborhood** of a node, including all nodes directly connected to it and the edges among those neighbors. Egonets are useful for understanding a node's local influence and network context.

Use Cases

- Analyzing influencers in a social graph

- Visualizing local business or communication networks

- Detecting fraud rings or cliques

How to Run Egonet in Neptune Analytics

```
CALL egonet(
  nodeId: STRING,
  edgeLabels: LIST<STRING>,
  direction: STRING
)
YIELD nodeId, edges
```

Parameters

Parameter	Description
nodeId	The center node of the egonet
edgeLabels	Labels of relationships to include
direction	"OUTGOING", "INCOMING", or "BOTH"

Example

```
CALL egonet(
  nodeId: "user567",
  edgeLabels: ["FOLLOWS"],
  direction: "BOTH"
)
YIELD nodeId, edges
```

This returns the immediate neighbors of user567, plus any connections among those neighbors.

Output

- A subgraph centered on the target node

- Optionally visualized in Jupyter notebooks or external tools

431

Comparing the Algorithms

Algorithm	Focus	Depth/Scope	Edge Weights	Common Use Cases
BFS	All paths from source	Fixed depth	✖ No	Friend suggestions, exploration
SSSP	Shortest path to all targets	Dynamic (weighted)	☑ Yes	Routing, latency minimization
Egonet	Local subgraph of a node	1-hop only	✖ No	Influence analysis, local neighborhood view

Visualization in Notebooks

Using the `%graph_notebook_vis_options` and `%visualize` magic commands in Jupyter, you can visualize paths returned from these algorithms:

```
%%oc
CALL bfs("userA", ["FRIEND_OF"], 2,
"OUTGOING") YIELD path


%visualize last_results
```

This renders the paths as an interactive graph for better understanding.

Best Practices

Best Practice	Why It Helps
Limit traversal depth in BFS	Avoids performance issues in dense graphs
Use SSSP with numeric weights only	Ensures correct path cost computation
Pre-filter nodes or edges	Reduces traversal load and memory usage
Visualize results	Easier debugging and analysis of path structures
Combine with centrality metrics	Find important paths from important nodes
Store frequent paths as relationships	Useful for caching or summarizing traversal results

Real-World Use Case: Financial Fraud Network

You're investigating suspicious activity in a financial transaction network. You can:

1. Use **BFS** to find all accounts connected within 3 hops of a known fraudulent account

2. Use **SSSP** to identify the **cheapest money path** between two entities

3. Use **Egonet** to extract and visualize the network around a suspicious account to see if it's part of a fraud ring

This combination provides rich context and allows fraud teams to act faster and with more confidence.

Summary

Amazon Neptune Analytics offers high-performance, built-in support for core path-finding algorithms:

- **BFS**: Broad exploration up to a certain depth

- **SSSP**: Weighted, cost-minimizing paths from a single source

- **Egonet**: One-hop subgraphs revealing local structure

These tools allow analysts and developers to explore, visualize, and act on complex relationships in massive graphs—quickly and at scale.

Chapter 38: Centrality (Degree, PageRank, Closeness Centrality)

In graph theory and network analysis, **centrality** refers to the importance or influence of a node within a graph. Understanding centrality allows you to identify key actors, optimize network performance, detect fraud, and enhance recommendation systems. Neptune Analytics provides built-in algorithms for computing **degree centrality**, **PageRank**, and **closeness centrality**, making it easy to analyze large-scale graphs without external tooling.

This chapter walks you through:

- The core concepts behind centrality metrics

- When and why to use each metric

- How to run these centrality algorithms in Neptune Analytics

- Tips for interpreting results and integrating them into applications

Let's dive into how Neptune Analytics makes graph centrality both scalable and simple to compute.

What Is Centrality?

Centrality measures aim to quantify how **"central"** or **"important"** a node is in a graph. Importance can be based on:

- **Connections** (how many neighbors a node has)

- **Influence** (how likely a node is to affect others)

- **Reachability** (how close a node is to the rest of the graph)

Each centrality metric has a different perspective on importance, and selecting the right one depends on your use case.

---

1. Degree Centrality

Degree centrality is the simplest measure: it counts how many edges are connected to a node.

- **In-degree**: Number of incoming edges

- **Out-degree**: Number of outgoing edges

- **Total degree**: Sum of in- and out-degree

Use Cases

- Identify influencers in a social network

- Detect hubs in a transportation system

- Spot anomalies in graph structure

Neptune Analytics Query

```
CALL algo.degree()
YIELD node, inDegree, outDegree, degree
RETURN node, inDegree, outDegree, degree
ORDER BY degree DESC
```

Sample Output

Node	InDegree	OutDegree	Degree
u123	100	95	195
u456	88	102	190

> **Tip**: Degree centrality is fast to compute and scales well even on massive graphs.

---

2. PageRank

PageRank measures a node's influence based on the number and quality of connections. It was originally developed by Google to rank web pages.

- Nodes earn higher scores if they are linked to by other important nodes.

- Scores propagate through the graph iteratively.

Use Cases

- Rank web pages, products, or users by influence

- Detect authoritative sources in a citation network

- Recommend trending items based on graph influence

Neptune Analytics Query

```
CALL algo.pageRank()
YIELD node, score
RETURN node, score
ORDER BY score DESC
LIMIT 10
```

Optional Parameters

```
CALL algo.pageRank({
  iterations: 20,
  dampingFactor: 0.85
})
YIELD node, score
RETURN node, score
```

- **iterations**: Number of times the algorithm runs (default: 20)

- **dampingFactor**: Probability of continuing traversal (default: 0.85)

Sample Output

Node	PageRank Score
p987	0.035
p234	0.033
p123	0.030

📊 **Interpretation**: Higher PageRank nodes are more "influential" or "visited" in the network.

---

3. Closeness Centrality

Closeness centrality measures how close a node is to all other nodes in the graph, based on shortest paths.

- Nodes with low total distance to others have high closeness.

- Ideal for identifying bridge nodes or information flow facilitators.

Use Cases

- Optimize logistics and routing

- Detect strategic nodes in communication networks

- Pinpoint brokers in social graphs

Neptune Analytics Query

```
CALL algo.closenessCentrality()
YIELD node, closeness
RETURN node, closeness
ORDER BY closeness DESC
LIMIT 10
```

Optional Parameters

```
CALL algo.closenessCentrality({
```

```
  sampleSize: 100
})
YIELD node, closeness
```

- **sampleSize**: For large graphs, approximates results by sampling paths

Sample Output

Node	Closeness Score
u456	0.082
u101	0.079

🔍 **Tip**: High closeness scores suggest fast reachability to the rest of the graph.

Comparing the Centrality Algorithms

Metric	Description	Fastest To Compute	Best For
Degree	Counts direct edges	☑	Simple influence detection
PageRank	Propagates influence scores	↓ (iterative)	Ranking nodes by quality of links
Closeness	Measures shortest-path proximity	✗ (expensive)	Reachability and flow

Performance and Scalability

Neptune Analytics uses an **in-memory execution engine**, making it highly efficient for centrality computations, even on large graphs (millions of nodes and edges).

Performance Tips

- Use `LIMIT` to view top results quickly

- Adjust **iterations** in PageRank for faster completion

- Use **sampling** in closeness centrality for large graphs

- Monitor memory usage for graphs >100M edges

Combining Centrality with Other Metrics

You can enrich your centrality analysis by joining it with node attributes.

Example: Top Influencers by PageRank and Follower Count

```
CALL algo.pageRank()
YIELD node, score
MATCH (node:User)
RETURN node.name, node.followers, score
ORDER BY score DESC
LIMIT 10
```

Use Case Scenarios

Social Networks

- Use **degree** to find highly connected users

- Use **PageRank** to find celebrities or influencers

- Use **closeness** to detect network brokers

Fraud Detection

- High **out-degree** with low **in-degree** may signal fake accounts

- Use **closeness** to find pivot nodes in transaction chains

E-commerce and Recommendations

- Use **PageRank** to prioritize products

- Combine with **vector search** to personalize recommendations

---

Query Variants and Filtering

You can target centrality to subgraphs or labeled relationships.

Example: Degree Centrality on "FOLLOWS" Edges Only

```
CALL algo.degree({
  edgeLabel: "FOLLOWS"
})
```

```
YIELD node, degree
RETURN node, degree
ORDER BY degree DESC
```

Example: PageRank on "Article" Nodes Only

```
CALL algo.pageRank({
  nodeLabel: "Article"
})
YIELD node, score
RETURN node, score
```

Storing and Using Results

After running a centrality algorithm, you can **store results**
as properties on nodes:

```
CALL algo.pageRank()
YIELD node, score
SET node.pagerank = score
RETURN count(*)
```

> 🧠 **Tip**: Persisting results allows future
> queries to sort or filter based on centrality.

Error Handling and Edge Cases

Common Issues

Problem	Cause	Fix
`OutOfMemoryException`	Graph too large	Reduce size or scale memory
`AlgorithmTimeoutException`	High iteration count	Lower iterations
`NoResultException`	Mismatched label or filter	Verify input criteria

Always review logs and **use sample queries first** to validate behavior.

Summary

Centrality is a fundamental concept in graph analytics, and Neptune Analytics makes computing it fast, flexible, and scalable.

Metric	Best For
Degree	Quick identification of highly connected nodes
PageRank	Influence and recommendation systems
Closeness	Reachability and optimization problems

Neptune's built-in `algo` procedures simplify centrality analysis—no need to build your own traversal logic or manage infrastructure.

Chapter 39: Similarity (Jaccard, Overlap, `neighbors.*`)

One of the most powerful capabilities in graph analytics is measuring **similarity** between nodes. In Amazon Neptune Analytics, you can evaluate how closely related two nodes are based on their **neighbor sets** — that is, the nodes to which they are connected. This technique underpins use cases such as recommendation engines, fraud detection, clustering, and link prediction.

This chapter covers how Neptune Analytics supports **set-based similarity algorithms**, including **Jaccard similarity**, **Overlap similarity**, and a family of functions under the `neighbors.*` namespace. You'll learn when and how to use each similarity function, understand their mathematical foundations, and apply them with practical openCypher examples.

What Is Graph Similarity?

Graph similarity is a measure of how alike two nodes are based on their structure, relationships, or properties. In Neptune Analytics, the focus is on **topological similarity** — based on shared neighbors.

The more neighbors two nodes share, the more similar they are likely to be.

> Unlike vector similarity (e.g. cosine distance using embeddings), **Jaccard** and **Overlap** rely entirely on the **connectivity of nodes**.

Key Similarity Functions in Neptune Analytics

Neptune Analytics provides similarity functions via the `neighbors.*` namespace, allowing you to easily calculate similarity between nodes using openCypher queries.

Function	Description
`neighbors.jaccard()`	Measures similarity based on ratio of shared to total neighbors
`neighbors.overlap()`	Measures raw count or ratio of shared neighbors
`neighbors()`	Returns the set of neighbor nodes for a given node

Let's explore each in detail.

Jaccard Similarity (`neighbors.jaccard()`)

The **Jaccard similarity** between two nodes is defined as:

$$J(A,B) = \frac{|N(A) \cap N(B)|}{|N(A) \cup N(B)|}$$

Where:

- $N(A)$ = neighbors of node A

- $N(B)$ = neighbors of node B

The result is a value between **0** (no shared neighbors) and **1** (identical neighbor sets).

Syntax

```
CALL neighbors.jaccard(
  sourceNodeId: STRING,
```

```
  targetNodeId: STRING,
  edgeFilter: MAP
)
YIELD similarity
```

Parameters

- sourceNodeId: ID of the first node

- targetNodeId: ID of the second node

- edgeFilter (optional): Specify relationship type and direction

Example: Jaccard Similarity Between Two Users

```
CALL neighbors.jaccard(
  'u1', 'u2', {type: 'FRIENDS_WITH'}
)
YIELD similarity
RETURN similarity
```

Output

similarity

0.6

This means that 60% of the total unique friends of u1 and u2 are shared.

Overlap Similarity (`neighbors.overlap()`)

Overlap similarity focuses on how many neighbors two nodes share, either in absolute count or as a ratio. It's useful when you care more about **shared connections** than proportional similarity.

Syntax

```
CALL neighbors.overlap(
  sourceNodeId: STRING,
  targetNodeId: STRING,
  edgeFilter: MAP,
  normalize: BOOLEAN
)
YIELD similarity
```

Parameters

- `normalize = true`: returns a ratio

- `normalize = false`: returns count of overlapping neighbors

Example: Overlap Count

```
CALL neighbors.overlap(
  'm1', 'm2',
  {type: 'RATED', direction: 'IN'},
  false
)
YIELD similarity
RETURN similarity
```

Output

similarity

12

In this case, 12 users have rated both movies m1 and m2.

Example: Normalized Overlap

```
CALL neighbors.overlap(
    'm1', 'm2',
    {type: 'RATED', direction: 'IN'},
    true
)
YIELD similarity
RETURN similarity
```

Output

similarity

0.35

Here, 35% of the raters are shared between the two movies.

Retrieving Neighbor Sets with `neighbors()`

You can also retrieve a node's full neighbor set using the `neighbors()` function. This is helpful for understanding the context around a node before calculating similarity.

Syntax

```
CALL neighbors(
  nodeId: STRING,
  edgeFilter: MAP
)
YIELD neighbor
RETURN neighbor
```

Example

```
CALL neighbors('u1', {type:
'FRIENDS_WITH'})
YIELD neighbor
RETURN neighbor
```

Output

neighbor

"u2"

"u3"

"u5"

This returns all node IDs connected to u1 via the
FRIENDS_WITH relationship.

Real-World Use Cases

1. Product Recommendations

Use Jaccard or Overlap similarity between products to find items bought or rated by similar users.

```
CALL neighbors.jaccard('itemA', 'itemB',
{type: 'BOUGHT_BY', direction: 'IN'})
YIELD similarity
RETURN similarity
```

2. Friend Suggestions

Find users with high Jaccard similarity based on mutual friends.

```
CALL neighbors.jaccard('u1', 'u5', {type:
'FRIENDS_WITH'})
YIELD similarity
RETURN similarity
```

3. Detecting Duplicate Accounts

If two accounts share a high overlap in transaction partners or logins, flag them for inspection.

```
CALL neighbors.overlap('acct1', 'acct2',
{type: 'SENT_FUNDS_TO'}, true)
YIELD similarity
RETURN similarity
```

Edge Filter Options

You can filter which edges are used in similarity calculations using:

- `type`: the relationship label (e.g., `FRIENDS_WITH`, `RATED`)

- `direction`: one of `IN`, `OUT`, or `BOTH`

Example: Only Incoming Ratings

```
CALL neighbors.overlap('m1', 'm2', {
  type: 'RATED',
  direction: 'IN'
}, false)
YIELD similarity
```

This evaluates only users who rated both movies.

Comparing Multiple Node Pairs

To compare many pairs of nodes, use a query with `UNWIND`:

```
UNWIND [['u1', 'u2'], ['u1', 'u3'], ['u1',
'u4']] AS pair
CALL neighbors.jaccard(pair[0], pair[1],
{type: 'FRIENDS_WITH'})
YIELD similarity
RETURN pair[0] AS node1, pair[1] AS node2,
similarity
```

Performance Tips

- Limit the neighbor set size with filters to improve performance

- Avoid calculating similarity on extremely high-degree nodes without purpose

- Cache neighbor sets in application memory for repeated comparisons

Troubleshooting

Problem	Cause	Solution
similarity = 0	No shared neighbors	Check edge direction or types
Long query time	High node degree	Use edge filters and pre-aggregation
No results	Node ID mismatch	Ensure you're using the correct id field, not internal ~id

Best Practices

- Use **Jaccard** when proportion matters (e.g., similar user behavior)

- Use **Overlap** when absolute count matters (e.g., common friends)

- Filter by **edge type** and **direction** for precision

- Pre-filter nodes by type to avoid invalid comparisons

- Combine similarity with other signals (e.g., vector, metadata) for hybrid models

---

Summary

Neptune Analytics makes it easy to compute graph-based similarity using powerful, built-in functions like `neighbors.jaccard()` and `neighbors.overlap()`. These tools allow you to go beyond basic queries and uncover nuanced patterns of similarity across your graph — whether you're finding lookalike users, recommending items, or spotting fraud.

By mastering these similarity functions and integrating them into your queries and applications, you'll unlock deeper value from your graph data.

Chapter 40: Community Detection (WCC, Label Propagation, SCC)

One of the most powerful applications of graph analytics is **community detection**—the process of identifying groups of tightly connected nodes within a larger network. Communities often reveal underlying structure and meaning in graphs, such as social circles, customer segments, topic clusters, or even coordinated threat groups.

In Neptune Analytics, community detection is made fast and accessible through a set of **built-in, memory-optimized algorithms**. This chapter focuses on three major algorithms you can use out of the box:

- **WCC (Weakly Connected Components)**

- **Label Propagation**

- **SCC (Strongly Connected Components)**

We'll cover:

- What each algorithm does and when to use it

- How to run these algorithms in Neptune Analytics

- openCypher query examples

- Interpreting results and applying them to real use cases

- Best practices and performance tips

What Is Community Detection?

Community detection is the task of discovering **groups of nodes** that are more **densely connected** with each other than with the rest of the graph. These groups are referred to as **components**, **clusters**, or **communities**.

Understanding these groupings helps uncover:

- Hidden relationships

- Subnetwork behavior

- Functional groupings (e.g., departments, customer types)

- Network boundaries or silos

🚀 Community Detection in Neptune Analytics

Neptune Analytics enables community detection through **Cypher procedures** that compute cluster identifiers for each node and **mutate the graph** by attaching a new property, such as componentId or communityId.

These algorithms are:

- **Read-only safe**: They don't change your original dataset

- **In-memory**: They scale to millions of nodes and edges

- **Easy to use**: Called via simple CALL neptunealgo.<algorithm> syntax

Each procedure returns a result set with each node and its associated group ID.

🔗 1. Weakly Connected Components (WCC)

What It Does

The **WCC algorithm** identifies clusters of nodes where **a path exists between any two nodes** in the same group if edge direction is ignored.

> Think: "Who's at least indirectly connected, even through reversed links?"

Ideal For

- Identifying **disconnected subgraphs**

- Spotting **islands** in communication or social networks

- Grouping **isolated customer segments**

Syntax

```
CALL neptunealgo.wcc.mutate()
YIELD node, componentId
RETURN node.id, componentId
```

- `componentId` is a numeric value assigned to each connected group

- Nodes with the same `componentId` belong to the same group

Example Use Case

You want to find all groups of users who are connected, regardless of the direction of the "follows" relationship.

```
CALL neptunealgo.wcc.mutate()
YIELD node, componentId
RETURN node.id, componentId
ORDER BY componentId
```

◎ 2. Label Propagation

What It Does

Label Propagation is an **iterative, unsupervised** algorithm where each node adopts the label most common among its neighbors. Over multiple rounds, natural communities emerge as nodes "agree" on a common label.

> Think: "I'll join the most popular group around me."

Ideal For

- **Social media clustering**

- **Behavioral segmentation** without prior knowledge

- **Emergent groups** in large graphs

Syntax

```
CALL
neptunealgo.labelPropagation.mutate({maxIte
rations: 20})
YIELD node, communityId
RETURN node.id, communityId
```

- `communityId` is the label each node settles into

- `maxIterations` is optional (default is 20)

Example Use Case

You want to discover communities of people who interact often.

```
CALL
neptunealgo.labelPropagation.mutate({maxIte
rations: 15})
YIELD node, communityId
RETURN communityId, count(node) AS size
ORDER BY size DESC
```

This gives a list of communities and how many nodes belong to each.

What It Does

SCC identifies **groups of nodes where every node is reachable from every other node in the group**, respecting edge directions. In other words, it finds **cycles** or **strong interdependencies**.

> Think: "Everyone in the group can reach everyone else, following the arrows."

Ideal For

- **Feedback loops** in systems

- **Transaction cycles** in financial networks

- **Mutual following** groups in social graphs

Syntax

```
CALL neptunealgo.scc.mutate()
YIELD node, componentId
RETURN node.id, componentId
```

- Like WCC, each node is assigned a `componentId`

- Only nodes in **strong cycles** are grouped

Example Use Case

You want to find tightly coupled systems where services call each other in loops.

```
CALL neptunealgo.scc.mutate()
YIELD node, componentId
RETURN componentId, count(node) AS size
ORDER BY size DESC
```

📎 Interpreting the Results

Each of the community detection algorithms adds a property to each node:

Algorithm	Node Property
WCC	componentId
Label Propagation	communityId
SCC	componentId

You can now use openCypher to filter, group, or visualize nodes by their assigned communities.

Filter by Component

```
MATCH (n)
WHERE n.componentId = 0
RETURN n.id
```

Count Nodes per Group

```
MATCH (n)
RETURN n.communityId, count(*) AS size
```

```
ORDER BY size DESC
```

Visualize Clusters (Notebook)

Use `%graph_notebook_vis_options` in Neptune notebooks to color nodes by `communityId` or `componentId`:

```
%%graph_notebook_vis_options
{
  "node_color_property": "communityId"
}
```

🛠 Best Practices

1. Run on Connected Data

Ensure that the graph has meaningful connections. Sparse or noisy graphs may lead to uninformative clusters.

2. Use Label Filtering

Target specific node types if your graph is heterogeneous:

```
MATCH (p:Person)
CALL
neptunealgo.labelPropagation.mutate({label:
"Person"})
YIELD node, communityId
RETURN node.id, communityId
```

Not all versions of the algorithm support label filtering—check current API docs.

3. Combine with Other Metrics

After assigning communities, apply other algorithms (like PageRank or centrality) within each group.

4. Rerun After Data Changes

Community structures are dynamic. If your graph changes (e.g., new nodes or edges), rerun the detection algorithm.

⚠ Limitations

Algorithm	Limitation
WCC	Ignores edge direction
Label Propagation	Non-deterministic; may vary each run
SCC	Strict—many nodes may end up as singletons

Label Propagation is fast but can yield different results on each run due to its randomized nature. If deterministic clustering is required, use WCC or SCC.

🌐 Use Case Ideas

- **E-commerce**: Group customers based on co-purchases or reviews

- **Cybersecurity**: Detect malware clusters or lateral movement groups

- **Telecom**: Identify subnetworks based on call graphs

- **Marketing**: Find influencers within tight-knit communities

Summary

Community detection is an essential tool for understanding the structure and dynamics of your graph. With Neptune Analytics, you can easily run WCC, Label Propagation, and SCC to detect clusters, group behavior, and identify connected ecosystems within your data.

Each algorithm serves a different purpose:

- **WCC**: Who's connected at all?

- **Label Propagation**: Who's in the same "neighborhood"?

- **SCC**: Who's tightly interdependent?

By incorporating these tools into your analysis, you can enrich your understanding of network behavior, optimize decisions, and uncover insights not visible through traditional data models.

Key Takeaways

- Neptune Analytics provides **three built-in community detection algorithms**.

- Each algorithm is run via **openCypher procedure calls** like `CALL neptunealgo.labelPropagation.mutate()`.

- Results are **written to nodes** as new properties (`componentId`, `communityId`).

- Use these properties for further queries, visualization, and analysis.

- Choose the right algorithm based on your **graph's directionality and clustering goals**.

Chapter 41: Miscellaneous Graph Procedures

Introduction

While most chapters in this book focus on the core features and algorithms in Amazon Neptune Analytics—like loading data, running graph queries, and analyzing structures—there are also several **lesser-known but highly useful graph procedures** that can simplify graph exploration, diagnostics, and manipulation.

These **miscellaneous graph procedures** serve as convenient tools for quick insights, metadata exploration, schema discovery, and basic graph transformations. They are especially helpful during data onboarding, prototyping, and iterative graph development.

In this chapter, we'll cover a variety of such procedures provided by Neptune Analytics, focusing on their usage, examples, and practical applications. These aren't full-fledged analytics algorithms, but rather **utility-style operations** that enhance your productivity when working with graph data.

What Are Graph Procedures?

In Neptune Analytics, a **procedure** is a built-in function you can call via OpenCypher-like syntax to perform utility operations on the graph. These may include:

- Listing all labels or relationship types

- Inspecting schema metadata

- Counting entities

- Performing lightweight sampling or diagnostics

These procedures are often **prefixed with** CALL, similar to procedures in other Cypher-like environments (e.g., Neo4j).

Procedure Categories

Neptune Analytics procedures can be grouped into several categories:

1. **Graph Schema Discovery**

2. **Label and Relationship Type Enumeration**

3. **Graph Statistics and Metadata**

4. **Sample Queries for Debugging**

5. **Utility Functions**

Let's explore each category with practical examples.

---

1. Graph Schema Discovery

Understanding the structure of your graph—its labels, relationships, and property keys—is crucial for effective querying. Neptune Analytics provides procedures to **automatically introspect schema components**.

List All Node Labels

```
CALL db.labels()
```

Returns: A list of all node labels (types) in the graph.

List All Relationship Types

```
CALL db.relationshipTypes()
```

Returns: A list of all relationship (edge) types used in the graph.

List All Property Keys

```
CALL db.propertyKeys()
```

Returns: A list of all distinct property keys (used on any node or edge).

---

2. Graph Statistics and Counts

Sometimes you need quick metrics to understand the graph's shape and scale.

Count All Nodes

```
MATCH (n) RETURN count(n) AS totalNodes
```

Count All Edges

```
MATCH ()-[r]->() RETURN count(r) AS totalEdges
```

Count Nodes by Label

```
MATCH (n) RETURN labels(n)[0] AS label, count(*) AS count ORDER BY count DESC
```

Count Edges by Relationship Type

```
MATCH ()-[r]->() RETURN type(r) AS type,
count(*) AS count ORDER BY count DESC
```

Count Distinct Property Keys Used

```
CALL db.propertyKeys()
```

This will help identify which properties are most frequently used and aid in query design or validation.

---

3. Sampling the Graph

Sampling is useful when you're exploring a new dataset or validating graph transformations.

Get a Sample of 10 Nodes

```
MATCH (n) RETURN n LIMIT 10
```

Get a Sample of 10 Edges

```
MATCH ()-[r]->() RETURN r LIMIT 10
```

Sample with Specific Label or Type

```
MATCH (p:Person) RETURN p LIMIT 5
MATCH (:Person)-[r:FRIENDS_WITH]->(:Person)
RETURN r LIMIT 5
```

These quick queries can be embedded in Jupyter notebooks or scripts to build initial understanding of the data.

---

4. Utility Procedures and Debugging Aids

While Neptune Analytics doesn't support user-defined procedures, it offers a few **graph-wide utility procedures** to aid with debugging and diagnostics.

List Unique Property Keys on a Label

```
MATCH (n:Person)
WITH DISTINCT keys(n) AS props
UNWIND props AS prop
RETURN DISTINCT prop
```

List Property Types (Manually Inferred)

```
MATCH (n:Person)
UNWIND keys(n) AS k
RETURN k, collect(DISTINCT typeof(n[k])) AS
types
LIMIT 20
```

Note: This requires using a helper function like `typeof()` or casting logic where supported.

---

5. Schema Exploration with Dynamic Queries

Though Neptune Analytics doesn't have a built-in schema browser, you can simulate one by writing meta-queries.

Find All Labels and Property Keys

```
MATCH (n)
WITH labels(n) AS labels, keys(n) AS props
UNWIND labels AS label
UNWIND props AS prop
RETURN DISTINCT label, prop
ORDER BY label, prop
```

Find Edge Types Between Labels

```
MATCH (a)-[r]->(b)
RETURN DISTINCT labels(a)[0] AS from,
type(r) AS edge, labels(b)[0] AS to
ORDER BY from, edge, to
```

This is extremely useful for generating data dictionaries and relationship maps for documentation or analysis.

Examples: Real-World Use Cases

Data Onboarding & QA

- **Check available node types**: Use CALL db.labels() to confirm expected labels.

- **Verify edge types**: CALL db.relationshipTypes() ensures expected relationships are loaded.

- **Confirm properties**: Use CALL db.propertyKeys() or custom meta-queries to

471

inspect attributes.

Visual Schema Mapping

Use the following query to build a high-level schema:

```
MATCH (a)-[r]->(b)
RETURN DISTINCT labels(a)[0] AS source,
type(r) AS relationship, labels(b)[0] AS
target
```

Feed this output into visualization tools or schema builders to generate diagrams.

Notes on Procedure Limitations

- Neptune Analytics procedures are **read-only** and designed for exploration and diagnostics.

- These are not stored procedures; they don't accept complex parameters.

- Results may be truncated or paginated depending on graph size and query limits.

Summary Table: Handy Procedures

Procedure	Description
`CALL db.labels()`	Lists all node labels
`CALL db.relationshipTypes()`	Lists all relationship types
`CALL db.propertyKeys()`	Lists all unique property keys
`MATCH (n) RETURN count(n)`	Counts all nodes
`MATCH ()-[r]->() RETURN count(r)`	Counts all relationships
`MATCH (a)-[r]->(b) RETURN DISTINCT labels(a)[0], type(r), labels(b)[0]`	Infers schema structure

Best Practices

- Use these procedures early when **onboarding a new dataset**.

- Store the output of meta-queries as part of **graph documentation**.

- Use sampling to **debug transformations** before full loads.

- Embed label/edge type checks into **automated validation** scripts.

Summary

Miscellaneous graph procedures in Neptune Analytics offer a lightweight, powerful toolkit for exploring, validating, and documenting your graph. From listing labels and relationship types to counting entities and inferring schema, these utilities save time and improve your confidence when working with complex data.

In this chapter, we explored:

- Common graph inspection procedures (`CALL db.*`)

- Metadata queries using OpenCypher

- Sampling techniques for quick graph exploration

- Schema inference and diagnostics

- Best practices for graph onboarding and validation

Vector Similarity

Chapter 42: Vector Indexing

As modern applications increasingly rely on **machine learning**, **semantic search**, and **recommendation systems**, the ability to work with **vector representations** of data has become essential. In graph systems, this capability enables a new dimension of analysis: **vector similarity** between nodes.

Amazon Neptune Analytics supports **vector indexing**, allowing you to associate nodes with vector embeddings and efficiently perform **top-K nearest neighbor searches** based on vector similarity. This makes it possible to integrate **AI-generated features**, such as sentence embeddings, image features, or product vectors, directly into your graph workflows.

In this chapter, we'll explore:

- What vector indexing is and why it matters

- How Neptune Analytics implements vector indexing

- Creating, updating, and deleting vector embeddings

- Performing top-K similarity search

- Use cases and best practices

- Real-world examples

What Is Vector Indexing?

Vector indexing is the process of associating each item (e.g., node) with a **multi-dimensional vector**, and then indexing these vectors to allow fast **approximate or exact nearest neighbor searches**.

Why Vector Indexing?

- Enables **semantic search** (e.g., "find nodes most similar in meaning")

- Powers **recommendation systems** ("users like you also viewed")

- Supports **anomaly detection, clustering**, and **embedding-based learning**

Each node in the graph can be enriched with a **vector embedding**, allowing similarity to be measured via **cosine similarity, Euclidean distance**, or other metrics.

Vector Indexing in Neptune Analytics

Neptune Analytics provides **built-in vector indexing** capabilities, including:

- **In-memory vector storage**

- **Upsert and delete operations for vectors**

- **Top-K nearest neighbor search**

- **Distance metrics**

- **Integration with graph query results**

Vectors are stored **separately from node properties**, optimized for efficient lookup and comparison.

Adding Vectors to Nodes

To add a vector embedding to a node, use the `vectors.upsert` procedure.

Syntax

```
CALL vectors.upsert([
  { id: "node1", embedding: [0.1, 0.2, 0.3]
},
  { id: "node2", embedding: [0.4, 0.5, 0.6]
}
])
```

Example

```
CALL vectors.upsert([
  { id: "movie_001", embedding: [0.9, 0.1,
0.4, 0.6] },
  { id: "movie_002", embedding: [0.8, 0.2,
0.5, 0.5] }
])
```

This associates each node ID with a vector of fixed dimension. All vectors in an index must be the same length.

477

Retrieving Similar Vectors (Top-K Search)

To perform a **similarity search**, use the
`vectors.topKByEmbedding` procedure.

Syntax

```
CALL vectors.topKByEmbedding(queryVector,
k)
YIELD nodeId, distance
RETURN nodeId, distance
```

Example

```
CALL vectors.topKByEmbedding([0.85, 0.15,
0.4, 0.6], 5)
YIELD nodeId, distance
RETURN nodeId, distance
```

This finds the **5 closest vectors** in the graph to the
provided query vector, ranked by distance.

Notes:

- **Lower distance = more similar**

- The default distance metric is **Euclidean**, but
  others may be supported depending on
  version/config

Deleting Vector Embeddings

If a node should no longer participate in vector search (e.g., it's deleted or outdated), remove its embedding:

```
CALL vectors.delete(["node1", "node2"])
```

This deletes the associated vectors without affecting the nodes themselves.

Best Practices for Vector Indexing

Best Practice	Why It Matters
Keep vector dimensions consistent	Inconsistent lengths cause errors during indexing
Normalize vectors (unit length)	Ensures better behavior with cosine similarity
Batch upserts for large volumes	More efficient than inserting one at a time
Store original vectors as node properties	Useful for backup or re-indexing
Update vectors regularly	Reflects latest ML model outputs or user behavior

Example Use Case: Semantic Product Search

You're building a **product recommendation system**. Each product has an embedding vector generated by a language model trained on product descriptions.

Workflow:

1. Store each product as a node in Neptune Analytics

2. Use `vectors.upsert` to add embeddings

3. At search time, generate a vector from a query (e.g., "eco-friendly kitchen appliances")

4. Use `topKByEmbedding` to find the most semantically similar products

5. Return the results to the user or continue querying with openCypher

Sample Code:

```
CALL vectors.topKByEmbedding([0.12, 0.88,
0.14, 0.51], 10)
YIELD nodeId, distance
MATCH (p:Product) WHERE id(p) = nodeId
RETURN p.name, p.price, distance
ORDER BY distance ASC
```

Combining Vector Search with Graph Patterns

Vector search is most powerful when **combined with graph queries**.

Example: Find the most similar users to "user123", **but only if they are in the same city**.

```
CALL vectors.topKByEmbedding([0.23, 0.77,
0.55], 10)
YIELD nodeId, distance
MATCH (u:User) WHERE id(u) = nodeId AND
u.city = "Chicago"
RETURN u.name, distance
```

This filters vector search results using openCypher conditions.

Performance Considerations

- Vector search in Neptune Analytics is **in-memory**, making it very fast even with millions of nodes

- Use consistent vector length (e.g., 128, 256, 512) across all embeddings

- Distance metric selection impacts accuracy and performance; choose based on use case

Distance Metric	Use Case
Euclidean (L2)	Geometric distance
Cosine Similarity	Semantic similarity (angle-based)
Manhattan (L1)	Sparse, grid-like spaces

As of writing, Euclidean is the primary supported metric; cosine can be approximated with normalization.

Real-World Applications

Domain	Use Case Example
E-commerce	Recommend products based on user embeddings
Social networks	Suggest friends with similar interests or behavior
Knowledge graphs	Link entities with semantically similar context embeddings
Document search	Semantic search over articles, papers, or FAQs
Cybersecurity	Cluster nodes based on threat profile embeddings

Summary

Vector indexing in Neptune Analytics opens the door to **AI-enhanced graph analytics**, where nodes are more than just IDs—they carry rich, learned representations. With native support for upserting, searching, and deleting vector embeddings, you can integrate modern ML techniques directly into your graph workflows.

Key capabilities:

- Associate nodes with fixed-length vector embeddings

- Perform fast top-K similarity search

- Combine with openCypher queries for powerful hybrid filtering

- Scale across millions of nodes with in-memory performance

Chapter 43: Vector Algorithms

Vector algorithms bring **semantic intelligence** to graph analytics by allowing you to represent nodes as **embeddings**—high-dimensional vectors that capture features like meaning, behavior, or similarity. Neptune Analytics extends the traditional graph model by integrating **vector indexing** and **vector similarity search**, enabling powerful hybrid use cases such as:

- Personalized recommendations

- Semantic search over graph nodes

- Fraud detection with behavioral embeddings

- Machine learning integration with node properties

In this chapter, you'll learn:

- What vector algorithms are and why they matter

- How vector indexing works in Neptune Analytics

- How to store and query vectors

- Built-in vector procedures: `topKByNode`, `topKByVector`, `distance`

- Real-world use cases and implementation patterns

Let's explore how Neptune Analytics enables next-gen graph analytics through vector-native computation.

What Are Vector Algorithms?

Vector algorithms operate on **embeddings**—numerical vector representations of graph entities (nodes). These vectors typically come from:

- **Machine learning models** (e.g., transformers, graph neural networks)

- **Text encoders** (e.g., BERT, sentence transformers)

- **Image/audio embeddings**

- **Behavioral logs** (e.g., clickstream data)

Each vector is usually a list of floating-point numbers:
`[0.23, -0.55, 0.88, ..., 0.01]`

By comparing vectors using **cosine similarity**, **Euclidean distance**, or **dot product**, you can find nodes that are "close" in meaning or behavior—even if they aren't connected by direct edges.

Vector Support in Neptune Analytics

Neptune Analytics supports:

- **Native vector storage**: Embed vectors directly into nodes

- **Vector indexing**: Automatic indexing for fast top-K queries

- **Hybrid graph + vector search**: Combine vector similarity with graph traversals

- **Built-in algorithms**: `topKByNode`, `topKByVector`, `distance`

Enabling Vector Search

You **must configure vector support at graph creation**:

```
aws neptune-graph create-graph \
  --graph-name "vector-enabled-graph" \
  --vector-search '{"dimension": 384}' \
  --provisioned-memory 256
```

Once enabled, Neptune indexes node vectors in-memory for high-speed retrieval.

> 🧠 **Tip**: The `dimension` (e.g., 128, 256, 384) must match your vector length exactly.

Storing Vectors in the Graph

Each node that participates in vector search must have:

- A `~id`

- A vector property (commonly named `embedding`, but flexible)

- The vector must match the declared dimension and be a list of floats

485

Example Cypher Insertion

```
UNWIND [
  {id: "p1", embedding: [0.1, 0.2, 0.3]},
  {id: "p2", embedding: [0.0, 0.1, 0.4]}
] AS row
MERGE (p:Product {~id: row.id})
SET p.embedding = row.embedding
```

> ☑ Ensure your vectors are **non-null**,
> **numerical**, and of fixed length

`algo.vectors.topKByNode`

This algorithm finds the **top K most similar nodes** to a given node, based on vector similarity.

Syntax

```
CALL algo.vectors.topKByNode({
  node: "p123",
  k: 5
})
YIELD similarNode, score
RETURN similarNode, score
```

Parameters

Param	Description
node	ID of the source node
k	Number of similar nodes to return

Output

similarNode	score
p234	0.989
p341	0.978

✎ **Interpretation**: Higher score = more similar. Uses cosine similarity by default.

`algo.vectors.topKByVector`

This procedure lets you supply a **raw vector**, without needing a source node.

Syntax

```
CALL algo.vectors.topKByVector({
  vector: [0.1, 0.2, 0.3],
  k: 3
})
YIELD similarNode, score
RETURN similarNode, score
```

Use Cases

- Compare custom vectors to graph entities

- Use external models for embeddings

- Feed user activity or preferences as live vectors

⧉ **Dynamic embeddings**: Use this to power live recommender systems or search inputs.

---

algo.vectors.distance

This procedure returns the **similarity score** between two nodes' vectors.

Syntax

```
CALL algo.vectors.distance({
  node1: "p123",
  node2: "p456"
})
YIELD score
RETURN score
```

Output

scor e
0.913

⟍ This helps validate the closeness between two entities explicitly.

Use Case: Personalized Recommendations

Let's say you have a user-product interaction graph and have generated **product embeddings** using a recommender model.

Query: Find top-5 similar products to one the user clicked on

```
MATCH (:User {~id: "u1"})-[:VIEWED]-
>(p:Product)
WITH p LIMIT 1
CALL algo.vectors.topKByNode({node: p.~id,
k: 5})
YIELD similarNode, score
RETURN similarNode, score
```

Use Case: Semantic Search

A user types a natural-language query like "wireless noise-cancelling headphones". Your application:

1. Encodes the query as a 384-dim vector using a sentence transformer

2. Runs a `topKByVector` search over products:

```
CALL algo.vectors.topKByVector({
  vector: [0.15, -0.03, ..., 0.22],
  k: 5
})
YIELD similarNode, score
```

```
RETURN similarNode.name, score
```

Combining Vectors with Graph Filters

You can filter results after computing similarity:

```
CALL algo.vectors.topKByNode({node: "p123",
k: 10})
YIELD similarNode, score
MATCH (similarNode:Product)
WHERE similarNode.category = "Electronics"
RETURN similarNode.name, score
```

Performance Considerations

- **Vector indexing is in-memory** → fast but memory-intensive

- **Preprocessing** vectors (normalize, dimensionality) is **your responsibility**

- Expect **sub-second performance** for vector queries on graphs with millions of vectors

Scaling Tips

Action	Effect
Reduce k	Faster results
Index fewer nodes	Save memory
Prune null/malformed vectors	Avoid runtime exceptions

Troubleshooting Vector Queries

Issue	Likely Cause	Solution
VectorIndexNotFound	Vector search not enabled	Recreate graph with --vector-search
DimensionMismatch	Vector size doesn't match graph setting	Match dimensions
Null score or missing results	Node missing vector	Check embedding property
Slow query	Too many indexed nodes or high k	Lower k or partition graph

Best Practices

- Use **same vector dimension** across all nodes

- Normalize vectors during preprocessing (e.g., unit length)

- Name your vector property clearly (embedding, vector)

Store vector results with nodes if reused:

```
SET node.topSim = similarNode.~id
```

-

Summary

Neptune Analytics' vector algorithms let you add **semantic similarity** and **intelligent retrieval** to your graph queries—at scale and with ease.

491

Key vector operations:

Procedure	Purpose
topKByNode	Find similar nodes to a specific node
topKByVector	Compare raw vector to indexed graph nodes
distance	Measure similarity between two node embeddings

These algorithms power the **next generation of graph analytics**, merging the symbolic reasoning of graphs with the pattern-learning strength of embeddings.

Chapter 44: VSS APIs (`.distance`, `.topK`, `.upsert`, `.remove`)

Amazon Neptune Analytics combines the power of graph traversal with vector search, allowing you to build **hybrid search systems** that understand both structure and semantics. This is made possible through **Vector Search Support (VSS)** APIs—functions that let you store, search, and manage high-dimensional vectors directly in your graph.

This chapter covers the core VSS APIs supported in Neptune Analytics:

- `.upsert()`: Add or update vectors on nodes

- `.topK()`: Find the most similar nodes to a given vector

- `.distance()`: Measure vector similarity or distance between nodes

- `.remove()`: Delete vector embeddings from nodes

We'll explore the syntax, use cases, best practices, and provide practical examples for each.

What is Vector Search?

Vector search is a technique for finding items that are similar to a given input vector. It's commonly used in:

- **Semantic search**

- **Recommendation engines**

- **Image or text similarity**

- **Anomaly detection**

Vectors are typically generated using models like BERT, CLIP, or FastText and represent the "meaning" or structure of an object in high-dimensional space (e.g., 384, 768, or 1024 dimensions).

Neptune Analytics lets you associate such vectors with nodes and run **approximate nearest neighbor (ANN)** searches directly using Cypher.

---

1. .upsert() – Add or Update Vectors

The .upsert() function associates a vector embedding with a node. You can use it to create new embeddings or update existing ones.

Syntax

```
CALL vectors.upsert(
  id: STRING,
  vector: LIST<FLOAT>
)
```

Parameters

- id: Node ID (~id) to associate the vector with

- vector: The high-dimensional embedding (length must match graph's configured dimension)

Example

```
CALL vectors.upsert("doc1", [0.12, -0.34,
0.98, ..., 0.05])
```

> ⚠ **Important**: The vector length must match the dimension configured when the graph was created (e.g., 384, 768). Otherwise, you'll get a validation error.

Batch Upserts (Recommended for Performance)

```
UNWIND [
  {id: "doc1", vec: [0.1, 0.2, ...]},
  {id: "doc2", vec: [0.3, 0.4, ...]}
] AS row
CALL vectors.upsert(row.id, row.vec)
```

---

2. .topK() – Find Nearest Neighbors

This function finds the top-K most similar vectors to a given **query vector**. It supports optional filters to narrow results.

Syntax

```
CALL vectors.topK(
  vector: LIST<FLOAT>,
  k: INT,
  filter: MAP
)
```

```
YIELD id, score
```

Parameters

- `vector`: The input query vector

- `k`: Number of top similar nodes to return

- `filter`: Optional map of Cypher-like filters on node properties

Example: Basic Similarity Search

```
CALL vectors.topK([0.1, -0.2, 0.4, ...], 5)
YIELD id, score
RETURN id, score
```

Example: Filter by Node Label

```
CALL vectors.topK([0.3, 0.7, 0.8, ...], 10,
{label: "Document"})
YIELD id, score
RETURN id, score
```

Example: Filter by Property

```
CALL vectors.topK(
  [0.5, 0.4, 0.9, ...], 3,
  {label: "Product", category:
"Electronics"}
)
YIELD id, score
```

Output

id	score
doc42	0.873
doc105	0.861
doc11	0.843

🔍 The `score` is based on cosine similarity by default (higher is better).

---

3. `.distance()` – Compute Distance Between Nodes

This function calculates the **vector distance** between two nodes in the graph.

Syntax

```
CALL vectors.distance(id1: STRING, id2:
STRING)
YIELD distance
```

Parameters

- `id1`, `id2`: The node IDs whose vectors will be compared

497

Example

```
CALL vectors.distance("doc1", "doc2")
YIELD distance
```

Output

distanc e
0.283

This is the **cosine distance** between the two vectors. A smaller value indicates higher similarity.

---

4. .remove() – Delete Vector Embeddings

You can remove vector embeddings from specific nodes using this function.

Syntax

```
CALL vectors.remove(id: STRING)
```

Example

```
CALL vectors.remove("doc1")
```

After removal, the node can no longer be matched in vector similarity queries.

Batch Removal

```
UNWIND ["doc1", "doc2", "doc3"] AS id
CALL vectors.remove(id)
```

Real-World Use Cases

Semantic Search Engine

- Convert user queries into vectors

- Use `vectors.topK()` to find semantically similar documents

Product Recommendations

- Store user and item embeddings

- Use `vectors.distance()` or `topK()` to find nearest products

Duplicate Detection

- Identify nearly identical entries with low vector distances

Hybrid Filtering

Combine vector similarity with graph filters:

```
CALL vectors.topK($vector, 5, {label:
"Article", language: "en"})
YIELD id, score
```

```
RETURN id, score
```

Error Handling and Validation

Error	Cause	Resolution
Vector dimension mismatch	Vector doesn't match configured dimension	Pad or slice your vectors to the correct length
Node ID not found	Trying to remove or compute distance on a missing node	Ensure node exists in the graph
Empty result	No matching vectors	Adjust filters or try larger k

Best Practices

- **Batch upserts** to reduce overhead

- Store a **timestamp** on vector updates if tracking versions

- Validate all vectors before upserting

- Use filters to **reduce search space** and increase performance

- Normalize vectors before upload if using cosine similarity

Monitoring and Debugging

- Monitor vector search latency and memory usage in **CloudWatch**

- Log vector API usage via **CloudTrail**

- For large-scale operations, break up upserts or removals into chunks

Summary

The VSS (Vector Search Support) APIs in Neptune Analytics offer an efficient way to build hybrid search systems that leverage both relationships and semantic embeddings. With `.upsert()`, `.topK()`, `.distance()`, and `.remove()`, you can manage high-dimensional vector data alongside graph structures to create more intelligent, contextual applications.

Best Practices

Chapter 45: openCypher Query Best Practices

Writing effective queries is essential to unlocking the full power of Neptune Analytics. While openCypher offers a flexible, expressive syntax for querying graph data, writing high-performing, readable, and scalable queries requires both **technical knowledge and practical habits**.

This chapter presents a collection of **best practices** for working with **openCypher in Neptune Analytics**, focusing on:

- Query performance optimization

- Readability and maintainability

- Query planning and debugging

- Patterns to avoid

- Useful functions and patterns for large-scale analytics

By following these best practices, you can ensure your queries are not only correct—but also fast, efficient, and production-ready.

---

1. Use Specific Pattern Matching

☑ **DO: Be explicit in patterns**

Use specific node labels and relationship types to narrow your matches and reduce computation.

```
// Good
MATCH (p:Person)-[:WORKS_FOR]->(c:Company)
RETURN p.name, c.name


// Bad (no labels or relationship types)
MATCH (a)-->(b)
RETURN a, b
```

> **Why?** Without labels or relationship types, the
> query engine must explore all nodes and
> relationships, which slows performance
> significantly.

---

2. Filter Early, Return Less

☑ DO: Apply WHERE filters as early as possible

```
MATCH (p:Person)
WHERE p.age > 40
RETURN p.name
```

> Filtering before a large MATCH saves memory
> and processing time.

☑ DO: Limit returned fields

Avoid returning entire nodes or unnecessary properties:

```
// Good
RETURN p.name, p.age
```

```
// Bad
RETURN p
```

Returning full node objects is slower and produces large result sets, especially over HTTP APIs.

---

3. Use `LIMIT` in Exploratory Queries

When exploring a dataset, always use `LIMIT` to avoid overwhelming the engine or network.

```
MATCH (n)
RETURN n
LIMIT 50
```

---

4. Avoid Cartesian Products

🚫 DON'T: Write unconnected `MATCH` clauses

```
// Bad: Creates a cartesian product
MATCH (a:Person)
MATCH (b:Company)
RETURN a, b
```

☑ DO: Connect patterns

```
MATCH (a:Person)-[:WORKS_FOR]->(b:Company)
RETURN a.name, b.name
```

Cartesian products multiply results needlessly.
Avoid unless explicitly needed.

5. Use Parameters in Reusable Queries

When executing queries via APIs or SDKs, always use
parameters to:

- Prevent injection

- Reuse queries

- Improve readability

Example:

```
MATCH (p:Person)
WHERE p.age > $minAge
RETURN p.name
```

Submit parameters via:

```
{
  "minAge": 30
}
```

Tip: Parameters make it easier to turn queries
into templates in apps or notebooks.

6. Use Aggregations Carefully

Aggregation is powerful, but misuse can hurt performance.

☑ DO: Aggregate only necessary fields

```
MATCH (p:Person)-[:WORKS_FOR]->(c:Company)
RETURN c.name, count(p) AS employee_count
```

🚫 DON'T: Over-aggregate or use unnecessary collect(*)

```
// Less efficient
RETURN collect(p)
```

---

7. Use OPTIONAL MATCH Judiciously

OPTIONAL MATCH is great for adding optional data (like friendships or secondary relationships) but adds overhead.

☑ DO: Use when truly optional

```
MATCH (p:Person)
OPTIONAL MATCH (p)-[:KNOWS]->(f:Person)
RETURN p.name, f.name
```

🚫 DON'T: Overuse it when MATCH is more appropriate

Excessive use can hide data issues and reduce performance clarity.

8. Avoid Overuse of `UNWIND` in Analytics

`UNWIND` is useful, but repeated or nested usage can bloat query time.

☑ **DO: Use for small arrays or parameter expansion**

```
UNWIND ['A', 'B', 'C'] AS letter
RETURN letter
```

🚫 **DON'T: Use for large-scale list processing in production queries**

---

9. Label Everything Clearly

Labels (`:Person`, `:Order`) help structure and index your graph. Use them:

- In all `MATCH` patterns

- When creating or filtering nodes

- To enforce logical grouping

  Even if a node technically works without a label, omitting one weakens performance.

---

10. Profile or Test Complex Queries First

Always test your complex queries on **small datasets** first. Look for:

- Excessive rows

- Cartesian joins

- High memory usage

  Neptune Analytics doesn't expose full
  `EXPLAIN` or `PROFILE` plans (yet), so start
  small and observe behavior.

Additional Best Practices

Use Meaningful Aliases

Instead of `MATCH (a)-[r]->(b)`, use:

```
MATCH (customer:Person)-[purchased:BOUGHT]-
>(item:Product)
```

Use `DISTINCT` to Eliminate Duplicates

```
MATCH (p:Person)-[:KNOWS]->(f:Person)
RETURN DISTINCT p.name
```

Performance Pitfalls to Avoid

Pitfall	Why It's Bad	How to Fix
No labels in MATCH	Slow traversal across all node types	Add specific labels
Full node returns	Memory-heavy results	Return only fields needed
Deep UNWIND chains	Inefficient row multiplication	Flatten logic or preprocess input
Overly long variable paths	Can explode in memory	Use *1..3 to limit range
Unbounded queries	Can overload query engine	Add LIMIT, use filters

Query Patterns to Know

Count All Nodes by Type

```
MATCH (n)
RETURN labels(n)[0] AS type, count(*) AS
count
```

Find the Most Connected Node

```
MATCH (n)-[r]->()
RETURN n.id, count(r) AS degree
ORDER BY degree DESC
LIMIT 1
```

Find Nodes with No Relationships

```
MATCH (n)
WHERE NOT (n)--()
RETURN n
```

Summary

Writing high-quality openCypher queries in Neptune Analytics involves more than just knowing the syntax. It's about understanding how the engine processes patterns, optimizing performance, and keeping queries readable and maintainable.

By applying these best practices, you'll:

- Avoid common mistakes that lead to slow queries

- Make your analytics pipelines more robust

- Create reusable, scalable, and secure queries

Key Takeaways

- Be specific with labels and patterns

- Filter early, return less

- Use parameters and aliases for clarity and safety

- Avoid Cartesian products and over-aggregation

- Always test on small datasets before running at scale

Tools and Utilities

Chapter 46: Nodestream

Introduction

In the evolving landscape of graph data systems, modern applications often require **streaming data ingestion and dynamic graph updates**. This is where **Nodestream**, an open-source framework, plays a powerful and complementary role to services like Amazon Neptune Analytics. Nodestream is designed for **building and managing property graphs from streaming data sources**, allowing you to define, structure, and enrich graph data in real-time.

While Neptune Analytics does not natively include Nodestream, the two can be used together in powerful ways. In this chapter, we'll explore what Nodestream is, its core capabilities, and how it can be integrated with Neptune Analytics to build scalable, real-time graph pipelines.

What is Nodestream?

Nodestream is an open-source, Python-based framework for **constructing, updating, and transforming property graphs from semi-structured and streaming data sources**.

Think of it as an **ETL (Extract, Transform, Load) engine for graphs**—purpose-built to transform raw records from sources like Kafka, Kinesis, or databases into structured graph elements like nodes, edges, and properties.

Core Features

- **Schema-driven**: Define graph structures declaratively using YAML configuration files.

- **Incremental ingestion**: Process and update graphs incrementally as data changes.

- **Pluggable architecture**: Supports a wide range of data sources and sinks.

- **Transformation engine**: Built-in functions for transforming data into graph models.

- **Supports multiple graph backends**, including Amazon Neptune and Neptune Analytics via OpenCypher.

Why Use Nodestream with Neptune Analytics?

While Neptune Analytics focuses on **high-performance querying and analytics**, it does not natively provide ingestion pipelines for streaming data. Nodestream fills this gap by:

- Enabling **streaming ingestion** from Kafka or Kinesis

- Transforming raw events into **Neptune-compatible graph structures**

- Allowing **declarative modeling** of entities and relationships

- Supporting **custom Python logic** for complex ETL steps

Together, Nodestream and Neptune Analytics provide an end-to-end solution for **real-time graph ingestion and analytics**.

Nodestream Architecture Overview

Nodestream is composed of several key components:

1. **Sources**
   Where the data comes from (Kafka, Kinesis, MongoDB, S3, etc.)

2. **Transformations**
   Convert raw input records into graph elements using mappings and logic.

3. **Graph Model**
   Defines how to map source data into graph shapes (nodes, edges, properties).

4. **Sinks**
   Where the graph data goes (e.g., Neptune, local files, stdout, etc.)

5. **State Management**
   Maintains progress across streaming runs using checkpointing.

Installing Nodestream

Nodestream is available as a Python package.

```
pip install nodestream
```

Once installed, you can run it using the `nodestream` CLI command.

Defining a Graph Model

Nodestream uses **YAML files** to define how incoming data should be transformed into graph objects.

Example: Graph Model Definition

```
graph_model:
  nodes:
    - label: Person
      key:
        - email
      properties:
        - name
        - age
  edges:
    - label: KNOWS
      source: Person
      destination: Person
      direction: undirected
```

This configuration says: if we find two records with the same `email`, create two `Person` nodes and connect them with a `KNOWS` relationship.

Example Use Case: Streaming Social Graph to Neptune

Let's walk through how Nodestream can be used to build a **real-time social graph** and stream it to Neptune Analytics.

Step 1: Source Setup

Configure a source like Kafka:

```
sources:
  - type: kafka
    topic: user_events
    bootstrap_servers: localhost:9092
    value_format: json
```

Step 2: Define the Graph Model

```
graph_model:
  nodes:
    - label: User
      key: [user_id]
      properties:
        - name
        - email
    - label: Product
      key: [product_id]
      properties:
        - title
  edges:
    - label: VIEWED
      source: User
      destination: Product
      properties:
```

515

```
      - timestamp
```

Step 3: Sink to Neptune

Define Neptune as the sink using OpenCypher:

```
sinks:
  - type: open_cypher
    url: https://g-
0123456789.region.neptune-
graph.amazonaws.com
    auth_mode: iam
```

Step 4: Run Nodestream

Run the job:

```
nodestream run --config social_graph.yaml
```

Nodestream will consume events from Kafka, transform them into nodes/edges, and send Cypher queries to Neptune Analytics for ingestion.

Advanced Nodestream Features

Custom Transformations

Nodestream allows you to write **custom Python functions** to manipulate incoming records before mapping to the graph.

```
def enrich_email(data):
    data["email"] = data["email"].lower()
    return data
```

Conditional Graph Logic

Add relationships only when certain conditions are met:

```
edges:
  - label: FOLLOWS
    source: User
    destination: User
    when:
      expression: event["action"] ==
"follow"
```

Multiple Outputs

Nodestream supports sending graph data to multiple backends—useful for **dual writing** or testing.

Integration Tips for Neptune Analytics

- **Use OpenCypher Sink**: Neptune Analytics supports OpenCypher over HTTPS—perfect for Nodestream's Cypher-based sink.

- **Leverage IAM Authentication**: Set `auth_mode`: `iam` in your sink config for secure access.

- **Monitor Query Performance**: Use query logging in Neptune Analytics to monitor updates from

Nodestream.

- **Batch Operations**: Nodestream sends batched Cypher statements for better performance.

Benefits of Using Nodestream with Neptune

Feature	Benefit
Declarative modeling	Quickly define and evolve your graph schema
Streaming ingestion	Process data in real time
ETL flexibility	Write complex logic in Python
Neptune compatibility	Supports OpenCypher format and IAM auth
Reusability	Use same pipelines for test and production

Limitations and Considerations

- **Not a native AWS service**: You need to host and manage Nodestream yourself (e.g., on EC2 or Lambda).

- **Cypher-based only**: Use Neptune Analytics with OpenCypher; not compatible with SPARQL or Gremlin backends.

- **Error handling**: Ensure retry logic is enabled when interacting with Neptune APIs.

- **Batch tuning**: Fine-tune batch size and concurrency for best throughput.

Summary

Nodestream is a versatile, open-source framework for building property graphs from streaming and structured data. By integrating it with Neptune Analytics, you unlock a powerful, real-time graph analytics platform that can handle dynamic, evolving data in near real-time.

In this chapter, we covered:

- What Nodestream is and why it matters

- Core concepts: sources, transformations, graph models, and sinks

- How to define and run Nodestream pipelines

- How to stream data into Neptune Analytics using OpenCypher

- Advanced features and best practices

Limits and Quotas

Chapter 47: Region Support

Understanding **region support** is crucial when planning, deploying, and managing your Amazon Neptune Analytics workloads. AWS Regions determine **where your Neptune Analytics graphs run**, impact **latency**, affect **data residency and compliance**, and dictate **availability of specific features**.

In this chapter, we'll walk through:

- What AWS Regions are

- Which Regions support Neptune Analytics

- How region choice affects performance and pricing

- Best practices for multi-region architecture

- Limitations and considerations

- Region-specific endpoints and features

What Are AWS Regions?

An **AWS Region** is a physical location in the world where AWS clusters its data centers. Each region is made up of **multiple Availability Zones (AZs)** to ensure redundancy and fault tolerance.

Neptune Analytics is a **regional service**, meaning your graph exists and operates within a single region's infrastructure.

Why Region Support Matters

Your choice of AWS Region can impact:

- **Latency** to users and applications

- **Data sovereignty and compliance** requirements

- **Integration with other AWS services** (e.g., S3, IAM, CloudWatch)

- **Service availability** – not all regions support all services

- **Pricing** – resource costs vary by region

- **Disaster recovery and fault tolerance**

Supported Regions for Neptune Analytics

As of early 2025, **Amazon Neptune Analytics** is available in the following AWS Regions:

Region Name	Region Code
US East (N. Virginia)	us-east-1
US West (Oregon)	us-west-2
Europe (Ireland)	eu-west-1
Europe (Frankfurt)	eu-central-1
Asia Pacific (Singapore)	ap-southeast-1
Asia Pacific (Tokyo)	ap-northeast-1

☑ Additional regions may be added over time. Always check the AWS Region Table for the most up-to-date list.

Choosing the Right Region

Your choice of region should depend on:

Factor	Consideration
Latency	Choose a region geographically close to your users or compute resources
Compliance	Certain regions support local data residency requirements (e.g., Germany)
Service Availability	Not all services or instance types are available in all regions
Pricing	Costs may vary for memory, storage, or data transfer
Integration Needs	Choose the same region as your S3 buckets, IAM roles, Lambda functions, etc.

How Region Affects Neptune Analytics

Neptune Analytics graphs are **region-bound**, meaning:

- Graphs cannot span multiple regions

- You must **create and manage** graphs separately in each region

- Queries, imports, and exports must interact with services **in the same region**

⚠ Cross-region operations (like loading from S3 in another region) require additional configuration or replication.

Creating a Graph in a Specific Region

Specify the region when creating a graph:

```
aws neptune-graph create-graph \
  --graph-name "sales-graph" \
  --region us-east-1 \
  --public-connectivity \
  --min-provisioned-memory 256
```

Every API and CLI operation must specify the region unless your AWS CLI default is already set.

Using Region-Specific Endpoints

Each region has **dedicated API endpoints** for Neptune Analytics. For example:

Control plane endpoint (graph management):

```
neptune-graph.us-east-1.amazonaws.com
```

-

Data plane endpoint (query execution):

```
g-abc123.neptune-graph.us-east-
1.amazonaws.com
```

-

If using **AWS PrivateLink**, endpoints are resolved **within the VPC** to regional service names like:

```
com.amazonaws.us-east-1.neptune-graph
com.amazonaws.us-east-1.neptune-graph-data
```

Working Across Regions

To support **multi-region architectures**, consider the following:

Option 1: Replicate Data
Export data in one region:

```
aws neptune-graph start-export-task \
  --graph-identifier g-xyz \
  --format PARQUET \
  --output-location s3://my-bucket-us-east-
1/exports/ \
  --role-arn
arn:aws:iam::123456789012:role/MyRole
```

•

Copy exported files to another region:

```
aws s3 cp \
  s3://my-bucket-us-east-1/exports/ \
  s3://my-bucket-eu-west-1/imports/ \
  --recursive
```

•

524

Import into a Neptune Analytics graph in another region:

```
aws neptune-graph start-import-task \
  --region eu-west-1 \
  --graph-identifier g-new \
  --source s3://my-bucket-eu-west-
1/imports/ \
  --format PARQUET \
  --role-arn
arn:aws:iam::123456789012:role/MyRole
```

•

Option 2: Independent Graphs per Region

For applications that require local reads and writes (e.g., latency-sensitive regional apps), maintain **separate graphs** and synchronize changes via Lambda or Step Functions.

> **There is no native multi-region Neptune Analytics replication** as of now.

Monitoring and Logging by Region

CloudWatch and CloudTrail logs are **region-specific**:

- To monitor Neptune Analytics in us-west-2, check:

  - **CloudWatch Logs** → us-west-2

  - **CloudTrail** → us-west-2

Ensure your **S3 buckets for exports/imports** and **IAM roles** also exist in the same region or are configured for cross-region access.

Compliance and Data Residency

Organizations subject to regulations such as GDPR, HIPAA, or financial standards may be required to store and process data in specific regions.

Use region selection to align with:

- **EU data sovereignty** (e.g., use `eu-central-1`)

- **APAC compliance** (e.g., `ap-southeast-1`)

- **US government workloads** (pending GovCloud support)

   Always validate your workload's legal requirements before selecting a region.

Limitations and Known Considerations

Topic	Details
Cross-region graph access	✘ Not supported
Cross-region S3 load/export	☑ Supported with manual data transfer or replication
Multi-region failover	✘ Not natively supported (use automation for DR)
Region feature parity	New Neptune Analytics features may appear first in select regions
IAM roles and endpoints	Must be created **per region**, not shared globally

526

Best Practices for Region Management

Best Practice	Benefit
Choose region closest to your users	Reduces query latency
Align with other AWS services	Simplifies networking, billing, and access control
Avoid cross-region data transfer	Minimizes cost and complexity
Use region tags in automation	Helps with tagging, budgeting, and traceability
Monitor each region separately	CloudWatch and CloudTrail are region-specific
Keep data locality requirements in mind	Ensures compliance with data regulations

Summary

Amazon Neptune Analytics is a **regional service** that runs independently in each AWS region where it's deployed. Choosing the right region is essential for performance, compliance, and reliability. Although multi-region architectures require some extra work, Neptune Analytics supports **export/import workflows** and **region-specific observability** to help you build global-scale solutions.

Key Takeaways:

- Neptune Analytics is currently supported in select AWS regions

- Each graph is **isolated to its region**—no cross-region queries

- Choose your region based on **latency, compliance, and integrations**

- Use **export/import pipelines** to replicate data across regions

- Monitor and manage each region's resources separately

Chapter 48: Parameter and Property Size Limits

As you build applications and analytics pipelines with **Neptune Analytics**, it's essential to understand the **limits** that govern the size and structure of graph elements and query parameters. These constraints help ensure optimal performance and memory management within the **in-memory engine** of Neptune Analytics.

In this chapter, you'll learn:

- The **maximum allowed sizes** for properties, parameters, and vectors

- How these limits affect **data loading**, **querying**, and **algorithm execution**

- Best practices for avoiding size-related errors

- How to handle and troubleshoot common size limit exceptions

Let's take a detailed look at the limits Neptune Analytics enforces and how to work within them effectively.

Why Limits Exist in Neptune Analytics

Neptune Analytics is optimized for **fast, large-scale, in-memory computation**. To maintain speed and scalability, it enforces hard and soft limits on:

- **Individual property sizes**

- **Query parameter sizes**

- **Vector dimensions**

- **List/map sizes**

- **Mutation and result payloads**

Understanding these boundaries is key to writing efficient, reliable queries and designing data models that scale.

Property and Parameter Size Limits

Let's break down the **most important limits** and what they mean in practice.

1. String Property Length

- **Maximum: 64 KB** (65,536 bytes) per string property

- Applies to node and edge properties stored as strings

  🧠 **Tip:** Use shorter identifiers or summarize large text fields before storing them in the graph. Store full documents in S3 and reference via URL or ID.

---

2. List Length (Property or Parameter)

- **Maximum list length: 100,000 elements**

This applies to:

- Lists passed as query parameters (e.g., `MATCH (n) WHERE n.id IN $ids`)

- List properties stored on nodes or edges

  ⚠ Avoid passing massive lists directly in queries. Use **UNWIND** or load external files for large batches.

---

3. Map Size (Number of Keys)

- **Maximum map size: 1,000 key-value pairs**

This limit applies to:

- Parameters of type `Map` (e.g., `$userMap`)

- Properties stored as maps (JSON-style)

  If you need larger maps, break them into multiple smaller maps or flatten your data.

---

4. Individual Property Count per Node/Edge

- **Maximum properties per entity: 1,000**

Each node or edge can store up to 1,000 property keys (regardless of value type).

- Ideal for metadata, labels, and ML features

- Not intended for storing deeply nested objects

☑ Use labeled edges and connected nodes to model complex or hierarchical data.

---

5. Vector Dimensions

- **Maximum vector dimension: 2,048**

You must specify the vector dimension when creating the graph (e.g., 128, 256, 384). All vectors used in that graph must match the dimension exactly.

🖻 Mismatches will trigger `DimensionMismatchException`.

Query Parameter Size Limits

Neptune Analytics allows parameterized queries, but the total **query payload** has limits.

Type	Limit
Total parameter size	~1 MB
Max list length	100,000
Max map size	1,000 keys
Max string per parameter	64 KB

Example (within limits):

```
WITH [1, 2, 3] AS ids
MATCH (n)
WHERE n.id IN ids
```

```
RETURN n
```

Example (too large):

```
WITH range(1, 200000) AS ids
MATCH (n)
WHERE n.id IN ids
RETURN n
```

> ☀ This would trigger a
> ParameterSizeExceededException.

Mutation Limits

Mutations include operations like CREATE, MERGE, SET, and DELETE.

Limit	Description
Max batch size	10,000 rows via UNWIND
Max single mutation payload	~1 MB
Max mutation time	60 seconds (default timeout)

Best Practice

- Break up large UNWIND blocks:

```
UNWIND $chunk1 AS row
MERGE (n:User {~id: row.id})
SET n.name = row.name
```

533

- For large inserts: Use **data loading via S3** or scripts

Query Result Limits

To avoid overwhelming clients or memory buffers:

Limit	Description
Max rows returned	10,000 (default)
Max row size	~1 MB
Max total result size	~10 MB

Use LIMIT and pagination for large result sets:

```
MATCH (n)
RETURN n
ORDER BY n.created_at
SKIP 0 LIMIT 1000
```

Avoid returning entire subgraphs in a single query.

Algorithm Limits (Vector, Centrality, etc.)

Algorithms in Neptune Analytics also enforce input size restrictions:

Algorithm	Key Limits
topKByNode, topKByVector	k must be ≤ 10,000
distance()	Works on two nodes with valid vectors

pageRank, labelPropagation	Will fail if memory overflows during execution

📊 Large graphs require enough memory provisioned (m-NCUs). Monitor usage via CloudWatch.

Exceptions Related to Size Limits

Exception	Cause	Solution
ParameterSizeExceededException	Parameter too large	Reduce input size
ListTooLongException	List > 100,000 elements	Use batching
MapTooLargeException	Map has > 1,000 keys	Split or flatten map
StringTooLongException	String > 64 KB	Store externally or truncate
DimensionMismatchException	Vector size doesn't match graph config	Reformat or pad vectors
PayloadTooLargeException	Mutation or query returns too much data	Limit results, break queries

535

Best Practices for Working Within Limits

1. **Validate data types and lengths** before loading or mutating

2. **Use batching** (e.g., with `UNWIND`) for large data operations

3. **Compress or normalize data**—avoid storing raw logs or long documents

4. **Monitor mutation sizes** in scripts and SDKs

5. **Avoid nested collections** when possible

6. **Test queries incrementally** before scaling input size

Monitoring Limits in Practice

Use **CloudWatch metrics** and **query statistics** to detect and prevent size issues:

- `QueryLatency`: Spikes may suggest oversized inputs

- `QueryFailureCount`: Investigate recurring exceptions

- `MemoryUtilization`: High usage may indicate oversized graph elements

Example: Reducing Payload Size

Instead of:

```
MATCH (n)
RETURN n
```

Use:

```
MATCH (n)
RETURN n.name, n.type
LIMIT 1000
```

Only return necessary fields to avoid result bloat.

Summary

Working within Neptune Analytics' limits ensures smooth execution, high performance, and system stability—especially when operating at scale.

Resource	Limit
String property	64 KB
List size	100,000
Map size	1,000 keys
Vector dimension	2,048
Query result size	~10 MB
UNWIND batch size	10,000 rows

By keeping your data, queries, and parameters within these thresholds, you'll avoid common exceptions and build a robust, efficient analytics pipeline.

API Reference

This chapter serves as a consolidated **API reference** for Amazon Neptune Analytics. It includes all the major functions, procedures, and endpoints you'll use when working with Neptune Analytics, including Cypher procedures, vector search APIs, administrative CLI commands, and graph lifecycle operations.

The reference is organized into the following categories:

1. **Graph Management APIs**

2. **Cypher Execution & Query APIs**

3. **Data Loading APIs**

4. **Vector Search APIs**

5. **Snapshot APIs**

6. **Monitoring & Metadata APIs**

7. **CLI Examples for Common Tasks**

---

1. Graph Management APIs

These APIs are used to create, list, describe, and delete Neptune Analytics graphs.

Create Graph

```
aws neptune-graph create-graph \
  --graph-name my-graph \
  --provisioned-memory 128 \
  --public-connectivity \
```

```
  --replica-count 1 \
  --region us-east-1
```

List Graphs

```
aws neptune-graph list-graphs
```

Describe Graph

```
aws neptune-graph get-graph \
  --graph-identifier g-abc123
```

Delete Graph

```
aws neptune-graph delete-graph \
  --graph-identifier g-abc123
```

---

2. Cypher Execution & Query APIs

Used for executing openCypher queries.

Execute Query

```
aws neptune-graph execute-query \
  --graph-identifier g-abc123 \
  --query-string "MATCH (n) RETURN n LIMIT
10" \
  --language openCypher
```

Query Parameters (Optional)

```
--parameters '{"userId": "u123"}'
```

In Notebooks (Python)

```python
from graph_notebook.neptune.client import
neptune
neptune.read("MATCH (n) RETURN n LIMIT 10")
```

---

3. Data Loading APIs

Used to import data into a Neptune Analytics graph.

Bulk Import (Empty Graph Only)

```
aws neptune-graph create-graph-using-
import-task \
  --graph-name my-graph \
  --source s3://bucket/path/ \
  --role-arn arn:aws:iam::account-
id:role/GraphRole \
  --format CSV \
  --region us-east-1
```

Batch Load (Existing Graph)

```
aws neptune-graph start-import-task \
  --graph-identifier g-abc123 \
  --format CSV \
  --source s3://bucket/path/ \
  --role-arn arn:aws:iam::account-
id:role/GraphRole
```

Monitor Import Task

```
aws neptune-graph get-import-task \
  --graph-identifier g-abc123 \
  --task-id it-xyz123
```

4. Vector Search APIs (Cypher Procedures)

These are Cypher-callable procedures built into Neptune
Analytics.

`.upsert()`

```
CALL vectors.upsert("doc1", [0.1, 0.2, 0.3,
...])
```

`.topK()`

```
CALL vectors.topK([0.1, 0.2, 0.3, ...], 5,
{label: "Document"})
YIELD id, score
```

`.distance()`

```
CALL vectors.distance("doc1", "doc2")
YIELD distance
```

`.remove()`

```
CALL vectors.remove("doc1")
```

5. Snapshot APIs

Used to create and manage point-in-time graph backups.

Create Snapshot

```
aws neptune-graph create-snapshot \
  --graph-identifier g-abc123 \
  --snapshot-name my-snapshot
```

List Snapshots

```
aws neptune-graph list-snapshots
```

Restore Snapshot

```
aws neptune-graph restore-snapshot \
  --snapshot-name my-snapshot \
  --graph-name restored-graph \
  --provisioned-memory 256
```

Delete Snapshot

```
aws neptune-graph delete-snapshot \
  --snapshot-name my-snapshot
```

---

6. Monitoring & Metadata APIs

Get Graph Summary

```
CALL db.stats()
YIELD nodeCount, edgeCount
```

Get Schema Summary

```
CALL db.schema()
YIELD label, property, type
```

Get Vector Config

```
CALL vectors.config()
YIELD dimension
```

7. Common CLI Tasks Reference

Task	CLI Command
Create graph	create-graph
Load data	start-import-task or create-graph-using-import-task
Execute query	execute-query
Create snapshot	create-snapshot
Restore graph	restore-snapshot
Delete graph	delete-graph
View graphs	list-graphs
Manage role	create-service-linked-role

Summary

This API Reference chapter provides a quick-access guide to the most essential Neptune Analytics operations—whether you're running queries, managing graphs, importing data, or building vector search solutions.

Keep this reference close at hand as you build with Neptune Analytics—it will serve as your command-line cheat sheet and Cypher helper for everything from graph creation to advanced querying.

Appendix

Useful Links and Further Reading

To help you deepen your understanding of Neptune Analytics, graph data science, and the broader openCypher and AWS ecosystem, this appendix collects a curated list of **useful links, references, documentation**, and **further reading materials**.

These resources cover:

- Official AWS Neptune documentation

- openCypher specifications and learning resources

- Graph algorithm theory and use cases

- Community forums and repositories

- Tools and utilities for working with Neptune Analytics

🔗 Official AWS Neptune Resources

These are your go-to links for official service documentation, feature updates, and supported tools:

- **Amazon Neptune Analytics Overview**

  https://docs.aws.amazon.com/neptune/latest/userguide/neptune-analytics.html

- **Neptune Analytics API Reference**
  https://docs.aws.amazon.com/neptune-analytics/latest/userguide/API_Reference.html

- **Neptune Analytics Pricing**

  https://aws.amazon.com/neptune/pricing/#Neptune_Analytics

- **Neptune Analytics Tutorials and Examples**
  https://github.com/aws-samples/amazon-neptune-samples

- **Amazon Neptune Product Page**
  https://aws.amazon.com/neptune/

🎨 openCypher Resources

Understanding openCypher is essential for querying Neptune Analytics effectively. These resources help you master the language:

- **openCypher Project Home**
  https://opencypher.org

- **Cypher Query Language Reference Card**
  https://neo4j.com/docs/cypher-refcard/current/

- **Cypher Language Specification (PDF)**

  https://s3.amazonaws.com/artifacts.opencypher.org/openCypher9.pdf

- **Cypher Query Language Tutorials**
  https://neo4j.com/developer/cypher

Note: Neptune Analytics follows **openCypher**, but not all Neo4j-specific extensions are supported.

📖 Graph Algorithms and Theory

Explore deeper concepts behind the algorithms you run in Neptune Analytics:

- **Graph Algorithms by Mark Needham and Amy E. Hodler (O'Reilly)**
  https://www.oreilly.com/library/view/graph-algorithms/9781492047674/

- **NetworkX Graph Algorithm Library (Python)**
  https://networkx.org/documentation/stable/

- **Stanford Network Analysis Project (SNAP)**
  https://snap.stanford.edu

- **Awesome Graph Algorithms GitHub Collection**
  https://github.com/ameya98/awesome-graph-algorithms

📁 Graph Notebook and Tools

For hands-on development with Neptune Analytics:

- **AWS Graph Notebook (Jupyter Extension)**
  https://github.com/aws/graph-notebook

- **Neptune Jupyter Notebook Quickstart**

  https://docs.aws.amazon.com/neptune/latest/userg

uide/notebooks-graph-notebook.html

- **Graph Visualization Libraries**

    - Cytoscape.js

    - D3.js Graphs

🎁 Sample Datasets

Use these public datasets to practice graph queries and algorithms:

- **Amazon Customer Co-purchase Graph**
  https://snap.stanford.edu/data/amazon0302.html

- **Facebook Social Circles Dataset**
  https://snap.stanford.edu/data/ego-Facebook.html

- **Citation Networks (Cora, DBLP)**
  https://linqs.soe.ucsc.edu/data

- **Movies & Actors Graph Dataset**
  https://github.com/neo4j-graph-examples/movies

🏛 AWS Developer Resources

- **AWS CLI Command Reference for Neptune Graphs**

    https://docs.aws.amazon.com/cli/latest/reference/neptune-graph/index.html

- **AWS SDKs**

  - Boto3 (Python)

  - Java SDK

  - Node.js SDK

- **AWS Data Engineering Blog (Neptune Articles)**
  https://aws.amazon.com/blogs/big-data/

🔔 Community and Forums

Join the conversation, ask questions, and stay informed:

- **AWS Discussion Forums – Amazon Neptune**
  https://repost.aws/t/neptune

- **Stack Overflow**

  https://stackoverflow.com/questions/tagged/amazon-neptune

- **LinkedIn Groups on Graph Databases**
  Search for "Graph Analytics", "Graph Databases", or "Neptune"

- **Reddit Communities**

  - r/aws

  - r/graphdatabases

📄 Further Reading and Inspiration

- **Gartner Report: Market Guide for Graph Database Management Systems**
  (Available to Gartner clients)

- **The Graph Database Landscape 2024 (DB Engines)**
  https://db-engines.com/en/ranking/graph+dbms

- **AWS Neptune Analytics Feature Announcements**
  https://aws.amazon.com/blogs/database/

- **"Graph Thinking" Blog Series** by AWS
  https://aws.amazon.com/blogs/big-data/tag/amazon-neptune/

☑ Recommended Next Steps

If you're looking to expand your journey:

1. **Try Neptune Graph Notebooks** with a sample dataset

2. **Run community detection** on a real-world graph (e.g., social, product, transaction)

3. **Experiment with graph algorithms** like PageRank or similarity

4. **Explore Cypher challenges or mini projects** from the openCypher community

5. **Join AWS re:Invent or AWS Summit sessions**
   on Neptune and graph analytics

Summary

The world of graph analytics is deep and dynamic. Whether you're learning openCypher, building complex analytical pipelines, or exploring the structure of networks, the resources in this appendix will help you keep growing.

Explore, experiment, and connect!